AFRICAN CHRISTIAN THEOLOGY

REVISITED

AFRICAN CHRISTIAN THEOLOGY

REVISITED

Dr. Richard J. Gehman

OASIS INTERNATIONAL LTD

INSIGHT BOOKS
African Issues
Africa's Authors

African Theology Revisited

ISBN 13: 978-1-59452-745-6
ISBN: 1-59452-745-8

Published by Oasis International Ltd, in partnership with Richard J. Gehman. Oasis International is a ministry devoted to fostering a robust and sustainable pan-African publishing industry. For more information, go to oasisint.net.

18 19 20 21 22 23 24 25 BPI 10 9 8 7 6 5 4 3 2 1

PRAISE FOR AFRICAN CHRISTIAN THEOLOGY REVISITED

"A combination of a long experience of ministry in Africa, a faithful commitment to the sufficiency of Scripture, a meticulous field research investigating African traditions, and the universal nature of Christianity gives undeniable credence to Dr. Gehman's attempt at theological reflection in Africa. This book treats you to a scholarly material that is systematically organized, exceptionally readable, thoroughly informative, and positively provocative. Read it!"

– **Dr. Alfred Muli,** Ph.D. - Adjunct Professor of Theology at Cairn University and Liberty University.

CONTENTS

INTRODUCTION

African Christian Theology began with the preaching of the Gospel in the vernacular languages and with the translation of Scripture into the mother tongues of Africa. Although many dismiss this as "missionary theology," the historic fact is that Africans participated in this process from the beginning. African evangelists and teachers were in the vanguard of proclaiming the Christian Gospel. They were the indispensable agents in the translation of Scripture. God's Word, translated into local African thought forms that are expressed in indigenous languages, is by definition the rudiments of African biblical theology.

Not until after World Word Two, however, did African Christian Theology begin addressing the African concerns that are so prevalent today; and that did not occur until Africans achieved higher education in western institutions and returned to Africa to teach in African universities. John Mbiti among the Protestants and Charles Nyamiti among the Roman Catholics pioneered in African Christian Theology. Desmond Tutu heralded African Liberation Theology in South Africa. Byang Kato arose among the evangelicals to sound the alarm and call for a return to biblical theology.

In 1978 the author published the book, *Doing African Christian Theology: An Evangelical Perspective*. Acknowledging the need for African Christian Theology, the book traced the history and methodology of African Christian Theology and encouraged a process of doing theology in Africa that was faithful to the Scriptures.

Forty years have passed since then, giving further opportunity to observe the direction of African Christian Theology. What began as a trickle of publications in the 1950s and 1960s has become a virtual flood-tide today.

The purpose of this publication is partly to update that 1979 publication. What is impressive is the significant contributions made by evangelicals in recent years. On the other hand, what is of great concern is the troubling failure of many other African theologians to remain faithful to the Scriptures.

In view of this disturbing trend, the purpose of this book moves beyond a mere updating of the 1978 publication. We seek to *revisit* the basic issues that make possible a biblical theology in Africa.

Chapter 3 lays down the foundation for being faithful in doing African theology. It critiques the methodologies of earlier African theologians and offers *Guidelines* for doing Christian theology in Africa.

Chapter 4 traces the *Historical Panorama of the Church's View of Scripture*. Many in Africa are unaware that unbelief in God's Word, that has sapped the vitality of many western churches and seminaries, is now seeping into African churches. One's presuppositions and preunderstandings shape and determine any theological reflection. When rooted in unbelief the results are disastrous. Tragically, these western naturalistic presuppositions have been embraced uncritically by many African theologians.

Chapter 5 addresses two profound questions that Christian theologians must face, whatever continent they live in: "Who is Jesus?" and, "Why was Jesus sent by the Father?" These questions demand a thoughtful and biblical response. The answers to these two fundamental questions should determine the direction of anyone's theological reflections.

Chapter 6 delves briefly into a number of key topics of African Christian Theology which need further reflection by evangelicals. Reflections on African culture, diversity of theologies, the influence of Greek philosophy on the early creeds, and the inclusion of African ancestors in Christian theology have all been largely shaped by those who do not submit to the authority of God's Word. A more thorough reflection from within the circle of faith is needful.

Chapter 7 offers several different paradigms for doing Christian theology in Africa. Using the African traditional value of communal sharing and learning, various models are presented in the hope of encouraging evangelicals to become more engaged in the wholesome and edifying work of reflecting on biblical teaching and applying it to life's situations in contemporary Africa.

The intention of this book is both negative and positive. On the negative side, African Christians must be alerted to the theological trends in Africa which are based on a faulty view of Scripture. Theologians who are halting between the authority of Scripture and a dependence on the higher critical views of Scripture need to reconsider their allegiance to Jesus Christ and his divine authority.

On the positive side, theologians in Africa are encouraged to fulfil their God given responsibility. Not only must the lost be evangelized, both outside and inside the churches, the people of God must grow in their obedience to Jesus Christ as they reflect upon God's revealed will in their particular context of life. Unless Christians search the Scriptures for themselves and seek to gain a knowledge of God's will for various issues that face them, they will fall into disobedience. And unless Christians become more and more a people of the Book, they will lose their evangelical fervency. Revival and renewal in the churches depend upon a prayerful meditation upon the Word of God.

This book is a clarion call for all African Christians to think through their Christian faith in the African context, but always under the authority of the Word of God. Erroneous theologies must be confronted and challenged with biblical teaching. The truth of God must be courageously defended. Let us seek to be genuinely and thoroughly African in our Christian theology, and absolutely biblical in our conclusions.

A word should be said about the title, "*African Christian Theology Revisited*." The nomenclature, "African Theology," most naturally refers to African traditional thought, not Christian theology. For this reason, "African Christian Theology" in the past was the preferred nomenclature for theology done by Christians. Hence, my previous book and this revision use the terminology, "African Christian Theology."

However, in recent years sentiment has changed and the title, "African Theology," has come into use even when referring to theology written by Christians in Africa. For purposes of this book, therefore, and within this book, we shall refer to "African Theology" as the broad category for Christians doing theology in Africa. Within this broad category we shall speak of three sub-categories: African Christian Theology, African Liberation Theology, and African Biblical Theology.

Since "African Christian Theology" in this book will refer to one strand of doing Christian theology in Africa, we will use "African Theology" as the broad category which includes three sub-categories of African Liberation Theology, African Christian Theology, and African Biblical Theology.

FOREWORD

Rev. Dr. Aiah Foday-Khabenje – General Secretary, Association of Evangelicals in Africa (AEA).

Christianity has gone full cycle and for the second time in the history of the Christian Church, Africa has become home for representative Christianity. As at the dawn of Christianity, when theology out of Africa nursed the church in other parts of the world, including Europe, the African Church is again in a position to contribute in revitalising and re-evangelising the once heartlands of the Christianity but now post-Christian Western hemisphere. The call is for the spread of the Apostolic and Catholic faith; once given and nurtured in Africa, albeit the stumping of the earlier church from flourishing in all Africa. The stump has now sprouted and the flourishing tree (Mt 12:33-35) ought to provide some shade for the global Church.

In spreading the gospel to all of Africa, Western missionaries may have erred by packaging the gospel in cultural cloaks, and at a time when their compatriots (colonial administrators) supressed the African peoples. However, it would be tragic and depraved for the African church to follow suit and veil the Good News of the Gospel in cultural outfits, contrary to biblical values and the Lordship of Jesus Christ.

In contemporary theological discourse in Africa, it would appear a dividing line has been drawn; a gapping furrow between biblical fidelity and nationalistic loyalty, Biblicism and Rationalism. The contention is between evangelicalism and liberal rationalism, especially in their view of scripture. The Evangelical view of the absolute divine authority of the Bible by faith, makes it the final authority for faith and conduct. The liberal view of Scripture at best, is a neo-orthodox view that the Bible is a record of human religious experience and only one among several sources for theologising.

The emergent "African Theology" as an academic theological discipline, has preoccupied the minds of African scholars and theologians since the mid-twentieth century. African Theology is borne mostly as a reaction to colonial and missionary denigration of Africans and their culture. Therefore, there is a tendency to romanticise and exalt African religious and cultural beliefs above biblical teachings. Whether this should in fact be "African Christian Theology" or "African Biblical Theology" or "Theology by Africans" is beside the point. The particular concern is about the liberal and rationalistic beliefs and the theological conclusions reached, as seen in many of the writings of the early proponents of African Theology.

A critical voice on the other side of the divide of these early pioneers of the debate was Byang Kato, the first African General Secretary of the Association of Evangelicals in Africa. Kato's clarion call to let "African Christians be Christian Africans" was an important call for biblical fidelity and from an evangelical view point. However, as the so called African Theology developed, the critical voice of evangelicals was missed by Kato's sudden and tragic death by drowning in the Pacific Ocean in Mombasa, Kenya. Over forty years after Kato's death, fresh questions are being asked about the direction of African Theology. It is heartening for me personally, that Kato's voice is being magnified; the stump of evangelical theology is sprouting and flourishing.

African Christian Theology Revisited by Richard J. Gehman is an important theological resource and a voice for evangelical theology in Africa. The key message is that culture must be subject to revealed Scripture in the Bible and reader must be willing to set aside beliefs that are inconsistent with Scripture. This is a call to be truly African and authentically Christian. Sound theologising is about conversion – turning around, transforming and altering in conformity with the teachings of Jesus Christ. This book could not have been written at a better time, when the call for sound theological education and biblical orthodoxy is in crescendo, not only in Africa but in the global Church as a whole.

Dr. Gehman provides a very helpful and comprehensive critical overview of the available literature on African Theology and leaves the reader with no doubt about the classical orthodox view on the various subject matters. Evangelical Theology is rooted in a life of obedience to the word of God and submission to the Lordship of Jesus Christ. Gehman's work is backed with a lived experience of a life time of thirty-seven years, as a missionary in Kenya and teaching at the Scott Theological College, for many of those years.

While the need for African Theology may not be in doubt, the Africanness of the theology espoused need not be esoteric, shrouded in mystery and ironically, embracing views developed in the catacombs of Western academia. An authentic theology for Africa is one that is tasks driven and truly responds to African realities for self-actualisation in accordance with God's purposes and glory. The kind of theologian who is out in the battle field, working in the trenches and engaged in spiritual warfare, establishing the Kingdom of God in the hearts of people and transforming their communities. Theologians who are engaged in evangelism, discipleship and teaching the people biblical truth as it applies to them in their context. Gehman calls this the "Task Theologian – one who knows biblical teaching and can relate it and apply it contextually to the believers in order to ground them in their faith".

A welcome contribution, in the quest for African Theology and warmly recommended for church leaders and as text for Bible Colleges and Christian Universities in Africa.

FOREWORD

Rev. Dr. Samuel Waje Kunhiyop, Ph.D. – Professor of Systematic Theology/ Ethics, ECWA Theological Seminary, Kagoro, Nigeria.

Dr. Richard J. Gehman is a retired veteran missionary with the Africa Inland Mission (A.I.M), for many years a distinguished lecturer and principal of Scott Theological College, Kenya, an active member of several boards and institutions and an accomplished academic who has authored numerous books while serving in Africa.

The author explicitly states the two critical aspects of African Theology, namely the role of Scripture and Context. He states. "Whenever the Gospel is communicated cross culturally, there must be a real measure of identification with the peoples. Christ must be presented in a manner that is both true to Scripture and meaningful to the people. True, Jesus Christ is Lord of all. But he is also Lord of each given people group. Christ must be seen and known and understood in the context of each culture. Even as the Eternal Spirit became incarnate as a human being in a particular culture, so Jesus Christ must belong to each society in a unique way...All believers everywhere struggle with problems which need resolution through theological reflection on the Scriptures" (p.14,15). In this highly thought-provoking and engaging book, the author interacts with the key rudiments of theology.

A good theology or a contextualized theology must be faithful in dealing with Scripture and relevant in the context of the people. His comprehensive historical survey on studies in African Theology reveals that the various theologies that have emerged in Africa in the last fifty years were constructed on "the quick sand of unbelieving western theologies," "faulty foundations," and a "faulty methodology" which "lead to faulty theology even as a poor foundations results in a poorly constructed building" (p. 88).

His conclusion after a thoughtful and scholarly interaction with all the theologies is very clear. "Much of what is called African Theology is premised on western philosophical and theological presuppositions. No one is able to do theology in vacuum. Because of the pervasive teaching of Existentialism and Post Modernism in western institutions, where African scholars have studied, much of African Theology is built on western thought and assumptions, conscious or unconscious" (p. 119). These theologies demonstrate that they have paid only lip service to African Christian Theology by intentionally ignoring the Scriptures which are the indispensable requirement of theology.

The author not only interacted with the poor theologies but articulates guidelines for developing African Theology. This section in Chapter 3 to me is really the major contribution of Dr. Gehman. Students of Theology, especially on African Theology will find helpful insights and guidance in developing theology, especially avoiding the pitfalls of the many theologies out there.

Dr. Gehman, though retired, has demonstrated through this book that he still has African Christianity at heart and is a great motivator to articulate a theology that is true to Scripture and relevant to the deep yearnings of the African Church. The author has also demonstrated that the right and proper thing to do is ***to scratch where one is itching***. In this book, Gehman has scratched where the African Church is itching. African theology must be rooted in the Scriptures and relevant to the culture.

In his words. "The book is a clarion call for all African Christians to think through their Christian faith in the African context, but always under the authority of the Word of God. Erroneous theologies must be confronted and challenged with biblical teaching. The truth of God must be courageously defended. Let us seek to be genuinely and thoroughly African in our Christian theology, and absolutely biblical in our conclusions" (p. 6).

The African Church desperately and urgently needs theologians who will take seriously the recommendations of Dr. Gehman and develop theologies on issues affecting the African Church in a biblical and relevant way. To that end, I strongly and enthusiastically recommend this extremely resourceful book to African theologians, theological students, research libraries and pastors. We have a saying in Hausa, a language spoken in Northern Nigeria that says, "*Ga Fili. Ga doki.*" ("Here is the horse. Ride it"). We have the book. Let us read it, apply it and write accordingly.

FOREWORD

Dr. Alfred Muli, Ph.D. - Adjunct Professor of theology at Cairn University and Liberty University, and former Lecturer at Scott Theological College, Kenya.

Dr. Richard Gehman is no stranger to Africa. In addition to teaching, Gehman pursued his research and writing interests. He authored twelve books and was manuscript drafter of six books on behalf of the Theological Advisory Group (TAG). Dr. Gehman founded TAG (composed of local church pastors and theological college lecturers, and Bible college tutors) to research topics which needed a Biblical solution from an African perspective.

In the pursuit of his interest in research, as well as concern for the church in Africa, Gehman has authored his finest book yet, namely, *African Christian Theology Revisited.* It is not an overstatement that the present volume is indeed Dr. Gehman's *magnum opus.*

This volume makes a significant contribution to the discipline of African Theology. It raises issues which sound discourse of African theology cannot afford to ignore. For instance, this book raises the issue of the relationship between the universal truth of the gospel and the local African context, warning against the possible confusion of gospel and culture. Also, the author points out the connection between African Christianity and the history of Christian thought and thereby demonstrating that African Christianity is not ahistorical but organically connected to historical and global Christianity.

Above all, Dr. Gehman's assessment of the methodology of doing African Theology, especially as found in chapter three, is without a doubt the single most remarkable contribution of this book. The author's careful interaction and analysis of African authors on the one hand, and his uncompromising assessment of their ideas and proposals in light of Scripture on the other, command authenticity. Emerging from this appraisal is the author's lament about the approach that treats the Bible and the African traditional heritage as equal sources of authority for African Christian Theology.

But what causes this problematic approach? In a word, it is presupposition. In every field of inquiry, our presuppositions determine our methodologies. And since study is a function of knowledge it behoves us to consider our presupposition in terms of epistemology. How do we know what we know? What is our *principium cognoscendi*? In other words, what is the source of authority for our knowledge? And since we are talking about a study that is qualified as Christian, there can be no other source of authority than the Bible.

The Bible attests to its own authority in that its primary author is the third person of the triune God, the Holy Spirit (2 Pe 1:21) who superintended human authors with his inspiration so that what they wrote was the exact product of what God intended (2 Ti 3:16). What this means is that the Bible, being the product of divine authorship, is the inerrant and infallible word of God. It is the objective propositional truth of God (Jn 17:17). Hence, the Bible is the final authority on all matters.

On the one hand, this view of Scripture necessitates the rejection of any hermeneutical procedure that disregards the rightful place of the Bible, such as the literary critical method since it denies the divine authorship of the Bible and instead treats it as a human book. On the other hand, this view of the Bible requires the utilization of the grammatical/historical method of biblical interpretation for it is most consistent with the Christian presupposition about the nature of the Bible. It observes grammatical rules, literary genre, textual context, and historical background. It is also the procedure employed in the historic Christian faith and stands the test of credible biblical interpretation.

What this means is that, while it is true that both the Bible and the African traditional heritage are important sources of theology in Africa, the two are not equal authorities. The former is primary and the latter secondary. The former informs the latter and the latter is subservient to the former and not vice versa. Therefore, any elements of African traditions, beliefs, and practices that are incompatible with biblical revelation must be rejected and replaced with a functional substitute. Therefore, whenever African Theological Reflection treats the Bible and African traditional heritage as equal sources of knowledge, it immediately fails in its task and inevitably produces a defective theology.

Dr. Gehman is right to sound the alarm regarding this danger. He is correct that the task of doing African theology should proceed from an unwavering faithfulness to biblical orthodoxy. It should affirm and uphold the Christian tradition of *sola scriptura*. This task should resist the temptation of sacrificing sound biblical teaching at the altar of cultural relevance. Indeed, while the gospel and culture are not mutually exclusive, they do not stand at par with each other. And while culture should be taken seriously, it should retain its subservient place in relation to the Biblical authority. The proper methodology of African Christian Theology is that which seeks to establish theological conclusions from the sound teaching of the Bible and then to articulate them in categories and symbols relevant to African traditional heritage. This entails the essence of true contextualization.

A combination of a long experience of ministry in Africa, a faithful commitment to the sufficiency of Scripture, a meticulous field research investigating African traditions, and the universal nature of Christianity gives undeniable credence to Gehman's attempt at theological reflection in Africa. This book treats you to a scholarly material that is systematically organized, exceptionally readable, thoroughly informative, and positively provocative. Read it!

FOREWORD

Professor James Kombo – D.Th., Associate Professor of Theological Studies and Deputy Vice Chancellor, Daystar University, Kenya.

The title of this book, *African Christian Theology Revisited,* befittingly speaks of a task its author Dr Richard Gehman was part of in the 1970s and which culminated in his 1978 voice of reason, *Doing African Christian Theology: An Evangelical Perspective.* Historically, the 1970s was the second decade of Africa's political independence. For the church, the epoch was marked by two important developments: the literal eruption of what became the African independent church movement on the one hand and the ensuing indigenization of the mission churches and its implications on the other hand. The latter was the concern of theological interlocutors of the day. They worried about the nature and the shape of the thought of the emerging African Christianity. For Richard Gehman who had been an Africa Inland Mission missionary (AIM) since 1967 and Principal of many years at the Africa Inland Church's (AIC) premier pastoral formation institution, Scott Theological College (now Scott Christian University), the strategic direction for this burgeoning church was the uncompromising answer to the enduring question: "Who is Jesus?" and, "Why was Jesus sent by the Father?"(See chapter 5).

This present publication revisits this 40 year old agenda as it incorporates significant evangelical contributions in the intervening period. He is not just interested in reiterating the voices of yore, but more importantly , he is keen at identifying, hearing and walking along side of new evangelical voices on this agenda because for him, "... the troubling failure of many other African theologians [is] to remain faithful to the Scriptures." His 'walking along side of new evangelical voices' in difficult and controversial areas identified in this book is particularly worthy of note. He, for instance in Chapter 3, critiques old theological methodologies that he believes had lapses in their theological architecture, and instead he offers what he sees as solid requisite ingredients for a faithful articulation of African theology. He also scans what he calls the "Historical Panorama of the Church's View of Scripture" (ch. 4), and concludes that the African theological discussants have naively and uncritically absorbed and implemented certain western theological models which he sees as downright hazardous.

But I have found Chapter 6 particularly interesting. In this short chapter, Gehman observes a range of things: he bring to the attention of his readers at least 6 active theological models or paradigms, all of which are of African extraction—an indication of attention to a robust contextual theological conversation; then he raises what he observes as the troubled culture-theology engagements notable in African theology in a manner that links the emerging dynamics to the age-old controversies around the Greek philosophy and the creeds of the early Church. Gehman's mode and tone in this chapter is clearly evangelical. This evangelical conviction is particularly troubled by what he observes as "... the inclusion of ancestors in Christian theology." His argument is that those who are prone to this practice "... have all been largely shaped by those who do not submit to the authority of God's Word." Although he takes this hard point of view, he is fairly magnanimous in granting that the ancestor talk within African theology may just be essential if we are to move towards "a more thorough reflection from within the circle of faith."

But Gehman's major contribution appears to have been saved for his 7th chapter. Here he identifies an important construct in the African mind – the value of communal sharing and learning. He proposes this as a significant resource which the African evangelical thought should actively explore and continually engage.

I take this opportunity to congratulate Gehman for sharing these deep thoughts. He has in this writing not only demonstrated his deep grasp of the African thought which is a product 50 years of active mission work in Africa, but he has also shared his deep heart and how he would have wished the African mind to relate to the matters of the Gospel, he has identified what he sees as gaps in African Theology for immediate engagement and he has by this book once again opened himself by placing an invitation for a continued walk and conversation with those of us who are still in the struggle for a biblical Christianity for Africa. For this contribution, I am truly grateful to Gehman – he is truly an African *mzee*.—always wise, clearly magnanimous, deeply reflective and very inviting to the next generation.

Perhaps in closing, I would have loved to see more African theology in this work—not theological methodology. After all, his 1978 voice of reason, *Doing African Christian Theology: An Evangelical Perspective*, already spoke to this. But perhaps more than anything else, we the theological educators should take seriously Gehman's proposal that the African traditional value of communal sharing and learning should be a hallmark "... in the hope of encouraging evangelicals to become more engaged in the wholesome and edifying work of reflecting on biblical teaching and applying it to life's situations in contemporary Africa." Might this also be our attitude towards engagement with the African theological thinkers who have chosen the more critical western theological models?

ACKNOWLEDGEMENTS

"No one is an island unto himself." We are all interdependent upon one another for whatever we do or become. As the Preacher said, "There is nothing new under the sun" (Ecc 1:9). We learn from others and stand on the shoulders of our mentors. After a prominent pastor had preached a sermon, he was asked, "How long did it take you to prepare that sermon?" "All my life," he answered. No experience or acquaintance in life is wasted. Everything and everyone contributes to our lives. The number of people to whom the author is indebted for this book is like the proverbial grains on the seashore:

- My parents who gave me life on this earth, led me to Christ, nurtured me in the Faith and left an indelible stamp on my life with their godly examples.
- My Church, the Bible Fellowship Church, which taught the Word of God faithfully, provided a family of faith which nourished me, and through their ministries I heard God's call to serve Him in Africa.
- Berean Bible School, our denominational institution, where I was grounded in biblical knowledge and where President Jansen E. Hartman encouraged me to attend Wheaton College after graduation.
- Wheaton College offered many marvellous role models, including President V. Raymond Edman who led chapel, and Dr. Kenneth Kantzer, my favourite teacher of all time, who taught theology with humility.
- Wheaton Graduate School where my exegesis of the Greek Gospels was honed through the memorable course with Dr. Berkley Mickelsen, and especially, the discipline of academic writing with my MA thesis.
- Gordon Divinity School and Westminster Theological Seminary where the elementary biblical knowledge of Bible School was deepened to a graduate level through giants in their fields.
- Flo Hilbert whom God our heavenly Father gave as my life's companion who served alongside of me, and faithfully loved me, helped me and encouraged me to fulfil my sense of calling in life.
- Rev. Sid Langford of the Africa Inland Mission who directed us to Scott Theological College where we had the marvellous opportunity of using the gifts for ministry which God had granted me.
- Desmond Hales, Principal of Scott, who asked me to teach "African Traditional Religion" and gave me three months to prepare in libraries for a course which had never been taught at Scott before.
- Africa Inland Church where I had the extraordinary privilege of training and working with dedicated servants of the Lord who taught me many lessons and in which I served as an assistant pastor for nine years.
- The School of World Missions, Fuller Theological Seminary, which afforded me the opportunity to study contextualization, and research a dissertation of 637 pages which resulted in three published books.
- The Theological Advisory Group which gave me the priceless privilege of working with godly, knowledgeable and seasoned pastors in research, and applying all that I had learned over the years.

- Above all earthly blessings, I acknowledge the Lordship of Christ in my life who has guided, protected, and enabled me to serve him, even providing in retirement the health and means to continue in ministry.

In addition to the general contributions mentioned above, individuals in particular have contributed to this book.

Access to the scores of books on African Theology was made possible by the gracious offer of Dr. Joseph Onyango, Associate Professor of Philosophy and Ethics at Asbury Theological Seminary, Dunnam Campus, in Orlando, Florida. Through his help I was able to borrow scores of books for reading.

Struggling to find a succinct, pithy title, I sought the counsel of a creative friend at our A.I.M. retirement centre, Mrs. Jean Olsen. *African Christian Theology Revisited* came to her mind and instantly we knew this was a winning title.

Darwin Dunham, the gifted A.I.M. artist who served his life time in Tanzania, crafted the front cover for which I am thankful.

Jeremy Johnson of OASIS International Ltd, the publisher of the *Africa Study Bible*, offered to publish all my books and ensure their continued availability after my translation to glory. This immediately struck a chord with me as an answer to prayer, and led me to think of the need to revise my earlier book, *Doing African Christian Theology: An Evangelical Perspective*, published in 1987 by Evangel Publishing House which has kept it in print. The Swahili translation by Rev. Charles Salalah was published in 1991. Without this offer by OASIS, I doubt whether this revision would ever have taken place.

Surely, all writers are indebted to the technical revolution and the development of computers. I can't even begin to imagine the trial of composing this book with quill and ink, or even a manual typewriter. But computers can also be the source of immense frustration. Nathan Gehman, our son, has helped me enormously with his expertise. On occasion I have also called on a neighbour friend, Randy Carpenter, who has assisted me with problems.

Common African wisdom is that it takes a village to rear a child. In the same way, it has taken a worldwide village of acquaintances and a long life of experience to make this book possible. To all those who have knowingly or unknowingly contributed to this volume, I owe a huge debt of thanks.

To God be the glory; Glory to God alone.

Et gloria Dei est; Soli Deo gloria (Latin)

Utukufu uwe kwa Mungu; Utukufu ni kwa Mungu pekee (Kiswahili)

Bo Jehovah torornatet and—ak; Torornatet kobo Jehovah inegei (Kalenjin)

Bo Katororet Jehovah; Katororet kobo Jehovah inegei (Nandi)

Duong' odog ni Nyasaye; Duong' en mar Nyasaye kende (Dholuo)

Ndaia ni kwa Ngai; Ndaia ni kwa Ngai eweka (Kikamba)

1

NEED FOR AFRICAN THEOLOGY

PERSONAL REFLECTIONS

The need for Christian Theology in Africa has gradually been impressed upon the author over the years. A couple of personal experiences may help us to understand this need.

Although I was reared in a Christian home and was converted at a young age, Christ did not seem very near to me. Somehow the person of Jesus Christ was distant. In contrast, God the Father as Spirit was real to me. I loved Him, read His Word faithfully, obeyed Him and tried to serve Him. As I grew older I became aware that Christ, the eternal Word of God, manifested in his human flesh the true nature of God. Why was it that God as Spirit I loved, but Jesus Christ, God manifest in the flesh, appeared to me less attractive?

After years of reflection on my personal experience I concluded that this was due to the image I had of Jesus Christ. His long hair and bearded face simply did not attract me to Him. Whenever I thought of Jesus Christ I thought of those portraits of Jesus Christ with a full beard and shoulder length hair. That simply was not the image of someone I could love.

Now as a matter of historical fact Jesus Christ probably did wear long hair with a beard. If we desire historical accuracy, then our image of Jesus Christ incarnate would surely include a bearded face. This raises the interesting question concerning those cultural experiences we have had which shape our ideal of what is valuable and good. No doubt many of our cultural values fall short of God's glory and we need to adjust our traditional values to conform to God's standards.

But in the communication of the Gospel we need to be oriented to the cultural heritage of the receivers if we are to communicate most effectively. To this day I find it advantageous to imagine Christ clean faced and with "properly cut hair." This may reflect my age and cultural background. But whatever it may reveal, the facts are that shoulder length hair and a full bearded face do not appeal to me even today.

This has cross cultural implications. Whenever the Gospel is communicated cross culturally, there must be a real measure of identification with the peoples. Christ must be presented in a manner that is both true to Scripture and meaningful to the people. True, Jesus Christ is Lord of all. But He is also Lord of each given people group. Christ must be seen and known and understood in the context of each culture. Even as the Eternal Spirit became incarnate as a human being in a particular culture, so Jesus Christ must belong to each society in a unique way.

Back in 1967, one year after arriving in Kenya as a missionary, my wife and I visited a church in Fort Hall (known today as Murang'a), decorated with remarkable Goyalike mural paintings by a Chagga artist called Elimo Njau. They depict the birth of Christ, his ministry and crucifixion. But Christ is an African, Mary and Joseph are Africans, and all the scenes are painted with an African landscape. My initial reaction was one of rejection, for the message communicated was contrary to the facts. Jesus, the son of David, the son of

Abraham, was a Jew. And Jews historically are not black. The scene of Jesus' birth was in Palestine, not in Africa.

Technically, that is all true. Yet over the years I have come to appreciate the dynamics which went into the painting of those murals. And my own experience with the image of Jesus confirmed that. Furthermore, I realized that the usual portraits of Jesus used in the West, such as Sallman's Head of Christ, are not truly reflective of Jesus either. Jesus Christ was from Palestine, a Middle Easterner with darker skin. Sallman's Head of Christ portrays him as an Anglo Saxon with facial features and colour, more representative of a West European.

We are confronted with two important issues: truth and application. Evangelicals have long been emphatic on maintaining the truth of the Gospel that is meaningfully revealed in Scripture. In our personal reflections we have observed that the facts are one thing. Jesus Christ, God incarnate in human flesh was not an African. Nor was he a European. We must seek to understand something of Jesus' personal appearance through historical research.

But the truth of the Gospel must be communicated to each person in his own culture. Christ must be understood and welcomed in culturally relevant ways. How does the Gospel truth apply to me? In a real sense, we are continually driven back to the Scriptures to answer that question. The meaning of the truth ultimately is determined by the inscripturated Word of God.

But we all live existentially with peculiar experiences, problems and needs. And so that truth with many and varied facets is applied to our own lives in a meaningful way, guided by the Holy Spirit through our cultural context. Our cultural eyes can only see Scripture clearly through the illumination of the Holy Spirit.

There is great need to communicate Jesus Christ to the African in such a way that we are both true to the Scriptures and meaningful to the African. Every believer must be made to feel at home with his Christian faith. This will necessitate a considerable measure of assimilation of traditional African culture into the expression of the Christian faith. Wherever an African tradition can be purified and retained for the glory of God, this should be done in African Christianity so that the Christian faith will have genuine marks of African indigeneity.

UNIVERSAL TRUTH OF THE GOSPEL

As evangelicals we believe in the relevancy of Jesus Christ and his Gospel for all peoples. God is the Creator of all men and women. We were all made in the image of God. We are all sons and daughters of Adam and Eve. And through Adam we have all fallen into sin. Our basic natures and needs are all the same. The Gospel by its very nature is relevant for all people.

The initial reaction of people who visit other cultures is shock over the differences. How different we behave. How different we live. And how frustratingly different are our values. These differences are the stuff of anthropology and the reason missionaries need training in cross cultural ministry.

But emphasis on differences can be overdone, even though I still admit to occasional frustration over the problems of communication that arise in ministry among peoples of a different culture. The facts are that people as human beings are very much the same. We have the same physical, social, psychological and spiritual needs. And we have the same potential for growth and development. We all need the Good News concerning Jesus Christ, the Saviour of the world, as taught in the Bible.

God created man and woman in His own image for his own glory to have a loving relationship of fellowship (Ge 1:26-28). Adam and Eve were created to glorify God with their minds, will and emotions. Fellowship with God is potentially possible.

Because of sin God has communicated his love and message of redemption through the Old Testament prophets and in these last days God has spoken through His Son, Jesus Christ (Heb 1:1). The Bible is God's inspired revelation of this Good News of salvation. And this divine revelation is intended for everyone.

The Gospel of Jesus Christ, as revealed in the Holy Scriptures, belongs to every person in every culture under the sun.

On the one hand, when Jesus Christ became man, He became a particular man in a particular culture. In this sense, Jesus is a foreigner to most peoples – a Jew from a tiny Middle Eastern country, born 2,000 years ago.

On the other hand, the locality of Jesus' birth and ministry is symbolic of the great truth that He belongs to every race, culture and language.

Palestine, the place of Jesus' birth and ministry, is on a land bridge connecting the three continents where all the ancient civilizations were located. Jesus was not born in Europe. Paul, the missionary, carried the Gospel to Greece and Rome from its home base in Antioch. Lydia became the first European Christian on Paul's second missionary journey (Ac 16:14). Jesus was not born in Asia. He was born in the Middle East. Nor was Jesus an African, though his home was so close to Africa that he found refuge with Mary and Joseph in Egypt when Herod the Great, the king of the Jews, sought to kill Jesus (Mt 2: 13ff).

In the providence of God the very place of Jesus' birth and ministry is parabolic of the fact that Jesus Christ and His Gospel belongs to the whole human race. Nor is there one race, nation or language which is closer to His heart of love than any other.

By the grace of God he has established one Holy Catholic Church built upon Christ Jesus the cornerstone. Everyone who is saved by grace through faith in Jesus Christ is a member of Christ's Church which is his Body (Eph 2:1-22). The word, "catholic," simply means "universal." The true Church is not identified with any visible organization in this world. Wherever men and women place their faith in Jesus Christ to save them from their sins, they have become members of the one Holy Catholic Church which is found throughout the world today. Those who were once strangers to one another, even traditional enemies, have become united in One Body with Jesus Christ as the Head (Eph 4:4-6).

As men and women, born by the Spirit of God (Jn 3:3-8), we are united in "one faith" (Eph 4:5). God has given to all believers the One Holy Spirit (Jn 14:25-26; 15:26-27; 16:12-14). And He has given to His Church various gifts, including pastors and teachers, to equip the saints so that we might grow up in the Body of Christ, "until we all attain to the unity of the faith" (Eph 4:7-13).

The emphasis in Scriptures is on the "unity of faith." God has one Gospel centring in One Saviour to be communicated to all peoples. The Bible, though written in different cultures by many men, from the Patriarch Moses to the Apostle John, spanning nearly 1,400 years, is yet marked by complete unity due to the superintending work of the Holy Spirit. "No prophecy was ever made by an act of human will, but men moved by the Holy Spirit spoke from God" (2 Pe 1:21). Thus the Bible contains all that God has wanted to communicate to mankind, and only what He wants to communicate.

We might compare the great diversity of human cultures with the bewildering array of Christian denominations. Beneath the amazing differences among people and their cultures, there is a unity. This unity is found within the people themselves who are more alike than their cultures because we all have one father and mother.

The Bible does not speak of a multitude of denominations, but it does speak of One Body of Christ. The Bible does not make distinctions between differing denominations, but it does distinguish between those who are saved and those who are not; between those who are dead in trespasses and sins and those who have been raised to a new life in Christ; between those who are children of God through faith in Christ and those who are children of the devil because of unbelief.

Born again believers are more alike throughout the world than their bewildering array of denominations might suggest because God is their Father by the Holy Spirit and Jesus Christ is their One Lord. Thus when we go beneath the wide range of Christian beliefs and practices found in the various denominations and learn to know the professing Christians themselves, we soon discover whether they know Jesus Christ personally or not. Those who truly know God through a personal faith in Christ are knit together with ourselves despite the denominational differences. We love the Lord Jesus Christ together, we pray together, and we witness together before others of our one faith in Christ, confident that Christ can change their lives even as He has done ours. We are one in Christ.

God's purpose for us as brothers and sisters in Christ is to study the Scriptures together to know his will for our lives. Herein is the shame of our divisions. Instead of sharing together in prayer and Bible study, we separate ourselves into contending groups, arguing and contending with each other. What we ought to do as brothers and sisters who disagree with our understanding of some biblical teaching is to seek God's will through mutual study of the Bible and in mutual love and respect.

God has given us His revelation in the Bible. Since God is the Author (2 Ti 3:16, 17), there is unity throughout the Scriptures, from Genesis to Revelation. Though different perspectives are found, reflecting different cultural backgrounds and personal experiences of the human authors, there is ultimate unity because the Holy Spirit is the One Divine Author.

We conclude, then, that God is One and that He has given the one Gospel to all men. As members of the One Body of Jesus Christ we earnestly seek God's will from His divine revelation, the Bible. In Scripture we find universal truth intended for all of God's people. Our responsibility is to develop and grow in our understanding, having our minds continually renewed by the Holy Spirit through the study of the Bible.

LOCAL CONTEXT OF THE GOSPEL

We have briefly sketched the universality of the Gospel and its relevance for all peoples. Our main concern, however, is to demonstrate that we need to apply and relate that Gospel to each context where people embrace Christ as Lord and Saviour. Each society understands the Word of God through their coloured glasses of a particular culture and historical context.

In the past, cross-cultural missionaries had sought to relate the teaching of the Bible to the local cultures. This was known as "indigenization." The word, "indigenous," is derived from Latin and means, "to bear or produce within." The intended idea was that Christianity must become "native," that is, "born, growing or produced within." Until Christianity is planted indigenously, until the Christian Church takes on the colouring of a given culture, Christianity remains foreign.

Missionary theory in the past generations included the idea of planting indigenous churches. This was summarized by the three-self formula: self-governing, self-propagating and self-supporting. The goal of the missionary endeavour was to plant churches which could multiply themselves within their own culture without the need for dependence upon foreign finance or personnel. Indigenization also included the utilization of traditional culture for the communication of the Gospel. The intention of this teaching on indigenization was autonomy and self-reliance of churches in every given culture instead of dependence upon the missionary sending churches.

The term, "contextualization," has come into popular use in the 1970s, supplanting the traditional use of the word, "indigenization." Shoki Coe and Aharon Sapsezian, directors of the "Theological Education Fund" (TEF), first used the word in 1972 with the publication of TEF's Third Mandate, entitled, *Ministry in Context*. Simply stated, contextualization is "the capacity to respond meaningfully to the Gospel within the framework of one's situation" (Coe 1972).

As presented by Shoki Coe and the Theological Education Fund Third Mandate, contextualization is not something radically different. It embraces everything which was meant by indigenization. Yet it is concerned with changing societies in the modern 20th century so that the Gospel is made relevant to modern day issues of justice, liberation, non-Christian religions, and economic power. Thus contextualization is concerned with the dynamic, changing context of present day culture, and not merely with an imagined static, traditional culture.

Because of the liberal theological perspective of many scholars who advocated contextualization, various evangelicals tried to avoid the use of the term. James Buswell rightly contended that "indigenization" is perfectly capable of bearing this enlarged meaning (Buswell 1978a: 17). After Bruce Fleming traced the historical development of contextualization with all "the implied theology," he advocated another expression, "context-indigenizing" (Fleming 1980).

Words can mean whatever we intend them to mean. Furthermore, the original definition given to contextualization by Shoki Coe and the TEF is perfectly acceptable to evangelicals: "the capacity of responding meaningfully to the Gospel within the framework of one's own situation." Therefore, we shall speak of contextualization with that definition in mind and with an implied evangelical theology.

As evangelicals we accept the Truth of God's revelation in the Bible. That Truth is of universal relevance. Wherever God communicates that Truth, peoples in their various cultures are compelled to make a decision: either believe and obey and thereby be born into the family of God, or reject and disobey and thereby remain under the judgement of God.

We also recognize that divine revelation becomes meaningful in different ways to different peoples under different situations. As a child I grew up in a sheltered Christian atmosphere. Having been saved at the tender age of five and having been preserved from gross sin by God's grace, I never really had a moving experience of conversion from sin. In my own experience the truth of God which bore deeply into my soul was the providential grace of God in calling me to his service and leading me step by step into ministry in Africa.

I can recall vividly over the years a certain measure of distress that the redemption of Christ from sin was not as meaningful to me as it ought to have been, so it seemed to me. God's presence was real. His sovereign control over my life was beyond dispute. With profound awareness I knew that God had separated me from my mother's womb to be his child and to serve him in Africa. There was no doubt. As a teenager I was reading the Scriptures and came across the words of the prophet, Isaiah. "The Spirit of the Lord God is upon me, because the Lord has anointed me to bring good news to the afflicted ..." (Isa 61:1). Never before had I seen that verse, but it expressed exactly what my experience had been. I knew that the Spirit of God was upon me and anointing me to preach the Good News. Consequently, I wrote in my Bible, "my life's verse." And so it has been ever since.

It was not until years later that God began to work in my own life, disclosing the utter sinfulness of my own heart before Him. These were not public sins, known and seen by all. But they were horrible sins before a holy God. Only as an adult believer, years after my new birth, did I become more and more conscious of the grace of Jesus Christ in my own life. Years after God had profoundly disclosed Himself as my Lord did He begin to reveal Himself as the gracious Saviour whose death on the cross was essential for my salvation.

Theologically, one might insist that the order should have been reversed. Should not I have been gripped by the grace of God in my salvation before moving on to a deeper understanding of God's will for my life? Logically, that may be true. But God is not restricted by our logic. He meets us where we are. He speaks to us where we currently need Him.

Contextualization is "the capacity to respond meaningfully to the Gospel within the framework of one's own situation ..." Not only is the Gospel true, it has profound meaning to us. And various parts of the Word of God have special meaning to different people in differing contexts.

Both truth and a meaningful application of God's Word are essential. "*All* Scripture is inspired by God and profitable..." (2 Ti 3: 16). The unbalanced emphasis of one Scripture while ignoring another counterbalancing truth is usually the cause for the distortion of the truth. Therefore, as Christians we are obligated to return again and again to Scripture to learn from God *all* that He has said to us, for all of it is profitable.

In our finite existence we are incapable of understanding and appropriating all of the truth of Scripture at once. We must learn line upon line, precept upon precept. And God usually speaks to us where we are – in our given historical and cultural context. Scripture becomes meaningful to us as the truth of God's Word interfaces with our own experiences. A child in first grade is hardly interested in those experiences of a university student. A man in Brazil is seldom interested in the experiences of a woman in Egypt. In like manner God has a meaningful word to speak to each child of God in his own given context. And that word is meaningful, not only because it is God's Word, but because of the context in which he finds himself.

HISTORICAL NEED FOR AFRICAN THEOLOGY

There is real need today for the Body of Christ in Africa, which is the Church of Jesus Christ, to think through various cultural questions in the light of God's Word. All believers everywhere struggle with problems which need resolution through theological reflection on the Scriptures. The problems we face in Africa are unique, owing to the unique circumstances in which we find ourselves. By the grace of God and through the course of time a growing number of mature, educated African believers are being produced in the churches who are able to study the Scriptures academically in the light of their context. They are able in consultation with all believers to arrive at a consensus as to what God is saying to His people in this particular context – how this text applies to them.

What a contrast to years gone by when theological beliefs were taught primarily by missionaries. Theological reflection was done by national believers along with the missionaries. But the colonial context did not provide that encouragement to allow the Christian nationals to study God's revelation for themselves. Whatever involvement there was by the African believers, and they were definitely involved, the final decisions of what Scripture taught on certain issues were usually made under firm missionary influence.

A few examples may help us to understand the African Christian historical background and point the way to our present urgent need for theological reflection by evangelical African believers.

United Missionary Approach

In Kenya the four main Protestant missions, which pioneered Christian witness from the beginning, were the Church Missionary Society, Church of Scotland Mission, the Africa Inland Mission and the United Methodist Mission. Though they came from different national and denominational backgrounds, they were united in their evangelical faith. Between 1909 and 1932 five Missionary Conferences were held, dealing with issues of mutual interest such as comity, mutual relations of the missions and the establishment of a United African Church. In the 1909 United Missionary Conference, Archdeacon Willis of the C.M.S. read a paper entitled, "The Desirability of a Single Native Church in British East Africa" (Cole 1957).

By the time of the United Missionary Conference was held at Kikuyu in 1913, there was a growing consensus that the Christian witness in British East Africa should be a united witness. Charles Hurlburt, Director of the A. I. M., had gone on record that the A.I.M. believed that "the church of the future should be on Church of England lines" (Cope 1979: 100).

Arising out of the Kikuyu conference of 1913, a Continuation Committee drew up proposals for an Alliance of Missionary Societies in British East African Protectorate. Their ultimate goal was a "United African Church within the Protectorate" for the purpose of presenting a visible unity among the Christians (C.C.K.C. 1918).

Because such a Church Union was thought to be premature at that moment, an Alliance of Mission Societies was formed in order to prepare the way for an eventual United African Church. Therefore, the Church Missionary Society, the Church of Scotland Mission, the Africa Inland Mission and the Methodists agreed to do everything possible to prepare for this eventual union. They developed the local church organizations along similar lines, sought to establish similar standards of discipline among the church members, respected the status of every Christian assigned to him by the branch of the Church of Christ to which he belonged, and sought to prepare the believers for eventual union (C.C.K.C. 1918).

The United African Church never was achieved. The first obstacle was the objection of the Anglo Catholics within the Anglican Church over the issue of apostolic succession of the priesthood (Cole 1957: 5). The concluding problem was the development of liberalism within several of the missions which alienated the A.I.M. from such a merger (A.M.S. 1922). Nevertheless, for many years there was consultation and agreement among the Protestant Missions as to their approach to various cultural problems faced by them.

This attempt to form a united Christian Church in Kenya by evangelicals played an important part in the united stand of the Protestant missions toward questions of African culture. Because these missionaries were all evangelical in their theology and because they were working together to present the Gospel with singular appeal, these missionaries tried to approach questions of African culture with one accord.

Participation of Nationals

To suggest that the missionaries made their conclusions by themselves without consultation with the African believers is to distort the historical facts. From the beginning there was in fact discussion and consultation between the expatriate missionaries and the national believers.

An example can be given from the Church of Scotland Mission. While the C.M.S. tolerated drinking of alcoholic beverages, the C.S.M. and A.I.M. advocated total abstinence. John W. Arthur, missionary leader of the Church of Scotland Mission, reported that both the missionaries and their Gikuyu Christians, advocated total abstinence. After a two-year experiment in which Africans were prevented from entering into the catechumenate if they refused to take a vow of total abstinence from alcoholic liquor, the young male Gikuyu Christians pressed Arthur to call a meeting to thrash out the question.

> *At our Church meeting on Saturday, the question was raised and fought out. It was entirely a native* shauri *and a straight fight between the young men, who were all on, not on only not to drink, but to forbid it in the buying of their girls etc., and two or three of the older Christians who made the opposition...*
>
> *In the end, there were two plain issues: - (1) that drinking or tasting of beer by Christians be prohibited. Only two or three of the older ones admitted to still taking it. The motion carried with only one discontent, 55 full Church members voting for it; (2) that beer in payment of buying a girl, or for work done, should also be prohibited (Arthur n.d.).*

One of the older Christians stated in the meeting that if the missionaries had ordered prohibition, he would have refused to obey. But since the "Native Church" desired it, he was willing to agree.

In another Conference of Kikuyu Church Elders, May 8-12, 1929, they all agreed that beer was evil and should be forbidden in all churches, and made a matter of discipline (C.K.E. 1929).

Not only were African believers given a decisive voice in many decisions of church practice, they themselves were the ones who frequently decided to give up many of the African customs. Various missionaries themselves contend that they did not force African believers to surrender their cultural practices, but that this was the choice of African Christians.

Linnell Davis, a missionary with the Africa Inland Mission and born in Kenya of missionary parents near the turn of the century, interviewed various older Christians and asked them why they took a particular approach to the Kamba cultural traditions. "Did the missionaries put this in your mind?" he asked them.

In almost every case they said that the more they studied the Scriptures, they came to their own conclusion.

In fact, the A.I.M missionaries in Ukambani had made the decision that any ruling about customs should be left up to the mature African Christians. They felt that the people had to decide for themselves. The fact that the African Christians had made the decision regarding their customs, ensured that the decision would be long lasting. No missionary could impose his will on the people with lasting results (Davis 1982: P.I).

The caricature of the older missionary these days is that of one who robbed the African of his culture and imposed the European culture on him. Mrs. Guilding, an A.I.M. missionary among the Kamba during the early part of the century, contends that the A.I.M. in Ukambani did not place pressure on the Africans to change their own culture. The missionaries felt their own responsibility was to teach the Bible, but not to force change.

For instance, the A.I.M missionaries in Ukambani never legislated against female circumcision (Guilding n.d.: T.I.). Martha Davis, wife of Linnell Davis and long-time missionary among the Kamba, affirmed that this is what she always had heard from the older missionaries. While the missionaries felt a responsibility to teach the Bible and advise, they placed no pressure on the African to change (Davis 1982: P.I.).

In fact an example can be given of missionaries forbidding the Africans to adopt European ways. Many early A.I.M. missionaries in Ukambani discouraged the wearing of European clothes, parting of hair and learning of English. They stressed the Kikamba Bible. Linnell Davis remembers a time when an African came into the church with shoes on and for this reason C.F. Johnston sent him out of the church (Davis 1982: P.I.). While this undoubtedly is an example of paternalism, it does reflect the desire of the missionaries not to encourage or even tolerate European enculturation.

The Kamba in fact resented Johnston's approach to European clothes and the learning of English. A case can be made for the belief that the Africans desired to emulate the missionary in his dress, behaviour and life style. When Mrs. Elwood Davis, mother of Linnell Davis, arrived in Machakos in 1911, she sensed the African resentment and therefore, began helping the women to sew their own dresses. She became renowned in Ukambani and greatly appreciated for this (Davis 1982: P.I.).

Eric Barnett, another A.I.M second generation missionary, maintains that in his experience the missionaries did not seek to change anything in the African culture except that which African Christians themselves said was evil. Nothing was said of dress or the food they ate. The Africans chose to wear the European clothes. Charms used to ward off evil spirits were removed. But almost always it was the African who forbad it (Barnett 1982: P.I).

Linnell Davis insists that it was the African who took the strict stand against polygamy. Some missionaries were more lenient. "In my knowledge," says Rev. Davis, "African church leaders tried to arrange for the men to give up all their wives except their first one, but only in a suitable way, so that the wives had houses provided for them and with an income to support them, or through marrying another man" (Davis 1982: P.I.).

Jean Baxter who arrived at Kapsabet among the Nandi as an A.I.M. missionary in 1936 speaks of the advice given her by Stuart Bryson, the senior A.I.M. missionary. "Speak not one word about Nandi customs," he said. "The Holy Spirit will do the correcting of the custom" (Baxter 1982: P. I.). Bryson advised her never to speak against female circumcision. And she does not recall missionaries speaking on the subject during those early days. Nor does she remember missionaries speaking against male circumcision.

These examples could be multiplied in greater number than this small book could contain. The fact is that in many places and under many circumstances the African believers did participate in the decisions made by the early Christian Church regarding African culture. A report on the Christian approach to the *kithitu* in Ukambani is a vivid demonstration that the church elders in fact did play a key role in deciding what should be done about some of the African traditions. Harmon Nixon, an A.I.M. missionary among the Akamba, gave this report to Ralph Davis, the A.I.M. leader in the States. The full presentation of the letter gives a balanced perspective on the subject.

> *The* kithitu *is a charm made from the horn of an antelope over which the Akamba take oaths in law courts. Up until very recently the local Government at Machakos would not allow Christians to take oaths on the Bible in civil law suits. To discerning Christians of which there is an ever-growing number, 'an idol is nothing in the world.' They laugh at people fearing a horn filled with trash. In civil law suits the crafty heathen have often defeated the unfortunate Christians who by ecclesiastical ruling were formerly prevented from swearing on the* kithitu. *Failure to swear on the* kithitu *is to the heathen tribunal elders 'prima facie' evidence of guilt. The Ukambani Regional Council ruled that Christians in Machakos District who had been sued at law by pagans could take an oath on the* kithitu.
>
> *In Kitui District the* kithitu *has much more sinister meaning than it does here (Machakos). Those taking the oath in Kitui must remove their clothes while taking the oath. Most Christians in Kitui still have a certain amount of faith in evil spirits and witchcraft. For a Christian in Kitui, to take an oath on a* kithitu *would be to defile his conscience. Furthermore, in Kitui, Christians can take oaths on the Bible which was not permitted in this district till after the above ruling was passed. I may say that the rule of the Regional Council applied to Machakos District only. Our oldest and most spiritual men unanimously supported it.*
>
> *Scripturally, I think it is better 'to swear not at all,' but for a Mukamba to lose a law suit just because of not being allowed to take an oath is unthinkable. Now that our Machakos people can swear on the Bible the* kithitu *need not 'be eaten'* (Nixon 1940).

This letter demonstrates that the African Christian elders participated in the decision making process. It demonstrates that the decisions regarding *kithitu* differed in Kitui and Machakos, showing that uniformity was not required by the missionaries. The different decisions arose in part from different circumstances and different perspectives of the Christians. Harmon Nixon reflects a sympathetic understanding of the African Christian's plight and an openness to various possible approaches.

Colonial Context

On the one hand, historical investigation demonstrates that African Christians from the beginning of the Church in Africa participated in many of the decisions regarding the biblical approach to their African culture. Furthermore, many missionaries did in fact value various aspects of African culture. Thus we affirm that the perspectives of such African scholars as Muga (Muga 1975: 100) and missionary scholars such as Cope (Cope 1979: 27) are not balanced. We cannot simply state that older missionaries considered African culture, religion and customs to be all of the devil. That is a stereotype and not factual.

On the other hand, this book would not be balanced if we concluded our discussion at this point. We must note that generalizations about missionaries and their approach to Africans and African culture are as dangerous as generalizations are in general. We must remember that missionaries differed greatly among themselves.

Take the question of clothes. We have seen that some missionaries tried to prevent Africans from adopting European clothes. Still other missionaries participated in the call for Africans to change their apparel. The A.I.M. missionaries among the Nandi are a case in point. The traditional dress was goat skins and beads. The missionaries encouraged the Nandi to remove the beads since they were dirty and filled with lice. Since the beads went up to the elbows and neck, it was not possible to wash the body with them on. Likewise, the goat skins were smelly, having been rubbed with fat. When Nandi women came to church with their traditional dress, the other African Christian ladies would move away from them because of their smelly skin coverings. The removal of such traditional garb was not mandatory but encouraged by the earlier missionaries. Later missionaries were more reticent in advising the Nandi to remove the skins and beads. But change did come (Baxter 1982: P.I).

Moreover, we cannot escape the whole colonial context in which the Gospel was first preached and the church planted here in Africa. Missionaries who came from the West had enjoyed many of the conveniences and advances in human knowledge which were not known in Africa. Missionaries had not been trained in cross cultural understanding of other peoples. Their reaction to African culture was therefore, in many ways, negative. That was part of the whole worldview of the westerner during the colonial era.

Apart from the culturally sensitized person today, our reaction is no different from theirs. African missionaries serving among "primitive" peoples today, who are naked and living with far fewer conveniences than back home, speak freely of their backwardness. Regrettably, there was an air of superiority among many missionaries who readily assumed the superiority of their own western culture and the inferiority of the African culture. Without the benefits of cross cultural studies preparing them for missionary service, they frequently failed to understand and appreciate the "strange" features of the culture.

It is doubtful whether we should presume today that we would have responded differently than did those early missionaries. The whole context from which they came and into which they were plunged lent itself toward an air of superiority. Elspeth Huxley describes the Kenya scene at the turn of the century.

> *By European standards Kenya in 1900 was 'wholly primitive.' Its scattered peoples, grouped into separate and mutually hostile tribes, were pagan, frequently nomadic, ignorant of the outside world and of such simple devices as plough, the wheel, the pump, the loom, the coin; they had evolved no alphabet, built no cities, made no roads; their tool was the digging stick, their dress the skin, their weapon the spear* (Huxley 1970: I, v).

Cagnolo, a Roman Catholic missionary to the Gikuyu, expressed "pity for those poor slaves of ignorance." He then declared, "It is an obligation upon us civilized peoples to put these phantasms to flight..." (Cagnolo 1930: 189). While Europeans have grown in their own understanding of the dark spots in their own western culture and gained new appreciation for the values of African traditional culture, the earlier missionaries did not enjoy these advantages. They were children of their age, even as we are today. As Huxley reminds us, almost every European held to the same belief.

"Civilization was good, barbarism was bad; Europeans were civilized, Africans were not; ergo, the European incursion that carried with it Christianity, literacy and the PAX BRITANNICA and an end to famines and epidemics could be nothing but a boon to Africans. It was as simple as that" (Huxley 1970: I, v). Only in this context can we understand the attitude and behaviour of those early missionaries. One can find all too many examples of crude superiority expressed in a variety of ways.

And so we can say that although the African believers often did play a significant role in various decisions regarding African traditional customs, all too often the missionaries were first among equals in the decision making process. Moreover, all too often critical questions with regard to African customs were imposed on the Africans instead of allowing the Holy Spirit over the course of time to develop a consensus among the believers.

We have previously seen that the Protestant Missions in Kenya were evangelical and sought to cooperate together on many policy decisions pertaining to African culture. We can find among those missions unfortunate examples of missionaries imposing their theological understanding on the African believers.

Example of Female Circumcision

One tragic example is that of female circumcision. All the Alliance Missions (C.M.S., C.S.M., A.I.M. and Methodist), without dissent, ruled that anyone who underwent female circumcision, or any Christian parent who consented to or assisted in the circumcision of the daughter would be disciplined. They all required that Christians before baptism take a vow against female circumcision (K.M.C. 1930). Female circumcision was frequently referred to as "sexual mutilation of girls." The missionary medical doctors were foremost in their opposition to this traditional practice. This consensus of missionary thinking against clitoridectomy was based on medical grounds, not moral. Because of the physical mutilation, the suffering and mental anguish imposed on the girls, female circumcision was opposed.

The Alliance was not alone. The Kenya Missionary Council, composed of all Protestant Missions working in Kenya, went on record that their conviction was that "it is the duty of the Christian Church to impress upon all its members and adherents that the sexual mutilation of girls or women is contrary to the teachings of Christ" (K.M.C. 1930).

The typed pamphlet in English and Kikuyu prepared for the Alliance of Missionary Societies by Dr. Philip of the Church of Scotland Mission on the subject of female circumcision was also submitted to the Kenya Missionary Council. In 1927 the K.M.C. agreed to print the pamphlet, "preferably by the Africa Inland Mission, Kijabe, for distribution throughout Kikuyu Reserve" (K.M.C. 1927).

Prohibition against female circumcision was enforced first of all through church membership requirements. Before baptism the Church of Scotland Mission asked the candidates nine questions, including this one:

> *Do you resolve anew to reject Satan and all his work, with all evil lusts; and that you will eschew all things not agreeable to the Word of God, such as things pertaining to departed spirits, witchcraft, divination, sexual immorality, intoxicating liquor, evil songs and female circumcision?* (C.S. 1926).

Once a person became a member of the church, he or she could be disciplined by either submitting to female circumcision as a girl or by permitting female circumcision as responsible adults. This was true both in the Africa Inland Mission and the Church of Scotland Mission (Barlow 1925).

Further pressure was brought to bear on the peoples by prohibiting female circumcision among girls registered in mission schools. This became a critical problem among the Gikuyu who first saw much of their good land taken by the colonialists. Later their traditional customs were threatened by preventing girls from attending mission schools if they underwent female circumcision.

To enforce this stand the A.I.M. drew up a document which all evangelists, teachers and other church and school leaders among the Gikuyu were required to sign. The A.I.M. was prepared to sacrifice a large portion of her membership in order "to purify and strengthen the church." Eventually, all the A.I.M. Gikuyu Christians were compelled to sign the loyalty pledge or be expelled from the church (Sandgren 1976:182).

The result of this united mission policy together with all the other grave problems related to land was the development of a crisis within Kenya during the 1920's. The A.I.M called for a special conference at Kijabe in October 1920 with no pre-arranged agenda and no closing date. The missionaries were to give themselves to prayer for revival until satisfied that God had heard their prayers. Included in the trouble that concerned the missionaries was "the Thuku Movement which for a time threatened to sweep the whole missionary movement in Kenya off its feet..." (Stauffacher 1927). Letters by the missionaries reflect the tension of those days. "These are critical days in Kenya," wrote Hulda Stumpf. "Lawlessness, insubordination, rebellion, disobedience and every other modifying term of sin in the catalogue among the people" (Stumpf 1927).

While the various Protestant missions took a uniform and steadily tougher line against female circumcision, various individual missionaries were uncertain about the approach they should take. John Stauffacher, an A.I.M. missionary among the Maasai, wrote this:

> *My opinion about female circumcision ... The whole of Kenya is stirred up, as it has now gone from the Church to the Government, an attempt having been made largely by the missionaries to make a civil law prohibiting it throughout the Colony. There is no question in my mind as to whether or not it should be stopped. It is a brutal custom ... but the question that is puzzling some of us is how to stop it. Some of the churches are expelling members wholesale, so that where there was a large congregation only four or five members remain. The Scottish Mission are I believe even demanding a thumb print signifying*

> *their opposition to female circumcision, or expulsion from the church. Kijabe I understand is taking the same stand, and I am told that we will soon be required to do the same, in which case as matters stand we will have no church at all. I agree that no one should be received into the Church who is in favour of it, and also that no one should be allowed to remain who had any part in it, but that men and women who have been in the Church for so many years, some as much as twenty, and all that time in good standing, and now suddenly should be told they must change their minds or get out, I can't quite make up my mind as to whether that is right or not. I feel that it is a bit too pre-mature, for to use a very poor argument these very men and women know that in some European congregations there are members who commit adultery, and no finger print is required of them. Of course what is wrong is wrong, but the fact that it has been allowed through a long period of years, seems to me requires care, lest we drive the mature Christians wholly away from us, at any rate let us begin first with the Europeans, for as some natives told me a few days ago, that if the white men will promise not to take their women for immoral purposes they will promise to stop circumcision, in fact many are using the argument that that is the very reason why the white men are demanding it, not very much of a compliment to the white race ...* (Stauffacher 1929).

Hulda Stumpf from Kijabe referred to a Joshua Mucai who along with others "was prohibited from teaching and was excommunicated FOREVER [emphasis original], the sentence read, unless he was willing to confess his wrong and swear allegiance to the white man and his rulings. The confession was sorrow for allowing his daughter to be circumcised" (Stumpf 1927). She observed that the teaching why some customs are to be avoided and others utilized while others should be purified has "to be done in LOVE [emphasis original], and not be legislation."

Indeed, this seems to have become the problem. The church in her sphere and the government in theirs used legislation to enforce the prohibition of female circumcision. Dr. Arthur of the Church of Scotland Mission resigned from the Executive Committee of the Legislative Council because they could not agree with him. John Stauffacher expressed concern that the Africans may believe "we missionaries are the law makers of the country" and that we are "responsible for laws which compel them against their will" (Stauffacher 1929).

For the A.I.M., the female circumcision controversy reached a crisis when Hulda Stumpf, 64 years old, was suffocated and forcibly circumcised in her own house at Kijabe on January 2, 1930, according to a post mortem report (KFCM 1930), though an AIM medical doctor who examined her body concluded that she had not been raped (Blakeslee 1956: 192). The irony of this tragedy is that Hulda Stumpf is the one who on several occasions raised doubts whether the mission policy concerning female circumcision was correct.

It is true of course that some African Christians also opposed clitoridectomy, though not without dissent. At the Conference of Kikuyu Church Elders in 1929 they agreed with one dissenting voice, that female circumcision is evil and should be abandoned by all Christians. They also agreed by a large majority that everyone submitting to the rite or requiring to submit to it, would be suspended from churches everywhere. Nine Kikuyu elders disagreed with this last resolution, advising the churches to go more slowly in this problem (C.K.E. 1929).

But this advice by the minority of Kikuyu church elders to move more slowly on the question was not followed. Instead, the decisions made to prohibit female circumcision were enforced. The A.I.M. Conference made the ruling that "all Church members and Catechumens who would not publicly declare themselves opposed to female circumcision, cut of [sic] their relation to Church and Class." When Stauffacher returned to Narok with this mission decision which needed implementation, he returned "with fear and trembling." He informed the Maasai Christians of this decision.

> *Imagine the horror that came over me when only two boys stood by us, and the rest in a mass withdrew, threating [sic] to take possession of the church, and organize to suit themselves, calling us false teachers, and that they alone stood for the truth. You at home who cannot see the defiant look on their faces, cannot possibly realize what this means to us, when men whose sincerity has never been doubted, and who have prayed and worked with us some of them more than twenty years, suddenly without warning turn and become our deadliest enemies* (Stauffacher 1930a).

> John Stauffacher lamented, ... *and I cannot help but feel sometimes that somewhere we have made a tremendous mistake, when it becomes necessary for us to force Christians (and I believe most of them are Christians) who have only so recently come out of the rankest heathenism. I don't see now how we can do differently, but I doubt if we should have done much harm if we had agreed that since female circumcision must go, we would be patient and work and pray against it, rather than that we should make a rule that severs them from church membership. I am afraid hundreds of them will never return* (Stauffacher 1930b).

While he states that the decision against female circumcision was "unanimous among all missionaries of all Societies," he declares, "I can't help but admit that my heart goes out strongly sometimes to the natives, although I know from our viewpoint they are wholly wrong." This "huge mistake" has played "terrific havoc" in the Church so that "as far as the human eye can see now our work here is a complete wreck" (Stauffacher 1930c).

The result was a massive exodus from all the Gikuyu churches and schools with only a handful of loyalists remaining. Githumu and Kijabe "were reduced to two or three loyal families each" (Sandgren 1976:237). Only a handful of children attended school. Only a few dozen Gikuyu families remained faithful to the A.I.M. in the early months of 1930, compared to 500 Gikuyu members in 1926. When 95% of the Gikuyu A.I.M. Christians had boycotted the church for the year 1930, attempts were made to rescind earlier decisions by allowing students to return to school without signing a pledge against female circumcision. But very few returned.

A cleavage had occurred within the mission founded churches, between the *kirore* (the older converts prior to World War I who had extended contact with the missionaries on the mission stations) and the *athome* (the Christians on the out-stations who became more closely identified with the Gikuyu in their concerns over European intrusion into Gikuyu land and customs). And this cleavage remained with permanent results.

The colonial policy regarding the land thus became the initial problem which led to agitation against colonial rule. But the mission policy regarding schools, used to enforce repudiation of female circumcision, became the torch that lit the fires which eventually led to the ouster of British rule and a massive exodus of Christians from mission founded schools.

Since missions were the exclusive administrators of schools among the Gikuyu, the people had nowhere to turn but to establish their own schools. The founding of independent schools went hand in hand with the founding of independent churches, all closely linked with the Kikuyu Central Association which advocated "no intervention of the white missionaries" (Leakey 1952: 91). The Gikuyu Independent Churches were a by-product of the independent schools, since schools and churches were inseparable (Murray Brown 1972: 141).

From our perspective today this mission policy regarding female circumcision was a tragic mistake. Instead of "purifying" the church, the churches were emptied. Instead of strengthening the Christians, they were weakened. For instead of attending churches where the Word of God was fully taught, they became adherents of the African independent churches. In the place of the mission churches and schools, the African Independent Pentecostal Church in Africa was formed in 1925 with their independent schools, and the African Orthodox Church was established in 1928 with their independent schools.

From the viewpoint of evangelicals who know these independent churches from within, there is a grave lack of spiritual vitality and a lack of faithfulness to the Word of God among these churches. Politics plays an important role in the life of these churches and we frequently read of clashes between parties within the churches, necessitating government intervention and supervision of the elections. Yet a very large portion of Gikuyu who once belonged to the mission founded churches, together with their descendants, are now identified with these African Independent Churches. And ironically, while female circumcision is strongly advocated by the older members, the practice is rapidly declining.

As evangelicals we firmly believe that the Spirit of the Living God indwells every believer. Jesus Christ is the Lord of His Body which is the Church. While conversion brings about radical change through the lordship of Jesus Christ, growth in grace is a slow process which involves a life time of maturing.

Female circumcision is unlike murder or adultery, sins specifically and clearly forbidden by the Word of God. Seldom did the mission ever try to base their objection to female circumcision on religious reasons. Rather, it was the physical aspect which brought on the opposition, the pain and suffering of the girls, the mutilation of the body, together with the psychological effects. The decision to oppose female circumcision was made primarily by the missionaries without due consideration to the conscience of the believers and their understanding of the will of God for their lives.

It may appear to some that the issue of female circumcision belongs to antiquity. The practice is disappearing. The government of Kenya occasionally speaks out against the custom. During some extensive research of mine several years ago I was led to believe by various individuals that female circumcision is indeed an irrelevant issue today. But such is not the case. Female circumcision may not be publicly acknowledged by many. Perhaps the practice is not known by many or not readily acknowledged. But recently we have come across reports of hospitals and private medical offices in which girls seek the operation of clitoridectomy. And we have heard of girls who feel so deeply the need for clitoridectomy, perhaps induced by their boyfriends, that they seek to operate on themselves with horrible physical and emotional effects. The Christian Church in Africa today needs to address itself to this issue. What does God have to say to Christian believers who still feel a need for this traditional rite? The missionaries gave their verdict years ago. What word of God do evangelical African believers have for those in our midst who feel a continued need for this traditional rite?

Herein is a most important reason for African Theology today. Each generation of Christians must consider anew God's will for their lives in their own living context. For the African Church today, there is an ever-greater need since many of the practices and beliefs of the churches today were made in the colonial context.

Example of Polygamy

Another example of this need for African Theology is polygamy. As the missionaries presented the claims of Christ to the Africans, the inevitable question arose over polygamy. It is of interest that the first recorded statement on polygamy by the Africa Inland Mission in 1903 is virtually identical to the decision of all the independent churches which have broken off of the A.I.M. founded Church, the Africa Inland Church. In 1903, soon after Charles Hurlburt arrived in Kenya, the new Director of the A.I.M., he made the following observations when there was an initial influx of Gikuyu converts at Kijabe. Hurlburt wrote:

> *Many problems are arising needing peculiar guidance. One is the question of polygamy. Kikuvi, for instance, has several wives, all bought before he knew the things of God. He was willing to put them all away, but by our advice kept them, because to drive them away would be cruel injustice, and would force them to lives of shame and slavery. His retaining them has led all but one to a definite, public acceptance of Jesus as Saviour. If driven away they must have hated the Gospel and its teachings. A large majority of the mission feels that the only right basis is to insist that converts take no more wives, if young, and that they marry but one, but the wives shall not be put away unless they are willing to go and marry another man. We may change this basis in after years, but this is our present light. While we shall set a premium on monogamy by withholding official privileges from those who have more than one wife* (H & D, VII, 4, 1903: 19).

We are here informed that the Director of the A.I.M. and the majority of missionaries in 1903 believed that monogamy was the Christian norm. But that no polygamist who became a believer should be required to put away any of his wives. In fact, the Director of the A.I.M. refused the offer by Kikuvi who was willing to put away his wives if that was required.

Within ten years this all changed. The Continuation Committee of the Kikuyu Conference in 1913 recommended that no person living in polygamy shall have the Lord's Supper administered to him (C.C.K.C. 1918). This indeed became the standard of all those mission churches which dreamed of merging to form one united Christian Church in British East Africa.

The reasons for this change are not known, though we can speculate. Whereas Martin Luther and Melanthon held that monogamy was not obligatory under every circumstance, that whatever was permitted by the Law of Moses, remained lawful today, John Calvin disagreed. Calvin forbade polygamy, saying that the patriarchs were guilty of sin (Barrett 1968: 19).

Now as a matter of historical fact, there was a close comradeship between the A.I.M. missionaries and those of the Presbyterian, Church of Scotland Mission. Their mission headquarters were relatively close together. At times the A.I.M. invited C.S.M. missionaries to speak at the A.I.M. missionary conferences. Dr. Arthur of C.S.M., a powerful person, became a prominent voice within the Alliance of Missionary Societies. It may very well be that the strong convictions of John Arthur, heir of Calvinism in the Church of Scotland, and prominent in the Alliance of Missions, made a strong impact regarding polygamy.

Whatever the reason for the united stand by Kenyan missions against polygamy, a very significant development has occurred. The African Independent Churches which have broken from the Africa Inland Church all agree in their dissent with the A.I.M. on their approach to polygamy.

The contemporary view of African Independent Churches by many scholars is that they represent truly indigenous Christianity. It is said that the Christianity brought to Africa was a westernized form which the Independent Churches are now Africanising. For instance, Muga affirms that "in the past few decades the Africans have rejected the over-westernized form of Christianity and this rejection has manifested itself in the formation of African Independent church movements which have all along reinforced national political movements" (Muga 1975: Preface).

A study of those African Independent Churches which have broken from the Africa Inland Church reflect only some modest adjustments with regard to belief and practice. There are no independent churches which broke from the Kalenjin A.I.C., none from the Luo A.I.C., though David Barrett erroneously reported that in 1954 The Voice of Salvation and Healing Church broke off from the Africa Inland Mission (Barrett 1973:188, 189). Almost all of the churches which broke from the Africa Inland Church are among the Akamba, except for the African Christian Church and Schools which broke from the Gikuyu A.I.C. in 1947 over the issue of inadequate emphasis on schools by the A.I.M. These Kamba African Independent Churches are four in number: the African Brotherhood Church, Good News Church of Africa, Ebenezer Gospel Church and the African Church.

All these independent churches follow basically the same doctrinal beliefs as the Africa Inland Church. One who worships in any of these independent African churches sees little difference from the pattern of divine worship practised in the Africa Inland Church. Furthermore, they adhere to the same approach to African customs and culture as the mother church and mission. There is one exception – their approach to the problem of polygamy.

None of these African Independent Churches embrace polygamy as the Christian ideal. Nor do they allow any polygamist to hold church office. But they all agree without exception that a polygamist who is converted can be baptized and admitted to the Lord's Table without being compelled to give up all his wives except his first. The striking thing is that they all agree so completely on this issue, and that this approach is what was first advocated by the Africa Inland Mission in 1903.

Today the problem of polygamy continually surfaces in the various councils of the Africa Inland Church and among other mission churches. Here is a problem that has been inherited by today's believers from the founding fathers of the missions and churches. What would God have His people do today concerning polygamy?

Traditionalism is a very real evil. To continue following a belief or practice simply because our forefathers did it in the church is not biblical. Each generation of believers needs to examine its own faith in the light of what God has taught in the Word of God. Because of non-biblical traditions, entrenched in the Roman Catholic Church, the Reformers found it necessary to contend for the faith and suffer the consequences of excommunication. What is necessary today is for Christian believers to turn to the Scriptures, time and time again, to have their understanding of these problems reformed by the Word of God.

Hindsight is always better than foresight. We are ever guilty of a kind of "generational-centrism" in which we judge past generations by our own standards and insights. Even as ethnocentric people judge other cultures by their own standards, thinking their own ways are the best, so every generation tends to weigh and assess former generations by their own values and standard of enlightenment. There are many today who wish the missions and their churches in Africa had not followed their course of action against female circumcision. And many wish that their approach to polygamy had been a bit different, perhaps that which is represented by the African Independent Churches mentioned above. But the past is past and cannot be undone.

We are reminded of a Kikamba proverb which says, "You can rear a ram, then it butts you." Where would we be today if the earlier missionary pioneers had not come to Africa? We are the rams which they have reared. It is all too easy for us, their children, offspring who owe our lives to them, to turn around and be ungrateful to them, butting them until it hurts. We pluck out the speck from their eyes, forgetting that we ourselves are not without the beams in our own eyes. Jesus said, "Blessed are the merciful, for they shall obtain mercy." We all stand in need of mercy. We would do well to display mercy to our forefathers, grateful for the rich heritage we have received from them.

Nevertheless, the Christian Church that has been planted in Africa is not bound by the teachings and convictions of her forebears. We are bound instead to Jesus Christ and His Word found in the Bible. We are responsible to shape our lives according to the will of God as we understand it in the Bible. God has no grandchildren. Each generation must be born again by the Spirit. And God's children cannot eat the manna from a generation ago. We ourselves must feed daily on the Scriptures and seek to understand God's will for our lives.

For these reasons African Theology is a necessity today for a vital, healthy, growing, effective church.

CONCLUSION

We now may summarize the many and varied reasons why African Theology is a necessity today.

1. The Holy Spirit who indwells the whole Body of Christ worldwide has promised to guide His people into a knowledge of God's truth.

The process of reflecting upon God's revelation in the light of one's context and then communicating that theological understanding to others has been a continuing process for the past 2,000 years. This process must also continue in Africa because the Holy Spirit will lead all of us into all truth. Jesus Christ is Lord of all and His Spirit indwells all of His people.

2. The Church of Jesus Christ in Africa must seek God's answer to her problems and needs unique to her own context.

Each individual Christian and each fellowship of believers finds itself in a unique stage of maturity. While we can learn and benefit from others in hearing what other Christians are doing about certain situations which confront them, we need not mimic them and parrot their solutions. Our solutions to our problems as we understand them from God's Word may in fact be similar to the solutions found elsewhere, but we should find those solutions through our own reflection on our context and in the light of God's Word.

While the Word of God is true for all people everywhere so that we all must conform to that one system of truth in the Word of God, each context has its own peculiar problems and potential. The African Christian Church has unique problems which are not faced by any other church in the same manner. Therefore, the African Christian Church must seek from God in the Scriptures through the illumination of the Holy Spirit the resolution to those problems.

3. The Body of Christ in Africa, through a reflection upon the Bible in their context, may be able to contribute to a fuller understanding of God's revelation for all people and thereby contribute toward a fuller, more balanced Christian theology for the Church universal.

Because of our own limitations in understanding the whole counsel of the Word of God, we tend to focus on certain truths which are made particularly relevant due to our own situation. Thus our own unique understanding of Scriptures may contribute to the understanding of Scriptures by the Church universal. In other words, our cultural and historical context may enable us to comprehend some truth of the Word of God which is not fully appreciated by other people of God in different contexts. Therefore, we have an obligation to contribute our understanding of God's revelation to the whole of theological reflection by the universal Church.

4. Church renewal, necessary for every generation of Christians, is dependent upon a prayerful study of God's Word within each given context of need.

Only through the study of the Word of God can each generation of believers be revived. Revival and renewal of each believer in each generation necessitates a reflection of their own lives in the light of God's Word. The end result will be a genuinely inspired African Theology which brings renewal and blessing by the working of the Holy Spirit.

As we study the history of the Christian Church we discover that unless each generation of believers comes to know God in a new and personal way, that branch of the church becomes stale in her love for God, stagnant in her spiritual growth and eventually sterile in her Christian life. Church renewal is absolutely essential in each generation. And that cannot take place apart from earnest prayer and a study of God's Word in each given context.

5. Christianity in Africa must be properly contextualized so that believers will feel at home with their Christian faith and non-believers will be attracted by its beauty.

Whether murals portraying the life of Jesus Christ should reflect an African background or not, it is essential that there be much continuity between traditional African culture and their newly found Christian faith. All that is good in traditional Africa and all that can be purified and utilized for the glory of God should be assimilated into the expression and communication of the Gospel of Jesus Christ.

Of course, everything must be measured by the standard of Holy Writ. But there is much truth and goodness in traditional African culture derived by the grace of God which can and must be incorporated into Christianity in Africa. The whole purpose is two-fold: to help believers find delight and joy in expressing their faith in Christ with true fulfilment and a sense of belonging; and secondly, to communicate the Gospel to the unbelievers in such a manner that they are drawn to Jesus Christ, the Saviour of the world, yes, and particularly of Africa.

6. The Body of Christ in Africa is directly responsible to Jesus Christ, the Head of the Church, and not to some foreign bishop or ecclesiastical body.

On the one hand, we as members of the Body of Christ, must be rightly related to the Universal Christian Church. We believe in the apostolicity of the Church, not based on external descent by ordination but on the internal assent to the teaching of the apostles of Jesus Christ as found in the New Testament. Any church that falls away from assent to that which has been taught by the apostles ceases to be part of the Holy Catholic Church.

On the other hand, the disciples of Jesus Christ are primarily and ultimately responsible to Christ Himself. We reject all forms of ecclesiastical imperialism whereby foreigners in one continent control the faith and practice of believers in another continent. Jesus Christ has granted to each believer and to the believers collectively in each particular church the priesthood whereby we have immediate access to the Father by the Spirit apart from any other human intermediary. We have divine illumination by the Holy Spirit as we seek to know God's will through His Word.

Having affirmed the necessity of African Theology we should note that it would seem better to speak of Christian theology (or theologies) in Africa rather than African Theology. What we want is a biblical theology properly related to each given context. So we would prefer to speak of Christian Theology in the context of Africa. Generally, we do not speak of European Theology or American Theology. There are many diverse Christian theologies in the west. Furthermore, Europe is as diverse as Africa with scores of "tribes" with traditional hostilities between them. And these diverse theologies in Europe seem to be unrelated to the cultural differences among the European "tribes."

We would call for a biblical theology for the African context which reflects the great evangelical truths which have united evangelicals through the centuries and apply these to the African context. We need to continue relating the great evangelical truths of biblical revelation to the ever-changing contexts found in Africa. Only as we take the written Word of God as our absolute and final authority will we conclude with an evangelical theology for Africa and rightly related to the historic creeds of Christianity.

However, what may happen more quickly is that various theological emphases represented in our evangelical churches will become incarnated in the African culture. Thus our evangelical theologies incarnated in the African culture, will be related to those great historic theological emphases in the universal church (i.e. Arminianism, Calvinism, Dispensational, Covenant etc.).

For these reasons, we prefer speaking of Christian Theology (or theologies) in Africa. Regardless of the term we may use, we have surely demonstrated that there are many reasons why the Christians in Africa need to address a host of issues which are specifically African in nature. African Christians also need to

communicate their theological reflections in a uniquely African manner for effective communication. Thus the Christian theology developed in Africa will have a distinctive African stamp while ever holding to the one apostolic faith. And in this sense we speak of African Theology.

2

HISTORY OF AFRICAN THEOLOGY

ORIGINS OF AFRICAN THEOLOGY

Missionaries Prepared the Way for African Theology

The foundations of what we call today, "African Theology," were laid by missionaries in several significant ways.

Preaching the Gospel to and by the Africans: When the Gospel was first preached by missionaries and the peoples believed it, African Theology was initiated. The Gospel took root in the hearts of the Africans as the Word of God was effectively communicated, meeting the needs of men and women. The African believers understood the Gospel, digested it and began to share their faith with others, using their own language and culture as the medium of communication. They began to formulate their Christian faith in African terms as they witnessed to others.

In any successful effort to communicate the Gospel to a people across cultural boundaries there must be some measure of relating biblical truths to the known practices and beliefs of the people. Without translation, no communication is possible. And theology is translation (cf. Sundkler 1960: 281).

Baeta observes, "My view is that if the gospel is being presented relevantly and with a full effectiveness, i.e., in such a manner that under African conditions and circumstances it is doing its gospel work – then its complete indigenization has taken place..." (Baeta 1964: 21).

Everyone recognizes the phenomenal growth of the Christian Church in Africa. In a very real sense the Gospel has been understood, received and believed. The Gospel has met deeply felt needs. Therefore, we conclude that a significant degree of indigenization of Christianity has taken place in Africa because the Gospel is doing its saving work of grace.

"Theology" is a discourse about God, a study of God, sometimes referred to as a science. Any "God-talk," any effort to speak about our understanding of God, is theology (Fashole-Luke 1974a: 100). In the Christian context theology is inseparable from the Scripture. The Christian Church has historically believed that the Bible is the Word of God. Thus theology is man's understanding of God's revelation of Himself in the Scripture. Theology may simply be defined as the application of the Word of God to all areas of life. Theology is done whenever people reflect on divine revelation and communicate their understanding of God's revelation to others.

As Adeyemo has said, Doing Theology for evangelicals "is an obedient spirit-led reflection upon God's revelatory words and acts, culminating in Jesus Christ, an honest application of the same to our lives, and consequent sincere communication of it for perfecting the saints for the work of the ministry (see Ezr 7:10; Eph 4:12)" (Adeyemo 1983: 147).

All too often theology is equated with professional scholars writing books on theology for one another. A measure of a theologian is his ability to interact with philosophers and theologians who study and write in many different languages. This view is reflected by Agbeti, who comments, "A 'theology' is not technically 'theology' when the experience about God had not been systematically, critically and scholarly interpreted or articulated" (Agbeti 1972: 7). If we restrict theology to elite Africans writing theology, then African Theology is of recent origins.

Teaching Africans to Read and Write: Doing Theology is done in varying stages. The most basic stage is when Africans hear the Gospel preached orally, understand it and embrace it by faith. A further stage is reached when believers are sufficiently educated so that they can read the Scriptures and think through their Christian faith on their own, and then enunciate this to others.

Missionaries were the ones who built primary schools to train Africans to read and write. Colonial governments depended on missions to do this. What initially began as two or three year schools designed to make Africans literate in order to read the Bible, developed into higher levels of education. No one can minimize the importance of schooling sponsored by missionaries. Literacy gave Africans access to the Bible and other reading materials which could only stimulate their thinking. In these little two-year elementary schools the Bible played a central role in their training. Thus the mission schools, taught by Africans, laid the foundation for nation building and providing an educated African Church – and initiated African Theology.

Translation of the Scriptures: No greater contribution could missionaries have made to African Theology than the translation of the Bible into the vernacular languages. This gave the literate African direct access to God's revelation independent of the missionary. The Bible in the hands of Africans meant that they were not dependent on the missionaries for their understanding of God's will for their lives.

As Tienou has observed, theology "is reflection on God's self-disclosure contained in the Scripture with the purpose of generating the knowledge of God and better obedience" (Tienou 1983: 98). As such, Africans have been reflecting on the Scriptures since the Bible was first translated into the vernacular languages.

All Bible translations are interpretations of the text from which the Bible is being translated. Anyone familiar with the dynamics of translation recognizes that there is no exact equivalence in any two languages. The translator must use his God given judgement to know how to express the words of Scripture in the African language. In every instance the Bible translations into the various African vernaculars were made with the assistance of African Christians.

A case in point is the translation of the Nandi Bible, the first complete Bible translated into a Kenyan vernacular language. In 1929 the Africa Inland Mission Field Council in Kenya appointed two men to translate the Nandi Bible: Stuart Bryson, the A.I.M. missionary, and Samuel Gimnyige, a Nandi pastor. They were co-workers in this task. For ten years these and other Nandi believers worked on the translation. They began with no Nandi grammar or any dictionary even of the simplest kind. In 1933 the Brysons, who then were the only A.I.M missionaries in Nandi land, were "still collecting Nandi words on scraps of paper which were kept in bundles in a biscuit-tin" (Bryson 1959: 74).

The Nandi Christians themselves played the pivotal role in the translation. Pastor Gimnyige worked steadily with Bryson all week long before bicycling back to Ndulele on the week-end to conduct the work at the school and lead in the Sunday services. Others shared in the work of translation including Reuben Arap Seroney and Reuben Arap Lagat. Sometimes they would struggle over the best way to translate the Bible. Throughout the days and weeks they would search for the best ways to communicate what God has said in the Bible. Sometimes the solution would be found suddenly while listening to the Nandi speak in the village or by observing some traditional practice.

The New Testament was published in Australia. Later in May 1939 the British and Foreign Bible Society printed the whole Nandi Bible, the first vernacular Bible in Kenya. While Bible translation may not appear at first glance to be doing theology, it is in fact nothing less. For the whole process of translating God's Word into the Nandi language necessitated reflection on what God meant in His Word and how best to communicate that to the Nandi in their culture.

"Oral Theology" is the interpretation of the biblical message through sermons, teachings, prayers, discussions, songs, witnessing and any oral communication. Mbiti says, "glimpses of African Theology may be found in the total African response, in word and action, to the gospel" (Dickson 1974: 205).

Many times the impression is given in missionary biographies that the expatriate missionaries were the chief ones who evangelized and spread the Good News of Jesus Christ. But this is contrary to the facts. The African believers themselves were the chief agents in the rapid spread of the Gospel.

The most important agent in evangelism in the Africa Inland Mission was the African Christian who served as evangelist and school teacher. From the earliest days of the A.I.M. there was the recognition that "evangelization must be done by the Africans themselves," as Peter Cameron Scott wrote in his diary (Miller n.d.: 43). The vision was to train the Africans to be pastors so that they could staff the stations in a few years and the missionaries be freed to move on to unreached territory (H & D, VII, 5, 1903: 12, 13).

John Stauffacher, the Extension Director of the A.I.M., gave an address to the A.I.M. Missionary Conference in 1912 in which he affirmed, "All we can hope for is to train those who shall do the work while we spread from tribe to tribe... Unless we hold continually before the native that the work is theirs, and we have come simply to show them how to do it, we shall never make much progress" (H & D, Oct. - Dec., 1912). Thus the number of evangelists, employed by the A.I.M., continued to grow. In 1922 there were 200 African evangelists, and by the late 1930's a reported 1,600 "native evangelists" working among 25 tribes in East and Central Africa.

Bible Schools played an important part in the preparation of pastors and evangelists. Within the Africa Inland Church in Kenya the strongest element by far is among the Kamba. The reason for this cannot be wholly attributed to the number of missionaries labouring in Ukambani, though that is one element. The fact is that 25 years after the A.I.M. began working in Kenya, the Gikuyu A.I.C. was the largest element in the Church, the Luo A.I.C. the second largest, and the Kamba the third largest. Many factors played their part.

A significant difference seems to be the Ukamba Bible Institute begun in 1928. The Kamba Church is the only part of the A.I.C. which has had its own vernacular Bible Institute for any sustained length of time. Moffat Bible School at Kijabe, begun in 1929, was taught in Kiswahili and intended for the Gikuyu, Maasai and Kalenjin. Furthermore, only a few Gikuyu attended in the earlier years because the launching of the Bible School coincided with the murder of Miss Stumpf and the crises over female circumcision. Though the Luo did have their own vernacular Bible School for a few years, it did not continue long because of the limited number of A.I.C. Luo students who attended. Kapsabet Bible School was not begun until 1954 and then it was conducted at first in

Nandi and later in Kiswahili to accommodate the Luo and other communities that attended.

The universal conviction of the older missionaries and the Kamba with whom I spoke, is that the strength of the A. I. C. among the Kamba is due to the Kamba pastors being trained in their vernacular tongue, studying theology and Bible in their own vernacular language for a sustained period of time since 1928. The truth of the Word of God was able to penetrate the hearts of the people more effectively because it was communicated in their own mother tongue.

Barrett stresses the strength and power found in the vernacular Bible translations. "Vernacular Scriptures have far greater power to communicate and create religious dynamic than versions in lingua franca such as Swahili ..." The vernacular translation enables the people group to grasp the inner meanings of such profound and intricate biblical doctrines. "The vernacular translation, if it were made, would enable the tribe to understand the deepest mysteries of the Kingdom of God..." (Barrett 1968: 133).

As these evangelists and pastors, trained in the Word of God, proclaimed the Gospel and called people to repentance and faith in Christ, oral theology developed of necessity. They reflected on God's revelation in their vernacular Bibles. They sought to communicate the meaning of that divine Word in relevant and effective ways. The gradual growth in the churches reflects the fact that the truth and meaning of God's Word was understood and believed.

We can affirm, therefore, that African Theology is not of recent origins, but began from the very beginning of the Christian Church in Africa. The Gospel met the spiritual needs of the African peoples – it was relevant. The size and strength of the Christian Church in Africa bears witness to this.

Publication of African Ethnologies: Gabriel Setiloane has observed that the missionaries were the first ones to demonstrate an interest in the religiosity of the African people. Missionary writings of their encounters with Africans provided the first literary records of African cultures and beliefs. "The most useful informative material are the records of the early missionaries, which in fact laid down the foundation for the study of social anthropology..." (Masoga 2017: On-Line). Ground-breaking studies were provided by missionaries such as Robert Moffatt, Samuel Broadbent, E.W. Smith, W.C. Willoughby, and Fr. Placide Tempels.

Through mission agencies, Africans were educated in Africa and a number were sponsored for overseas studies. Resulting from their graduate studies came pioneer African ethnographies by J.B. Danquaah, S.M. Molema, Jomo Kenyatta, and J.H. Soga.

Missionary Goal of Indigenous Churches: Not to be forgotten is that mission agencies had declared that their goal was an indigenous Church. Henry Venn (1796-1873) of the Church Missionary Society in England, and Rufus Anderson (1796-1880), Foreign Secretary of the American Board of Commissioners for Foreign Missions are generally recognized as the originators of the "three-self" philosophy of missions – self-supporting, self-propagating, and self-governing. This implied that educated national clergy would lead their African churches independent of overseas control. Indigenous, self-governing churches has been the goal of all Christian missions, despite their difficulties in implementing their vision (Shenk 2000: 999).

REASONS FOR CONTEMPORARY DEVELOPMENTS

African Independence

African Theology took a dramatic leap forward when independence swept through Africa in the 1950s and 1960s. Seismic changes occurred not only politically, but culturally and religiously.

When the imagination of independence gripped the minds of Africans, missions began more serious efforts to prepare Africans for autonomous leadership of the churches. Africans were sent overseas for training. Theological colleges were planted in Africa. Both missionaries and national Christians began thinking anew of the relationship between the Gospel and African culture. The catchword at that time was "indigenization."

In May 1955 a Conference was held in Accra, Gold Coast, sponsored by the Christian Council. The topic of discussion was "Christianity and African Culture" (Christian Council 1955). Eight lectures were presented by theologians, churchmen and sociologists, both African and missionary. Professor Busia stated the importance of the Conference in a few words. "For conversion to the Christian Faith to be more than superficial, the Christian Church must come to grips with traditional beliefs and practices, and with the world-view that these beliefs and practices imply" (Christian Council 1955: iii). Various topics of the African worldview were discussed from a Christian perspective. Unfortunately, the perspective was only a generally Christian, though a genuinely Christian perspective, without any attempt to search the Scriptures and come up with a biblical theology of African culture. This tragic lack of biblical study in the 1950's has become the unfortunate hallmark of most conferences and consultations on African Theology ever since.

In 1960 Bengt Sundkler, a Lutheran missionary to South Africa, wrote a book entitled, *The Christian Ministry in Africa* (Sundkler 1960). One chapter of the book treated the topic, "Towards Christian Theology in Africa." Sundkler stressed the need for relevancy, interpreting Christ in terms of the African experience. Theology as translation is an "ever-renewed reinterpretation to new generations" (Sundkler 1960: 281).

A number of key issues motivated Africans to develop an African Theology.

Confusion of Gospel and Culture

A major problem during the colonial era and widely recognized today was the popular equation of Christianity with western civilization. Western culture was thought to be the embodiment of Christian values. During the first half of the twentieth century missionaries easily contrasted "the dark continent" with their "Christian homelands."

Complicating the problem was the relationship of the missionaries to the colonial masters. By their race, nationality, culture and religion the missionaries were identified with the colonial masters in the eyes of the African population. Regardless of the many differences, and regardless of the frequent hostilities between the colonial powers and the missionaries, there was an inevitable cultural bond that drew the missionaries to the friendship of the colonialist. And the Africans recognized this. The missionaries together with the colonizers, all from "the enlightened West," were seeking to uplift the African population from their "primitive" life.

"In line with the general outlook of the times, even in religiously indifferent matters, Western cultural patterns were rated far superior to African ones and were accordingly insisted upon within the church" (Baeta 1964: 20). Thus culture and the Gospel were confused.

In Kenya the Alliance of Missionary Societies appointed the Native Customs Board to consider various African customs. One such issue was dowry. Even though the patriarchs in the Old Testament paid dowry for their wives (e.g. Ge 24:59, 61; 29:24), and the Bible never raises objections to the practice, this African custom did not find favour with missionaries because it was strange by western standards. After making a study of the matter, The Native Customs Board reported back to the Alliance in January 1919. They agreed that the Societies should urge the African Church Councils to teach their converts not to demand dowry in the marriage of their daughters. But they felt it was impractical to require baptized bachelors not to pay more than a certain maximum as dowry. In the end "the ultimate disappearance of the dowry be looked for more as a result of Christian teaching than government prohibition or regulations."

Some years later in a strange reversal, the Church of Scotland Mission and the Africa Inland Mission actually required that half of the bride price be paid before any marriage. Marriage of communicants before half the bride price was paid constituted grounds for church discipline (Barlow 1925).

The fact is that the whole colonial mentality prior to African independence was that of missionaries from "Christian nations" taking the gospel to peoples and nations living in total darkness. It was all too easy for the missionary to confuse his own cultural values with the supra-cultural values of Scripture. As Dickson observed, "In the early days of missions in Africa no clear distinction was drawn between the gospel and Christianity" (1974: 199). "And Christianity, as it was brought to Africa, was the gospel together with a cultural encrustment of a Western nature" (Dickson 1974: 199).

Many African theologians (cf. Fashole-Luke 1974a: 98) recognize that there must be "aspects of discontinuity between the Gospel and any culture," and that this discontinuity is ignored in "ethnic theologies." That is, there are parts of any culture which must be abandoned by Christians because it falls under the judgement of God. If the Gospel is domesticated by being unduly accommodating to culture, it will lose the authority of the Word of God. If the Gospel is accommodated to a culture through compromise of the fundamental aspects of biblical teaching, then that gospel parts company with Christianity.

However, "Christianity always comes with a cultural conditioning, but what those engaged in the task of producing an African Theology are claiming, is that this 'cultural conditioning' must be African and not Western. Furthermore, it is being argued that African Christians must produce a theology which bears the distinctive stamp of African thinking and reflection" (Fashole-Luke 1974a: 98). African Theology "involves steeping oneself in the patterns of thought of traditional African religions and studying Christianity in the light of that heritage, thus endeavouring to find points of contact between African traditional beliefs and Christian beliefs, so that Christianity can be more effectively and relevantly proclaimed to the African situation" (Fashole-Luke 1974a: 100). This study of traditional religion is to be "positive" and not "negative," according to Fashole-Luke, instead of the negative approach so characteristic of the past.

Denigration of African Culture

Missionaries found it all too easy to reject African beliefs and practices without adequate understanding. "Ignorance of the real facts created many false images of Africa, and inadequate observations often led to exaggerations. Religion was one of the aspects of African life which suffered from misunderstanding and distortions" (Hassing 1971: 510). As a result, Fashole-Luke complains that, "African religious customs, rites, practices, and beliefs were rejected without being properly evaluated" (Fashole-Luke 1974a: 97).

Dietrich Westermann, a western missionary, wrote, "The Africans have been treated by us as having no religion, no language, no traditions, no institutions, no racial character of their own, as empty vessels to be filled with European or American food" (Goreham 1975: 233).

In many ways Fashole-Luke and Westermann seem unduly harsh, though they are representative of most contemporary scholarship on the subject. Their opinion certainly does not reflect the assessment made by the older missionaries themselves. The older A.I.M. missionaries were renowned for their mastery of the vernacular language. Some of these like Linnell Davis, Ken and Herb Downing, Earl Anderson, George Rhoad, Paul, Eric and Bill Barnett learned the language while growing up in Kenya as missionary children. They learned by listening, observing and doing. Furthermore, up until the 1940's the language policy of the Africa Inland Mission required mastery of the vernacular, not the trade language, Kiswahili.

Thus for instance C.F. Johnston with a mastery of Kikamba would sit with the elders at the *thome* and talk with them for hours into the night. Some of these missionaries knew the older and deeper vocabulary better than the younger generations of Africans. Would not this knowledge of African languages enable them to penetrate with understanding the African customs and culture?

When talking to these older missionaries, it becomes quite apparent that they understood and valued many of the traditional ways of the Africans. To say that the A.I.M. was negative on all the African customs and culture, as some scholars maintain, is quite inadmissible. Various aspects of African culture which they appreciated include family cohesiveness where the child always belongs and is accepted; respect for the elders; decorum and self-restraint; feeling of mutual responsibility; decency in dress, speech and behaviour; social security for the aged in their own homes; hospitality was so genuine that people never prepared much food for a journey; fraternity and communal relationships were so strong that they cared for one another; apart from severe famines, people never died of poverty for the food was shared; family solidarity was so strong that divorce was rare and orphanages unnecessary; crime was limited, nothing like it is today.

Yet it is illuminating to talk with the Africans who knew and appreciated some of these missionaries, Africans who until this day love and respect those missionaries. From their perspective missionaries only had a superficial knowledge of African customs and culture, depending upon the Christian African to explain the meaning. One of the earliest converts in Machakos observed, "It seemed that missionaries saw so much darkness in the old days that they did not seek advice. Only today when there is light do missionaries seek advice."

One may ask, "Why did the early missionaries avoid certain African traditions without researching them?" Those missionaries were struggling to establish a Christian church among a peoples who rejected Jesus Christ. What these early

A.I.M. missionaries did was similar to the practice of the early Christian Church, struggling to plant a Christian witness in the midst of European paganism. We read in the *Teaching of the Twelve Apostles*:

> *My son, flee from all wickedness and from everything like it... My child, do not be an observer of omens, for this leads to idolatry; or engage in witchcraft, astrology or ritual ablutions. Do not even desire to see these things (or hear them), for from all these idolatry is born (Schopp 1947: 173).*

To avoid the temptation of returning to sinful practices, both African believers and missionaries advocated separation from and avoidance of many traditional practices, in much the same way as the missionaries did in early church history when they evangelized the pagan Europeans.

Failure to Address African Issues

Whatever one's perspective of the missionary era may be, the consequence is undeniable. African customs and beliefs were not adequately addressed by the Word of God. Little theological reflection was done on how the Gospel related to traditional culture, except to reject various customs. The colonial mentality did not encourage mutual theological reflection by both missionaries and national believers. Thus, African culture was not penetrated by the Word of Jesus Christ. And missionaries to a distressing extent were influenced by their own cultural perceptions derived from their western nations of origin instead of from the biblical worldview.

The result of this whole colonial mentality was that the Gospel was not preached with as much relevancy as it deserved. Baptized Christians and "marginal Christians" did not always "feel at home" in the institutional church planted by the missionaries with its foreign hymns and formal liturgy. Nor were all their spiritual needs addressed because the Gospel had not been applied to those areas where they hurt and where they struggled. Christians lived "split-level" lives. One level was Christian and the other level was traditional. The African Christian

> *suffered from a form of religious schizophrenia. With part of himself he has been compelled to pay lip service to Christianity as understood, expressed and preached by the white man. But with an even greater part of himself, a part he has been often ashamed to acknowledge openly and which he has struggled to repress, he has felt that his Africanness was being violated* (Tutu 1978: 366).

Arising out of this failure is a need to answer the questions which the Africans are asking, questions not asked during the colonial era. Instead of a monologue with the teacher instructing the peoples what he thinks the questions and answers are, we need dialogue in order to discover from the African believers themselves a better understanding of their felt needs. And then together we should search the Scriptures and reflect upon God's revelation in the African context. "The African theologian's task is to understand the modern African and his past and relate the Gospel to him and his needs" (Gelzer 1970: 1092).

Africanising Christianity also involves the contextualizing of her worship and witness. This includes contextualizing the African churches' hymnody, musical instruments, liturgy, vestments and architecture. Worship must involve the whole inner being. What stirs the westerner's soul is quite different from what stirs the African's soul. Anything in our "worship services" which hinders true worship from the heart should be removed in favour of that which is more relevant. There are very few western hymns sung in our churches which stir the heart like those written locally. And the beat of those western hymns which are readily accepted in Africa is quite different from the stately hymns of the faith from the West. African Theology must think its way through the whole biblical teaching of worship in the African context.

A case in point is the Christian approach to sickness. One of the greatest reasons for African converts turning back to traditional religion is illness. In traditional African culture there was high mortality. Sickness frequently led to death. Because sickness is often not understood and because it frequently leads to death, African believers sometimes become very frightened at the prospect of illness.

The people traditionally turned to diviners for assistance. He was always there to help. Illness was never explained solely through natural means. There were reasons behind every illness that were rooted in their traditional worldview. The cure generally required more than natural herbs. Treatment included help from the spiritual world in dealing with the spiritual causes of the illness.

With the coming of the missionaries two developments took place: (1) western medicine was sometimes introduced in dispensaries and hospitals with a natural explanation for all sickness and healing; and (2) many missionaries treated former diagnoses of sickness, as superstition, unworthy of belief. Whether these messengers of the Christian Faith were conscious of the problem or not, they were presenting a western approach to sickness and healing which minimizes the supernatural in all healing. The impression was given that sickness is caused by microscopic organisms and the sick will become well through natural medications.

We are well aware of the tremendous spiritual impact that missionary medicine has had upon African peoples. Hospitals and dispensaries sponsored by evangelicals have always integrated the spiritual aspect of life with physical healing, but the integration has sometimes been inadequate. Doctors and nurses are often overworked and may feel unable to devote extra time to patients with spiritual needs. African chaplains have performed an admirable ministry of caring for the spiritual needs of patients, sharing the Gospel with them, praying with them and leading many to faith in Christ.

But the problem remains. Many an African believer is willing to receive treatment from western style dispensaries, hoping for a cure. But if they are not healed, they do what most people do, namely, seek help from other sources. In Africa those sources are traditional religion and the diviner. Sickness is one of the greatest causes for African believers to return to the traditional diviner who communicates with the spirit world.

The Gospel simply has not penetrated the soul of many Christians in Africa because the heart of Africa was not seriously reflected upon from the Christian view point. What does God have to say to people immersed in the African traditional worldview where sickness is always the result of malignant personal agents? We need a biblical theology of divine healing within the African context.

Dehumanizing of Africans through Colonialism

National rivalry between European nations in the nineteenth century led to a scramble for African colonies. Europeans sought raw materials from the continent and a market for the goods they processed in Europe. For economic reasons, “imperialism” or “the lust for territory” was born. The European nations signed “the Congo Basin Treaties” in 1885 which marked on the African map their “spheres of influence. This date marks the beginning of the “Scramble for Africa” (Dixon 2000: 46).

In the process of seeking economic gain, the Europeans violated not only the rights of the Africans, but robbed them of their dignity. For financial profit the Europeans alienated the Africans from their land and herded them elsewhere like cattle. Europeans compelled them to work on settler’s farms and taxed them to pay for the administrative expenses. Each African was required to carry identification papers called a *kipande* in Kenya.

In all these cases the Africans were treated differently from the European settlers. Africans were made to feel inferior, not only because of their culture but because of who they were – Africans. Dehumanizing the African was the greatest injury inflicted on the African. Africans with their African culture were made to feel inferior.

It should therefore be no surprise that Africans began pushing back after independence and affirming their dignity. African Theology is related to the African's assertion of his own “Africanness.” In reaction to the negative feelings toward himself and his culture which he imbibed from the colonial era, the African theologian reasserts his own dignity and self-worth. Recent developments in African Theology cannot be understood apart from the historical context of oppression through the slave trade and European colonization. In the 1930’s there was an awakening of African consciousness. L.S. Senghor advocated Negritude, a pride in the rediscovery of African culture, religion and language. African Theology is a quest for African self-identity:

> *African Christian Theology, as it is developing, might be considered as a theology of selfhood, not only in recognition of the changed status of much of Africa, from the colonial to the post-colonial period, but also as a symbol of the desire of the Church in Africa to be in a position to present Christ as one who knows and understands the hopes and fears of Africans...* (Dickson 1975: 45).

“The focal point of African theology would remain the same: an expression of the Christian faith which does justice to the African's humanity and God-given ways of life and thought” (Dickson 1975: 45).

African Theology is in many ways a reactionary theology. In the process of asserting their own self-worth and making a distinctive contribution to theology, there is a tendency toward reaction against what has been taught them by the missionaries prior to independence. As Desmond Tutu declares, “Most of what is subsumed under the heading ‘African Theology’ is the result of reaction against cultural and ecclesiastical colonialism” (Tutu 1978: 364). Much time is devoted to the criticism of past missionaries and missions for their failures. Attempts are made to construct a new theology based on a new methodology which is distinctive from all other past theologies.

The dynamics of cultural dissimilation are well known. People, wanting to be different, assert their uniqueness by different means. A church which desires to assert her own uniqueness may do so by developing distinctive differences in her theological beliefs or church practices. Cultural dissimilation has been used to explain the theological differences which have surfaced in the history of the Christian Church. No doubt this process is at work many times through the development of African Theology.

At the time when Africa was gaining independence, Baeta commented, "The present reaction, usually referred to as the African Cultural Renaissance, is therefore bound to confront the churches with a number of problems" (Baeta 1964: 20). Customs were restored to respectability, such as the pouring of libations in Ghana, "not necessarily because its original religious value is still acknowledged or believed in, but rather because it is the genuinely African framework for saying prayers and for otherwise communing with the supernatural world" (Baeta 1964: 20).

As the African peoples have thrown off the political yoke of colonialism, as they are now seeking to deal with the economic yoke of neo-colonialism, so the Christian Church is seeking to deal with the ecclesiastical yoke of missionary Christianity. It is reactionary, but it can also be positive. As Fashole-Luke has said, "African Christians must produce a Theology which bears the distinctive stamp of African thinking and reflection" (Fashole-Luke 1974a: 97). While the African Christians react to those trappings which appear to them foreign and non-African, they have the obligation with all Christians to abide by what God is teaches in the Scriptures in order to make the Christian faith their own faith.

Conclusion

In certain ways the recent development of African Theology is a mark of maturity in the African Church. African Christians are thinking for themselves and addressing issues that concern them.

> *African Christian theologians rightly feel that, so far, they have lived a theology which they have not reflected on by themselves, but which the missionaries thought for them and brought ready baked from their homes. Having become mature, African Christian theologians legitimately aspire to rethink theology for themselves* (Daidanso 1983: 66).

We may say then, that the "transplanted theology" which lacked total relevancy for the Africans was the gunpowder that exploded. The fire which ignited the gunpowder was the movement toward independence. World War Two quickened the pressure for independence, politically, culturally, and religiously. Only after World War Two did significant numbers of Africans undertake advanced theological study overseas. As they returned to their home churches in the 1950s, 1960s and 1970s with many of their churches in the process of receiving independence from their founding missions, these young educated leaders began "to examine their inherited theology in the light of the present and to begin reformulating their thinking in the setting of their own culture" (Gelzer 1970: 1091). "African theology – in the sense of theology 'done' by Africans – is relatively new. Indeed African theologians as a recognizable professional group did not exist until rather recently" (Gelzer 1970: 1091).

A BRIEF INTRODUCTION TO AFRICAN THEOLOGY

Contributions to African Theology by Africans began as a trickle in 1960s with Harry Sawyerr of Sierra Leone, Bolaji Idowu of Nigeria and Vincent Mulago of Congo/Zaire as pioneers. *Biblical Revelation and African Belief*, edited by Kwesi Dickson and Paul Ellingworth, resulted from a pioneering conference of African theologians in 1966 held in Ibadan, Nigeria.

The pace of publications picked up in the 1970s until today there is a plethora of articles and books on the subject. They not only prove to be numerous, but also diverse. They differ in perspectives, agendas and venues. In fact, so diverse are they that classification is difficult.

Classification of African Theologies

Bediako observes that two trends emerged in African Theology after independence. The first pertained to issues of social justice during the struggle for political independence, leading to a theology of liberation. The second pertained to "a theological exploration into the indigenous cultures of African peoples, with particular stress on their pre-Christian (and also pre-Islamic) religious traditions" (Bediako 2004: 49). This is the common division of African theologies.

For purposes of this book, however, we shall add a third category: (1) African Liberation Theology, (2) African Christian Theology, and (3) African Biblical Theology. We readily admit that serious objections can be raised against this classification.

First, we should note what all three have in common. The authors all identify as Christian. They all declare the importance of the Bible in doing African Theology. The authors are all African and are proud of their identity as African. They all believe that the theology which they were taught by missionaries was deficient. Furthermore, they propose to Africanize and contextualize theology for Africa. If they have so much in common, why seek to categorize them in different camps?

Secondly, in practice it is difficult to place every author in one of the three categories. Not all authors fit neatly in one category. There is an overlapping between the categories.

So why choose to demarcate one group over another? For purposes of this book it is important to underline a significant and fundamental difference between them. While all the African authors are united on many concerns, they divide on one issue, namely, the final source of authority for doing their theology. Where does the authority lie? Although everyone acknowledges the importance of the Bible for doing African Theology, they differ significantly in their view of the Bible. As a result, the final authority lies with the scholar who picks and chooses what he or she thinks is of value for African Theology. This will be demonstrated in Chapter 3.

Following is a look at a few representatives found in each of the three classifications in order to provide a flavour of what each group teaches.

African Liberation Theology

The category of African Liberation Theology is a broad umbrella that includes all theologies that resist oppression, whether it is political, cultural, or patriarchal rule. Liberation Theology in South Africa found its roots in Black Theology in the United States. John Mbiti notes that Black Theology is a painful phenomenon in the history of the Church because it is "a judgement on American Christianity...Ideally there would be no reason for Black Theology. It was forced into existence by the particularities of American history" (Wilmore 1979: 477).

Influence of James Cone: The Civil Rights Movement in the United States began in the 1960s with Rev. Martin Luther King Jr. leading the non-violent resistance to segregation. The Black Theology movement developed after King's murder on April 4, 1968. The following year the National Committee of Black Churchmen on June 13, 1969, defined "Black Theology as "a theology of black liberation...It is the affirmation of black humanity that emancipates black people from white racism" (Wilmore 1979: 101).

James Cone (1938 – 1985), an ordained minister in the African Methodist Episcopal Church in America, became the leader of American Black Theology. He was the one who "made the word *liberation* the organizing principle of an emerging black perspective on theology" (Cone 1986: 106). Black Theology in South Africa drew its inspiration from Cone's book, *A Black Theology of Liberation* (Cone 1970).

His brand of theology was militant and separatistic. James Cone claimed that "Black Theology is Christian theology and possibly the only expression of Christian theology in America...there can be no theology of the gospel which does not arise from an oppressed community...Black Theology believes that the black community itself is precisely where Christ is at work" (Cone 1970: 23-24). With his truculent attitude, Cone wrote, "Black theology must realize that the white Jesus has no place in the black community, and it is our task to destroy him. We must replace him with the Black Messiah...a messiah who sees his existence as inseparable from black liberation and the destruction of white racism" (Cone 1970: 79).

Cone was deeply influenced by the existential theologians, Karl Barth and Paul Tillich, though he preferred Tillich who developed theology by asking questions that arise from the cultural situation of man and shaping the answers according to that situation (Cone 1970: 52f). According to Cone, "The meaning of Scripture is not to be found in the words of Scripture as such but only in its power to point beyond itself to the reality of God's revelation; and in America, that means black liberation" (Cone 1970: 69).

Though he believed it was important to take the biblical witness into account, the Bible is not the revelation of God; only Christ is. Nor is the Bible an infallible witness. God is not the author of the Bible, Cone wrote. Emphasis on verbal infallibility leads to unimportant concerns. Scripture is not a guide which makes our decisions for us. "It matters little to the oppressed who authored Scripture; what is important is whether it can serve as a weapon against the oppressors" (Cone 1970: 67).

James Cone repeatedly says that Scripture is important for doing theology but he finds many sources for theology, including: Black Experience, Black History, Black Culture, Revelation, Scripture and tradition. In his opinion, it is difficult to know which of these sources is most important because they are all intertwined (Cone 1970: 54-69).

Though he maintains that Scripture is important for theology, he states in effect that his reason is pragmatic – in order to gain a hearing from the African Americans. Cone believes that American radicals have not gained a hearing from the African Americans because they do not take seriously the religious character of the blacks. "It is not possible," he writes, "to speak meaningfully to the black community about liberation unless it is analysed from a Christian perspective which centers on Jesus Christ" (Cone 1970: 78).

We conclude that Cone's view of Scripture falls outside the bounds of orthodoxy. He only finds value in the Bible as it helps him with black liberation. What the Bible actually teaches is set aside because the writers of the Scriptures were culture bound and shaped by different ideologies.

Desmond Tutu: Desmond Tutu (born 1931), recipient of the Nobel Peace Prize in 1984 and six honorary doctoral degrees, is an icon for peace worldwide. As Archbishop of the Anglican Church in South Africa, he became an avowed black theologian of liberation (Tlhagale 1987: 45). He called for the Church to be a "Community of Liberation" to be active politically (Goba 1987: 66). In the view of Tutu, political liberation should be "a serious preoccupation" of the church and this should not be seen as "an alternative to personal salvation in Jesus Christ" (Mutloatse 1983: 76). He affirms that the "Church exists primarily to worship and adore God," but this should never become a form of escapism (Mutloatse 1983: 84). "Christianity knows nothing about pie in the sky when you die, or a concern for man's soul only. That would be a travesty of the religion of Jesus of Nazareth, who healed the sick, fed the hungry etc." (Mutloatse 1983: 85). Because of the incarnation, Tutu insists that "Christians can no longer afford the luxury of compartmentalizing life so that they may think that religion should keep to its boundaries and not impinge on the things beyond its ken and competence" (Maimela 1987: 44).

Though Archbishop Tutu is an advocate of liberation, he parts company with James Cone in several ways. Unlike Cone who advocates hostility and separation from the whites, Tutu advocated reconciliation and peace. He desired to create "a new, non-racial, just and peaceful South Africa, by dismantling apartheid..." (Maimela 1987).

Drawing from American Black Theology, Tutu sees both Black Theology and African Theology "giving the black man a proper pride in things black and African" (Tutu 1979: 488). But he gives this thrust a more biblical perspective than James Cone. In a sermon entitled, "What Jesus Means to Me," the Archbishop delivers a moving and compelling argument for Africans to find their self-esteem in Christ.

"The Good News is that God loves me long before I could have done anything to deserve it" (Mutloatse 1983: 138). "I am loved. That is the most important fact about me and nothing, absolutely nothing, can change that fact. All I do now is an expression of my gratitude for what God has already done for me in Christ Jesus, my Lord and Saviour" (Mutloatse 1983: 139). "Victims of injustice and oppression" need not suffer from "a slave mentality by which they despised themselves and went about apologizing for their existence. They would know that they matter to God, and nothing anybody did to them could change that fundamental fact about themselves" (Mutloatse 1983: 141).

One positive contribution that Black Theology has made, in Tutu's opinion, is its "wonderful service in rehabilitating the African religious consciousness." African Theology has discredited the western lie that "the worthwhile religion in Africa had to await the advent of the white man" (Tutu 1979: 488-499).

Whatever positive things we may note about Archbishop's role in tearing down the South African Apartheid regime, and his commitment to reading the Bible daily, we must note that his view of Scripture is faulty. The Bible, he says, is not a single book but a library of books with contradictions. They must be interpreted by using methods of Social Sciences in order to unravel the early social world of the Bible. "There are certain parts which you have to say no to. The Bible accepted slavery. St Paul said women should not speak in church at all and there are people who have used that to say women should not be ordained. There are many things that you shouldn't accept" (Tutu 2017: Wikipedia). With this approach to Scripture, Desmond Tutu becomes the final authority of what should be accepted or rejected.

Because every culture and community has a different perspective on life's experiences, just as the diverse writers of the Bible had different perspectives, Bishop Tutu said that there can be no universal theology. The western idea of "a universal theology" is "thoroughly erroneous." "For theology can never properly claim a universality which rightly belongs only to the eternal Gospel of Jesus Christ" (Tutu 1979).

Desmond Tutu was a moderating representative of Black Theology of Liberation from South Africa among others. Tutu shares with other African theologians a sharp contrast to American Black Theology in his desire for fellowship with the whites. Manas Buthelezi wrote that what is unique about the Christian Gospel is that the "love of God in Jesus Christ transforms strange neighbours into loving brothers." God's love leads to fellowship (Bosch 1979: 231). E. Baartman wrote, "This is the difficult demand...'TO LOVE THE WHITE MAN.' We cannot hate our fellow man. God created us in love because He loved us, He so loved us that He chose death. It is difficult to love whites. It is costly to love whites, yet the black man must...The Gospel directs us all to unity. Those in Christ must be one in Christ" (Bosch 1979: 231).

But Desmond Tutu built his theology on a faulty foundation of a flawed Bible that led to more radical views of African Liberation Theology.

Itumeleng Mosala (born 1950 in South Africa), is a Methodist minister, a social activist, President of Azanian People's Organization (AZAPO) and Vice-Chancellor of Technikon North West. AZAPO became the voice of the Black Consciousness Movement after the Black People's Convention (BPC) was banned and one of its founding fathers, Stephen Bantu Biko, was murdered in 1997.

As an anti-apartheid activist, Mosala uses the Bible as an instrument in the struggle against the black oppressors. "Black theology's exegetical starting point," Mosala states, "expresses itself in the notion that the Bible is the revealed Word of God" (Mosala 1989: 15). Since the Bible is the witness to God's self-disclosure in Jesus Christ, "the black experience requires that Scripture be a source of Black Theology" (Mosala 1989: 15).

But his understanding of Scripture is skewed, influenced greatly by his Marxist ideology of class struggle. The proper way of reading the Bible, according to Mosala, is through "the black experience of oppression and exploitation" in order to "perceive the God of the Bible as the God of liberation" (Mosala 1989: 15). Black Theology does not believe in "a nonideological appropriation of the Scriptures." One must get behind the words of Scripture through a sociological and ideological hermeneutic. For example, the struggle between Yahweh and Baal in the Old Testament is not a struggle between the only true God and a pseudo-god. It was

> *a struggle between the God of Israelite landless peasants and subdued slaves and the God of Israelite royal, noble, landlord and priestly classes. In other words, the Bible is rent apart by the antagonistic struggles of warring classes of Israelites society in much the same way that our world is torn asunder by society's class, cultural, racial and gender divisions* (Mosala 1989: 16).

Black Theology cannot claim the *whole* Bible for that ignores "the results of biblical scholarship over the last century and has its roots in ruling-class ideology." The "ruling-class ideology" refers to the attempt by the dominant ruling classes to establish a dominant control over other classes through an effort to universalize the ethic of the ruling classes.

The Christian Church has always been the church of the bourgeoisie, Mosala says. Therefore it is a grave mistake for Black Theology to adopt the Church's biblical hermeneutics for that always protects bourgeois theological interests. Such theology is "pro-humanity but anti-black-working-class and anti-black women" (Mosala 1989: 19).

What Black Theology needs, according to Mosala, is "a *new* exegetical starting point" if it is to grip the black working-class and peasant masses. The starting point "must itself be grounded in a materialist epistemology that is characterized, among other things, by its location of truth not in a world beyond history but indeed within the crucible of historical struggles" (Mosala 1989: 21).

We can only conclude that Mosala has no serious commitment to Christ or his Word. His main allegiance is to the atheistic, materialistic philosophy of Marxism which had gripped many of the radicals in South Africa.

Musa W. Dube (born 1964), a mother, lay preacher in the United Methodist Church, and a Professor of New Testament Studies at the University of Botswana, is engaged in women's liberation. She has written on a wide range of biblical topics, but mainly from the feminist and post-colonial perspectives. Gender and gender discrimination are her focus (Dube 2017: Internet).

Her interpretation of the Scriptures is influenced by her belief that biblical texts have multiple meanings, as many as the readers of the text and the methods which they use to interpret the text. The choice of the method of interpretation is determined by the social conditions of the readers who interpret the Bible.

Dube believes that most Africans are not schooled in "the critical reading of the Bible." The problem is that "biblical scholarship has become a highly specialised and sophisticated science." By interpreting the Bible with the "historical critical method," she says, the reader only learns of the original meaning of the text with little or no import for the modern reader. By limiting yourself to the "historical critical" hermeneutic, she believes, the Bible is kept as the property of intellectual readers only.

As an illustration of her effort to interpret and appropriate the Scripture, she uses the encounter of Jesus with the Samaritan woman at the well (John 4:1-42). The woman told Jesus that she had been married to five different husbands. Dube compares her experience with the African woman's experience of being "married" to poverty and starvation, violent civil and ethnic wars, oppressive international financial policies, HIV and AIDS.

Professor Dube is an illustration of a one-sided approach to Scripture. Desperate to find meaning and application for the present, she allegorizes the text by applying it to the social problems oppressing African women today. But in the process she fails to listen to what the Scriptures actually teach – a woman thirsty for water, living in a life of sin, and Jesus offering her living water that satisfies forever and wells up to eternal life. By failing to listen to the Scripture, Dube misses what God offers to every human being, the satisfying and fulfilling presence of the Holy Spirit within the life of a believer who worships God in spirit and in truth.

Mercy Oduyoye (born 1934) is from an earlier generation. As a married woman in Ghana, a pioneering feminist activist, the Youth Education Secretary and staff member of the World Council of Churches, she expressed the same women's concerns as Professor Dube has done: oppression, poverty and impoverishment, marginalization from the global technological culture, exploitation that results from unjust global trade and economic arrangements (Oduyoye 1994: 167). She added marriage, procreation, womanhood, purity and a feminist view of life. It is very true, as she mentions, that women who read the Bible often hear what is unheard by men. But the serious question is this: do these feminists hear what the Bible is saying or is the Bible simply an echo chamber which repeats back to them what they themselves are saying?

Liberation Theology Diffused: In 1991 when the African peoples of South Africa overcame Apartheid and they gained majority rule, Liberation Theology dissipated, but it did not disappear. Liberation Theology continued with the theme of liberation against western oppression, neo-colonial rule, and economic policies of the West toward Africa. Concerns for Liberation also became absorbed in African Christian Theology (Bowers 2001).

One such example is **Laurenti Magesa**, a priest in the Tanzania Roman Catholic Church and lecturer in the Catholic University of Eastern Africa in Nairobi. He identifies himself with African Liberation Theology. "African liberation calls for 'reclamation' of the African dignity founded on the unconscious and subconscious religious, social, political and cultural values so long suppressed" (Bujo 2003: 233). He believes that African Theology, "if it is to be worthy of the name," must make "an original contribution of its own to Christian thinking at the level of the universal Church." This "original contribution" is "part and parcel of liberation" to express "African identity that has its roots in African religion" (Bujo 2003: 235). Though a Roman Catholic who adheres to "a normal and healthy development of Catholic doctrine," he draws heavily from his African traditional culture and religion.

Magesa reflects the concerns of other African theologians who focus on the horizontal needs of the African peoples: African identity, "the African person's *anthropological* poverty," "the ill effects of globalization, oppression and exploitation." He promotes a "holistic" worldview which includes the community of the living and the living dead, the visible and invisible worlds. Left in the shadows of neglect is the biblical view of sin, its consequences and God's provision to resolve this human predicament.

African Christian Theology

While African Liberation Theology and Black Theology found its origins in South Africa with its resistance to Apartheid, African Christian Theology began earlier throughout the rest of Africa. It was concerned with African culture, African identity, and a dialogue between Christianity and African Traditional Religion, as well as with classical theological themes.

The relationship between Liberation Theology and African Theology has been a point of contention. John Mbiti argued, "Black Theology cannot and will not become African Theology. Black Theology and African Theology emerge from different historical and contemporary situations... [African Theology] grows out of our joy in the experience of the Christian faith, whereas Black Theology emerges from pains of oppression" (Mbiti 1979: 482).

Desmond Tutu on the other hand believes that Black Theology and African Theology are "bound together by close bonds on three levels at least." They are united by "our blackness (of all shades)," they are bound to "mother Africa," and are united "through our baptism and through our membership in the Body of Christ which makes us all His ambassadors and partakers in the ministry of reconciliation" (Tutu 1979: 483-485).

Despite the disparate views of how these two streams of theology relate, history suggests that they are merging together with similar emphases.

A Survey of African Christian Theology: Contributions began as a trickle in the 1960s, expanded significantly in the 1970s and thereafter exploded exponentially. In this brief survey we can only mention the beginnings and examine a few representatives of African Christian Theology.

In 1960 Bengt Sundkler, a Lutheran missionary to South Africa, wrote a book entitled, *The Christian Ministry in Africa* (Sundler 1960). One chapter of the book treated the topic, "Towards Christian Theology in Africa." Sundkler stressed the need for relevancy, interpreting Christ in terms of the African experience. Theology as translation is an "ever-renewed reinterpretation to new generations" (Sundler 1960: 281).

Sundkler's book stimulated others to think along similar lines. Harry Sawyerr (1926-2013), a Canon in the Anglican Church in Sierra Leone and Professor of Theology in Fourah Bay College, Sierra Leone, wrote a response to Sundkler, expressing gratitude for Sundkler's "lucid and precise" presentation (Sawyerr 1963). Interestingly enough, Sawyerr wonders whether Sundkler has overrated the African myths by calling them "original revelation" and thereby minimizing the Old Testament. This is one of several examples where African theologians have tended to be more conservative than their missionary colleagues. Sawyerr proceeded to suggest several lines of approach to theology for Africa, "based on the life setting and thought-world of the African" (Sawyerr 1963: 269).

The following year in 1964, Professor Christian Goncalves Baëta (1908-1994) of the University of Ghana, stated that one of the two most important issues facing the Younger Churches is "the relation of Christian faith to local cultures and how the Younger Churches may achieve a distinctive self-hood of their own" (Baëta 1964: 19). Baëta speaks of African Christian Theology in terms of its relevancy, effectiveness and indigeneity.

In 1965 the All Africa Conference of Churches co-sponsored with the Theological Education Fund (TEF) a Theological Consultation at Ibadan. These papers were eventually printed in book form (Dickson 1969). It contains eight papers by Africans on belief in sacrifices, priesthood, man, ethics, vital participation and the spirit world. The consultation reflects deep interest in African beliefs, but fails to interact with the Scripture. The one exception is the article written by John Mbiti on Eschatology (Dickson 1969: 159-184).

In 1966 Donald Jacobs, a Mennonite missionary in Tanzania with his Ph.D. researching the Kamba of Kenya, mimeographed a course on theology for private circulation (Jacobs 1966). This is a reasonable effort on the part of an evangelical Christian theologian in Africa to deal with African questions in a course on theology. In the preface Jacobs wrote, "I became aware of some of the great blind spots while teaching Theology in Africa ... the Church in the West has simply not tried to answer questions which it has not first asked" (Preface). This is an experimental effort on the part of a missionary to make theology more relevant for Africa.

In 1968 the venerable professor of theology in Fourah Bay College, Sierra Leone, Harry Sawyerr (1926-2013), made a major contribution in his book entitled, *Creative Evangelism*. In the book the author wrestles with a new Christian encounter with Africa, seeking fresh approaches in doctrine and liturgy. Canon Sawyerr repudiates that historic Christianity which holds that "the Bible is infallibly authoritative" (Sawyerr 1968: 69). In this he becomes representative of many theologians in Africa today.

Harry Sawyerr wrestled with the problem, "What is African theology?" He is somewhat troubled with the word, "African." While he recognizes that Africans understand the culture of the soil on which they are nurtured better than most foreigners would, he also deplores any attempt to define Theologia Africana, "as specifically devised and produced for Africans per se" (Sawyerr 1971: 22). He prefers to adopt the suggestion "that the term 'African' is primarily a mythological term, expressive of love for a continent or commitment to an ideal" (Sawyerr 1971: 23). Sawyerr concludes by saying, "In spite of the difficulties inherent in the term Africa, there is a strong case for a Theologia Africana which will seek to interpret Christ to the African in such a way that he feels at home in the new faith" (Sawyerr 1971: 24).

In 1969 The Lutheran World Fellowship's Department of Theology sponsored a theological consultation which convened at their Lutheran seminary in Makumira, Tanzania (Peterson 1970). Theologians from nine African countries and many different denominations met. They spoke of "Christian Theology in Africa Today," reflecting both a reserve for the term, "African Theology," and the lack of popular usage of that label. They sensed an urgent need for more African theologians since two-thirds of the theologians present were expatriates.

In that same year John Mbiti of Kenya (born 1931) published his first major treatise, *African Religions and Philosophy* (1969) and began his apologetic efforts to restore African Traditional Religion to respectability and acceptance. Mbiti became a prolific author of international repute.

Theology in Africa began in the 1960's, but not until 1971 did African Christian Theology come of age with a greater frequency in the use of African Theology. The year 1971 was significant in that the greatest number and most significant contributions to date were published in that year. One might say that the need for African Christian Theology was rooted in the African Christian Church from the earliest years. The post-World War Two years, which brought independence to Africa, saw a greater interest and respect for traditional culture. Christians, living in this nationalistic context, began to relate their Christian faith more and more to their traditional African culture which is infused with African religion.

By 1971 a flood tide began sweeping the continent with African contributions on the subject of African Christian Theology. Authors included John Mbiti, Charles Nyamiti, John Pobee, Kwesi Dickson, Jean Marc Ela, Justin Ukpong, Eboussi Boulaga, Mercy Oduyoye and Joseph Mugambi.

Two conferences were held in East Africa on Black Theology and African Christian Theology (Mshana 1972). The Conference of Black Churchmen sponsored by the African Commission of the National Committee of Black Churchmen in the United States was held in Dar es Salaam, Tanzania, in August 1971. They accepted no white participants on the basis that "If you're white, you can have no way of knowing what it is to be black" (Mshana 1972: 20). The major thrust of the conference was the need for black people to re-educate themselves in order to understand themselves, and to communicate creatively with Blacks in Africa and elsewhere.

In January 1972 The Theological Consultation in African Theology and Church Life was sponsored by the Department of Religious Studies and Philosophy of Makerere University and held in Makerere University. Their concern was the development of a relevant theology for Africa. African Christian Theology emerges from the life, culture, traditions and faith of the African peoples.

In 1974 further steps were taken to clarify what African Christian Theology really is and why it is needed (Fashole-Luke 1974a; Dickson 1974; Mbiti 1974a).

Fashole-Luke developed one of the themes of African Christian Theology, namely, ancestors, and attempted to baptize this traditional element into the Christian Church (Fashole-Luke 1974b). In that same year "An Institute on Ancestor Veneration and the Communion of Saints" was sponsored by the Association of Theological Institutions in East Africa in Nairobi, Kenya.

By 1984 Justin Ukpong in his survey of African theologies (Ukpong 1984) could declare, "'African Theology' is a household expression today in theological circles all over Africa. Yet, when we get down to defining what it really is, it is sometimes not easy to get a clear answer" (Upkong 1984: 4). He surveys the African theologies under three categories: South African Black Theology, African Liberation Theology and African Inculturation Theology.

By the 1980s African Christian Theology had evolved into a diverse and sophisticated effort to create a Christian theology that is truly "African." We cannot detail all contributions that have been made. The plethora of diverse African writings is best tracked, as Paul Bowers mentions, "through ongoing bibliographic surveys such as those found in the *Revue Africaine de Théologie* (Congo/Zaire) and the *International Review of Missions* (Switzerland), and through the abstracts and reviews offered in journals such as *Missionalia* (South Africa) and *BookNotes for Africa* (Zambia)" (Bowers 2001: 30).

In 1978 Okeke wrote, "It is merely a waste of paper writing on the failings of the earlier missionaries. Today is our time to put right those things we find undesirable in their missionary methods and practices" (Okeke 1978: 49). Numerous African theologians have taken up that challenge and have offered their proposals. We shall examine a couple of select writers of African Christian Theology to see what they offer.

Agbonkhianmeghe Orobator, born in Nigeria, is a Jesuit priest who teaches at Hekima College Jesuit School of Theology in Nairobi, Kenya. In his book, *Theology Brewed in an African Pot*, he probes the question of how to make Christian theology intelligible to Africans. As a Christian he considers the Bible as "a guide for our talk about God." As a Roman Catholic he adheres to the Vatican Council II pronouncement that "the Bible should be the very soul of any theology." The Bible *contains* the Word of God and narrates the *experience* of the people of God (Orobator 2008: 18f).

In his doing of theology in the African context he keeps in mind three issues:

First, he considers the *Scripture*. His aim is not to quote chapters and verses to support his theological position but to learn from the Bible "the experience of our ancestors in faith. How did they experience God? How did they express their experience in words and actions?" (Orobator 2008: 14).

Second, he highly regards the *traditions* of the church, "the deep well of insights" over 2000 years.

Third, he considers the *context*. "My underlying assumption," Orobator says, "is that our African background has a lot to contribute to our faith seeking understanding, love and hope" (Orobator 2008: 14).

Then Orobator added a fourth source, Chinua Achebe's novel, *Things Fall Apart*. He recommends that the reader should first read this novel before proceeding with his book and doing African theology. In his opinion, Achebe's novel "contains such a profound source of wisdom, narratives, and events that can enrich, structure, and enlighten theological reflection from an African perspective" (Orobator 2008: 20f).

He then examines various aspects of Christian thought. For our purposes we shall only examine what he says about the Trinity. Orobator notes that the Trinity is a confusing concept. It is a unique way for Christians to speak about God. "We know God the Father, Son, and Spirit only because Jesus came to save us in the power of the Spirit and show us the way to God (see John 14)" (Orobator 2008: 36).

He refers to New Testament texts that refer to God the Father, Jesus Christ and the Holy Spirit. Though the way we speak of the Trinity today is biblical, it was not until the fourth century that the doctrine of the Trinity was developed during the Trinitarian controversies. Christian theologians at that time "created terminology (language) for talking about the Trinity. Unfortunately, this language drew heavily on the dominant forms of abstract and speculative Greek philosophy, namely, neo—Platonism. Our ways of talking about the Triune God today bear the burden of this Greek legacy" (Orobator 2008: 37). Consequently, this technical way of speaking of the Trinity does not fit with our modern context.

Therefore, he inquires, "As an African how do I understand the idea of the Triune God? Is there anything in my African background that gives me a unique insight into the meaning of three persons in one God?" (Orobator 2008: 37f). As a Nigerian he draws on a traditional figure of a woman among the Yoruba people. Her name is *Obirin meta*, meaning "three woman." This is a woman who combines strength, character, and personality. "*Obirin meta* is a woman with many sides, a many sided character. She is a multifunctional woman of unmatched density and unbounded substance" (Orobator 2008: 38).

Orobator believes that this African character, *Obirin meta,* helps Africans to think of God in an African way. What kind of God would he look like? "Not a majestic high God enrobed in terrifying inapproachable light. Rather, *Obirin meta* allows us to form the idea and open up to the experience of a God who combines many sides, many personalities, many realities, many relationships, and many qualities *at the same time and as the one and the same God.* Another way of putting it is to say that *Obirin meta* symbolizes the abundant and radical open-endedness of God in God's self and in our encounter of God" (Orobator 2008: 39).

Apparently, he does not take seriously the Scripture which repeatedly speaks of God as awesome in his majesty. Has he never read Exodus 19-20 where God appeared to the Israelites on Mt. Sinai, covered with fire, smoke and with a deafening noise, so terrifying that the Israelites "trembled with fear?" Moses later declared, "For the LORD your God is a consuming fire, a jealous God" (Dt 5:24). The writer of Hebrews refers to that epiphany by saying, "*The sight was so terrifying that Moses said, 'I am trembling with fear*" (Heb 12:21). We dare not domesticate God to suit our sensibilities!

Orobator says that this African way of viewing God "makes sense to me." As a result of naming God in this way "the mystery blocking our imagination and understanding disappears. God comes closer to us in the reality of everyday living. There is no mystery here – only God who is all things to us, inside and outside, the radically open-ended One" (Orobator 2008: 40).

Westerners have made similar efforts to explain the Trinity. One analogy is water which has three manifestations: vapour, water and ice. Or the Trinity is like an egg, one egg composed of a shell, a yoke and the egg white. St. Patrick, the missionary who evangelized Ireland, compared the Trinity to the shamrock, a member of the clover family of grass with three small, green leaves on a single stem. The problem with all these efforts to make sense of the Trinity is that they fall short of conveying the truth found in the Scriptures. If taken literally, they teach heresy.

There are multiple problems with this proposal by Orobator. First, he contradicts himself. On page 35 he spoke of the Trinity as a symbol which "points beyond itself to something larger and fuller than our imagination can comprehend." Five pages later he states that his African analogy of *Obirin meta* eliminates the mystery of the Trinity. The biblical fact is that the Trinity has always been and always will be a mystery. God is transcendent and infinite in his Being. The human mind cannot grasp a full understanding of God.

Another problem is that *Obirin meta* is a Yoruba tradition, not a pan-African tradition. *Obirin meta* is foreign to most of Africa and would need to be introduced as a foreign concept.

More importantly, his African analogy replicates the heresy of Modalism that the Church condemned. In the fifth century Modalism was proposed in order to resolve the mystery of the Trinity by saying that the one true God appeared to the Old Testament saints as Yahweh, in the Gospels the same God appeared as the Son, Jesus Christ, and in the book of Acts He appeared as the Holy Spirit. For Orobator God manifests different sides of his character to people at different times. God appears as an *unbreakable stone* when we need God to be strong for us. He appears as the *eye that sees the four corners of the world* when we are overwhelmed by the complexities of our existence. He also can appear as the *river that never ceases to flow* when we need God to shower us with blessings (Orobator 2008: 40).

The fundamental problem with Orobator's theologizing is that he minimizes the role of Scripture and the Nicene Creed which all Christians have supported, and he maximizes the importance of African culture. He urges readers to read first the novel of Achebe, but he never encourages the reading or studying of the Scriptures.

The early church fathers wrestled with the truths revealed in Scripture. Jesus Christ, the Son of God, talked to God the Father. They had an "I-Thou" relationship. The Father and Son were two "Persons" who communed together. God the Father spoke to the Son at his baptism, and the Holy Spirit descended on the Son. The Father, Son and Spirit had attributes of personality. Therefore, the Scriptures cannot be reconciled with the *Obirin meta* analogy Orobator proposes.

The doctrine of the Trinity is not illogical. It does not deny the law of non-contradiction, because orthodox theologians do not say that God is One and that He is Three in the same sense. That is illogical. To say that the earth is one planet and at the same time say that the earth is three planets makes no sense. The doctrine of the Trinity states, rather, that God is One in one sense, and that he is Three in another sense.

The Westminster Confession, for example, states: "There is but one only, living, and true God, who is infinite in being and perfection..." It further declares, "In the unity of the Godhead there be three persons, of one substance, power and eternity..."

One of the presuppositions of Orobator is that the Bible is not a unified Book but has many contradictory theologies. It is true, as Orobator says, "These Gospels do not *primarily* tell a history...Their primary purpose is not history for the sake of recounting and relating concrete and objective data and facts. The primary purpose is faith" (Orobator 2008: 69). We fully agree that the purpose of the Gospels is not *primarily* to tell history. Nevertheless, the Gospels do record historical accounts of factual events that actually took place in history; and they tell it in a complimentary fashion without error. Eyewitnesses can tell accurately what they saw, but from a different perspective and without contradiction.

For Orobator, however, "each of the early communities had its own Christology or Christologies." The interpretations by each of the four Gospels, he says, should be treated in the light of modern advances in theological and scriptural research as "partial rather than absolute theological statements or exclusive biblical interpretations" (Orobator 2008: 69f).

This approach to African Theology by the Roman Catholic Jesuit priest is consistent with others who are writing African Christian Theology.

Victor I. Ezigbo, a Nigerian by birth, is Associate Professor of Contextual and Systematic Theology at Bethel University, St. Paul, Minnesota. His book, *Re-Imagining African Christologies: Conversing with the Interpretations and Appropriations of Jesus in Contemporary African Christianity*, joins a large number of African efforts to forge a new African Christology.

Ezigbo observes that many African theologians seek to "deconstruct Missionary Christology" and in its place "re-explain the Christ-event within the indigenous cultural and religious thought." However, he believes that they fail to answer the questions which lay Christians are asking today. "Consequently, an unwarranted dichotomy exists between the contextual Christologies that many theologians are developing and the existing grassroots" (Ezigbo 2010: 18). He argues that the perennial challenge of African theologians is not Missionary Christology but how to engage *the new contexts* in which African peoples now live" (Ezigbo 2010: 19f). African theologians, Ezigbo contends, have constructed Christologies that are not written with the laity in mind but are designed for Western academia. "Most of these Christologies are peer-driven and escape some key existential Chrisological questions that the majority of lay Christians are asking" (Ezigbo 2010: 20).

The view that Jesus Christ is the "solution to the problems that confront humanity" is faulted by Ezigbo. In contrast to the "solution-oriented" Christologies, Ezigbo proposes the Revealer Christology. In his words, "I argue that the Christology that aims to engage with both the Christ-Event and the complex contexts of Africa should construe Jesus the Christ simultaneously as a *question* and an *answer* to the theological, cultural, religious, anthropological, spiritual and socio-economic issues which confront, shape and inform these contexts" (Ezigbo 2010: xiii). Jesus not only answers the painful questions which Africans ask, but Jesus is the questioner who shapes and reforms their questions.

The Christ-Event may sometimes upset, unsettle, critique, and reshape the solution-oriented Christologies. This is because Jesus Christ critiques and judges our preconceived notions. He reforms our preconceptions of God and the spirits. As the one who has both the questions and answers, "Jesus Christ confronts us as *revealer* of divinity and humanity. Therefore, he mediates and interprets divinity and humanity for the purpose of enacting and sustaining a relationship between God and human beings" (Ezigbo 2010: xiv).

For example, African Christians with a colonial mentality may feel incomplete, inferior or cursed by God. But the questioning of Jesus Christ helps those Christians to rediscover the teaching of Jesus on the dignity of human beings as God's creatures (Mt 6:25-32).

Throughout the book he distances himself from the existing Christologies in Africa, including the views of Yusufu Turaki, Tokunboh Adeyemo, and Byang Kato, fellow Nigerians. He believes that it is a "theological mistake to see Jesus as the revealer of the propositional truth of God and humanity." Instead, "the Christ-Event also provides a unique way for human beings to experience and encounter God." The key motif here is *relationship*. "The aim of the Christ-Event is not to provide human beings with a mere clear, comprehensive, intellectual, and exhaustive knowledge of God, other spiritual beings and human beings, but rather to provide a revealer through whom human beings can have a meaningful relationship with God, and to judge their preconceptions and understandings of other spiritual being, human beings, and the human world" (Ezigbo 2010: 154f).

In seeking to relate the Revealer Christology to the religious quests of African peoples, he considers three major issues for most Nigerians. *First*, the African quest to understand the relationship with the spiritual world. *Second*, the African attempts to manoeuvre and manipulate the spiritual world to work in their favour. *Third*, the search for a medium who can disclose the meaning of the events that happen to the Africans. While Africans use diviners in their quest to deal with unforeseen problems of life, "The Revealer Christology model that is proposed in this book presents Jesus Christ as the being who reshapes radically the content of these quests" (Ezigbo 2010: 166).

The key question of this book is: what would Jesus look like when he is explained in the categories that synchronize with the worldviews and experiences of African peoples?" But he finds this way of contextualizing Christology one-sided. Contextual Christology should "also be a constructive process of reinterpreting the indigenous religious beliefs and experiences of Africans in the ways that synchronize with the meaning and purpose of the Christ-Event." This means that a contextual theologian is misleading if he only asks the question, "What would Jesus look like in Africa?" He also needs to ask the question, "What would the worldviews and experiences of the people look like when they are examined in the light of the Christ-Event?" (Ezigbo 2010: 175f).

He concludes the book by making an astute observation.

> *It is an error to assume that the peoples of Africa cannot truly experience Jesus Christ unless he is described by a local metaphor, for example, as ancestor. Some theologians who construct culture-oriented Christologies are guilty of this error. It is important to point out here that ironically this assumption is suggestive of a derogatory view of African peoples as incapable of understanding the complex teaching of Christianity about Jesus Christ if he is not explicated with a local metaphor. The primary issue that confronts African Christianity is the perception of Jesus Christ merely as a solution to peoples' problems...Therefore, the Christology that will befit contemporary Christianity must be able to inspire a contextualization and counter-contextualization proceeds in which Christians begin to construe Jesus Christ as the divine and human being who questions their perceptions of their problems and solutions as well as redefines and solves their problems* (Ezigbo 2010: 304).

In this rather brief and inadequate summary of Ezigbo's Revealer Christology, the reader is left somewhat befuddled and air-born in abstract theologizing. The book could have been written more simply and made more practical. After reading the book, taking copious notes, and reviewing what Ezigbo says, he leaves me with bewilderment and confusion. We conclude with several questions and observations.

To address the question of Christology without basing it on the Scriptures is a tragic error. Surely, the meaning of the Christ event is to be found in Scripture and not in African culture. A theologian must seriously engage with the biblical text if he is to expound a Christian theology. The significance of the incarnation cannot be discussed without considering the purpose of his coming, namely, to die as the sin-bearer, as the Lamb of God, in order to save lost sinners. Nowhere do we find in this book on Revealer Christology anything bearing on this subject.

He never deals with the basic question, "How does Jesus Christ reveal himself to us?" This is "Revealer Christology." By what means does Jesus reveal himself? We assume that Jesus cannot reveal himself in Scripture because the Bible is not the Word of God; it only *contains* the Word of God. How do we determine who Jesus is from an errant book? What is wheat and what is chaff? What is truth and what is error? Who is this historical Jesus? Only the readers have the authority to decide who Jesus is since they must determine what is true and what is not.

This old modernist view of the Scriptures was succeeded by the existentialist view that the Bible *becomes* the Word of God as the reader experiences a revelatory event. In either case, the process of Christ revealing himself to his people is subjective and depends on the reader. Some may encounter Christ in one way, another in a different way. The result is many Christologies, potentially conflicting theologies.

Ezigbo is an enigma. He teaches in Bethel University, St. Paul, Minnesota, a self-identified evangelical institution. Yet one searches in vain for evidence of Ezigbo's evangelical credentials. According to him, the criteria for determining an adequate representation of Jesus Christ lies in the "spirit" and not the "letter" ("letter" refers to the different biblical images of Jesus Christ).

> *The collection of images of Jesus Christ in the New Testament can point to him, and guide in constructing a Christology, it does not exhaust the significance of Jesus Christ. The 'spirit' of our inquiring of biblical writers should stimulate or inspire us to imagine Jesus Christ afresh as we encounter Jesus Christ* (Smith 2017: Internet).

For Ezigbo the Scriptures are not the Word of God but "a witness or expression of God's revelation" (Ezigbo 2010: 191). He denounces those who, although they express the need to interact with the indigenous cultures and religions when designing a Christology for Africa, "insist on the supremacy of the Bible and the Christoloical formulations of the early church in the matter of Christology" (Ezigbo 2010: 19).

Ezigbo repudiates those, like Byang Kato, who say that there is no salvation outside of Christ. Ezigbo writes, "According to Kato, it 'is not arrogance to herald the fact that all who are not 'in Christ' are lost.' It is rather 'articulating what the Scriptures says'" (Ezigbo 2010: 39).

On the one hand, Ezigbo believes our theology should not contradict the Holy Scriptures (Smith 2017: Internet). On the other hand, he contradicts the Scripture which clearly teaches that there is "no salvation outside of Christ." Ezigbo picks and chooses what he believes from Scripture.

For this reason we have identified Ezigbo as an African theologian who is aligned with all those mentioned above under the category of African Christian Theology.

African Biblical Theology

The third type of African Theology, as we would classify it, is African Biblical Theology. Although the authors are similar in many respects to those doing other types of African Theology, they differ in one crucial area: their final source of authority. Both African Liberation Theology and African Christian Theology use the Bible along with other sources, but it is the African authors themselves who are the final authority as they pick and choose what pleases them from the various sources to craft their own version of African Theology.

Though the authors of African Biblical Theology do not agree theologically in various areas, they all agree that the Bible has the final word. When disagreements arise concerning interpretations of Scripture, they turn to Scripture as the final authority to resolve the disputes. God's inerrant Word, divinely inspired by the Holy Spirit, should be interpreted through the normal methods of grammatical-historical hermeneutics, not the historical-critical hermeneutic which undermines the integrity of the text, nor should the Scriptures be "deconstructed." Whenever differences of interpretation occur, the Bible retains the final authority.

Similar Concerns of Evangelical Theologians: These African theologians who grant to the Scriptures final authority concur with their other African colleagues in many of their concerns.

Dr. Byang Kato, who might be called the "Father of Evangelical Theology," has been much maligned by liberal African theologians who feel that he is irrelevant to the conversation of contextualization. But Kato felt great sympathy for those under any kind of bondage. He called "the enslavement of Africans by the whites" as "probably the worst evil done by one class of people to another. It may be surpassed only by Hitler's massacre of six million Jews" (Kato 1975). (Though we must also say that all races, including Africans, have historically engaged in the inhumane practice of slavery.)

In his major treatise, *Theological Pitfalls,* Kato urged the need to relate the Gospel to the context when he declared: "Evangelicals who hold the Bible as their basic source for Christian theology must learn to move beyond the divinely revealed source to the human dimension where the action is. They must discover how best to relate the human situation in all areas including the socio-economic arena" (Kato 1975: 151).

Kato agreed with John Mbiti that missionaries were not prepared to "face a serious encounter" with traditional religions. Because the missionaries did not address the issues troubling the Africans, "the Church in Africa is suffering from theological anaemia due to the failures of the past" (Kato 1973). Therefore, he said, "I see the need of Christian theology addressing itself specifically to the African situation...African theologians today should also make their own contribution to theology for the benefit of the church universal" (Kato 1976). Christian doctrine should be expressed in terms that Africans can understand. "Whatever would promote the glory of Christ in His Church in Africa and make the African feel 'this is my faith,' should be promoted."

Dr. Samuel Ngewa, professor in Africa International University and prolific author, laments that missionaries ignored African sacrifices when preaching the Gospel. He urges greater effort in utilizing traditional beliefs and practices when "communicating the Biblical themes to the African peoples" (Ngewa 1987: 79). One of the many qualities of an African Christian theologian should be "a sincere respect for the African culture. He sees it not only for what it is worth, but also takes pride in that it is his heritage" (Ngewa 1987: 7-8).

Dr. Samuel Waje Kunhiyop, former General Secretary of ECWA, Nigeria, and visiting Professor of Ethics at Brigham University, Karuu, Nigeria, declared: "The principal challenge facing African Christianity is making Christianity relevant enough so that it addresses African existential problems and biblical enough so that it is consistent with God's revelation" (Kunhiyop 1997: 3). He agrees with Jean-Marc Ela's "insightful remark" that African Theology must "take into account what is actually lived in particular experience of African local communities" in order to be relevant (Kunhiyop 1997: 4).

Because of his commitment to the authority of Scripture, Dr. Kunhiyop concludes that "the actual expression of theological truth will differ from culture to culture. However, the content, namely, the basic theological truths, will not change" (Kunhiyop 1997: 16).

Dr. Aiah Foday-Khabenje, General Secretary of Evangelicals in Africa stated: "Too much of our theological reflection in Africa is informed by Western thinkers and their understanding of Scripture. Ignorance and ethnic arrogance have resulted in the African worldview and African religious beliefs being dismissed as primitive and heathen" (Kunhiyop 2012: Foreword).

Slow Beginnings of African Biblical Theology: Conservative evangelicals in Africa were slower in training Africans at higher levels of theology than the ecumenical missionaries. Byang Kato alluded to the fact that most missionaries from evangelical churches in the West had limited education. Their primary concern was evangelism and church planting, while neglecting education and preparation of African leadership.

Furthermore, when African independence arrived in the 1960s, the World Council of Churches through the Theological Education Fund provided scholarships for hundreds of Africans to take advanced training overseas, almost always in liberal institutions. By contrast the evangelicals had limited funds. Nor did they have many men and women trained at degree level who would have been capable of profiting from such scholarships.

As a result, African Biblical Theology had a slow start. When comparing the number of articles and books that are published today by African theologians, it would appear that the gap has not yet been filled. Most African Protestant denominations were founded as conservative, evangelical, Gospel preaching churches, but as the parent denominations in the West became liberal, this influence has filtered into many Protestant denominations in Africa. Most publications by African theologians are liberal.

Practical Nature of African Biblical Theology: The nature of the contributions made by evangelicals is strikingly different from the ecumenical scholars. Of the scores and scores of tomes written on African Liberation Theology and African Christian Theology, they tend to be academic, serving as scholarly contributions that engage their peers. They represent an elite class separate from the masses.

As Orobator commented in 2008, "Theology in Africa remains confined largely to a group of people I call 'professional Christians,' mostly men – there are a few women too – who make a living as ministers of the church: priests, religious, sister, and brothers. Seminaries and institutions of religious formation serve as the privileged setting for doing theology" (Orobator 2008: 9).

Many of these books are obtuse, opaque and abstract. They are actually boring. These books are not written for the masses but for scholarly pursuits. They theorize and postulate about what African Theology should be or what themes could be.

In contrast, the contributors of African Biblical Theology are practical and make a genuine impact on the growth and maturing of the African Church. The practical contributions of evangelical scholars in the past fifty years are quite impressive. Much of it began with the founding of the Association of Evangelicals of Africa and Madagascar (A.E.A.M.) in 1966 and the impetus given by Dr. Byang Kato, the first African General Secretary of the A.E.A.M. "Although Kato lived a relatively short life, he has remained the most influential Evangelical theologian in Nigeria and arguably in Africa" (Ezigbo 2010: 55).

Contributions of African Biblical Theologians: Although evangelicals were late in their efforts to facilitate African leadership and scholarship, amazing advances have been made.

Association of Evangelicals of Africa: Two large missionary societies in North America (the Interdenominational Foreign Mission Association [I.F.M.A.], and the Evangelical Foreign Missions Association [E.F.M.A.]) became concerned that the World Council of Churches was influencing many national African churches through the five to six million US dollars they designated for scholarships in the 1960s. Hundreds of Africans were given scholarships between 1960 and 1965 averaging $13,000 each. Numerous African evangelicals accepted these scholarships for study in liberal institutions and the missionaries feared that they would not return to Africa for ministry, or if they did, they would return as liberal pastors and theologians (Breman 1996: 7-8).

Steps were taken that led to the Africa Evangelical Conference in Limuru, Kenya in 1966. The convener was Rev. Kenneth Downing, the General Secretary of the Africa Evangelical Office which had been started earlier in 1962. Downing was born in Kenya, fluent in Kikuyu and a veteran missionary of the Africa Inland Mission who had traversed the continent of Africa to promote and establish Evangelical Fellowships.

On the fifth day of the Conference Dr. Aaron B. Gamedze of Swaziland proposed the creation of an African Evangelical Association (A.E.A.M.). This was overwhelmingly approved and the Association of Evangelicals of Africa and Madagascar was formed. Later the name was shortened by eliminating the name, "Madagascar" (A.E.A.). African officers were appointed.

This pan-African Evangelical Association began as a small organization comprised of 11 National Fellowships of Evangelicals that had been formed through the itinerating ministry of Ken Downing. Today the National Evangelical Fellowships throughout Africa number 40. A Constitution was formed and a statement of faith adopted from the Evangelical Alliance which was founded in Great Britain in 1846. The first article of faith reads: "THE HOLY SCRIPTURES, as originally given by God, divinely inspired, infallible, entirely trustworthy, and the supreme authority in all matters of faith and conduct" (Breman 1996: 489).

The term, "evangelical," means many things to many people. It is an elastic term that incorporates a disparate range of beliefs. "The Declaration of Nigerian Evangelicals 1975," mainly the work of Byang Kato, enumerates what Nigerian Evangelicals considered basic, core beliefs of Evangelicals.

(1) The Divine inspiration of the Bible, its infallibility, and its final authority on all matters of faith and conduct;

(2) The One eternal God, Creator and Lord of the universe, Father, Son and Holy Spirit.
(3) Jesus Christ the God-man, and His Lordship in every area of the believer's life.
(4) The Holy Spirit as a person, and His constant indwelling in the life of the believer.
(5) The Creation of Man perfect in the image of God, and his subsequent fall, and total depravity.
(6) The redemption from the penalty, the power and ultimately, the presence of sin solely through the sacrificial death and the resurrection of Jesus Christ.
(7) The future physical and personal return of Christ.
(8) The eternal dwelling of believers with the Lord in heaven and the eternal punishment of unbelievers in hell (Breman 1996: 31).

Rev. Kenneth Downing served as General Secretary of the A.E.A.M., 1966-1970, while Rev. Dr. Samuel Odunaike served as President 1969-1991. At the Second General Assembly at Limuru, Kenya, in 1973, Dr. Byang Kato was unanimously elected A.E.A.M.'s first *African* General Secretary. Though his time of service was shortened by his untimely drowning off the coast of Kenya in 1975, his influence on evangelicals in Africa was profound (Breman 1996: 40-51).

In the paper that Kato read to the Second General Assembly of A.E.A.M. in 1973, he articulated the errors of various African Theologies and then proposed an evangelical response. He urged that certain projects of training and the promotion of national evangelical leadership "should be embarked upon right away." Included was the recommendation that two theological schools at university level be established, one in Francophone and one in Anglophone. The recommendation was agreed upon. African religions and philosophy were to be taught and irrelevant subjects scrapped. More emphasis was to be placed on the Scriptures and the unique nature of Christian revelation" (Kato 1973).

Graduate Schools of Theology: Byang Kato stressed the need to "concentrate effort on the training of men in the Scriptures, employing the original languages to facilitate their ability in exegeting the Word of God in depth" (1975: 182). He emphasized the importance of sound theology and Bible knowledge in evangelical churches in Africa to thwart the danger of syncretism and universalism infesting the pastors and their churches. "Training on African soil would mean that the teaching was suited for Africa" (Breman 1996: 254). The purpose of theological training at university level in Africa was to provide contextualized education appropriate for African church leaders.

The Bangui Evangelical School of Theology for Francophone Africa was established in 1977 in Bangui, Central Africa Republic, and the Nairobi Evangelical School of Theology for Anglophone Africa was established in Nairobi, Kenya, in 1983. N.E.G.S.T. became chartered by the Kenyan Government in 2011 as a Chartered Private University known as the Africa International University.

It is significant that within the By-Laws of the Graduate School in Kenya one objective stated:

> *To provide courses which in every case, to whatever degree is practicable and necessary, will be oriented to Africa and its circumstances, problems and needs. To present the unchanging*

> *Christian faith to students through the perspective of African culture and world-view. To develop a sufficient awareness among church leaders of the relevant philosophies, ideologies, and problems that will enable them to contextualize the Gospel and apply it to the life situation of their people. To incarnate the eternal and unchanging truth of God in the lives of the people in Africa thus making it meaningful and readily applicable to every need. To relate all taught theology to the contemporary and local culture and African thought processes. To present biblical truth in its relation to African questions and problems and those that are relevant to Africa. To ensure that every aspect of the training given shall contribute to these goals, without making the course parochial or neglecting world-wide theological problems and the worldwide commission of the church* (NEGST By-Laws p. 1).

Though the objective as stated above was not composed by the late Byang Kato himself, he would have heartily supported this goal for the Evangelical Graduate School. Indeed, the whole task of proclaiming "the unchanging Christian faith" to the peoples "through the perspective of African culture and worldview" was the burden of Kato and all those evangelicals who share his evangelical convictions. Kato together with all evangelicals on the African continent are seeking to establish an African Christian faith which will be, in Kato's words, "truly biblical and truly African."

As we all know, the task of implementing our ideas is not easy. Evangelicals have no private access to the royal road of contextualizing the Gospel. Their dreams are more dramatic than their actual implementation. But the fact is that evangelicals, like Byang Kato and the members of the Association of Evangelicals of Africa and Madagascar and others of like mind, are busily engaged in the task of making the Gospel incarnate in African culture.

***Accrediting Association of Theological Education in Africa* (ACTEA)**: In 1976 the Executive Council of the AEAM decided to establish ACTEA with the aim to "assist evangelical theological schools and programmes throughout Africa in their quest for excellence and renewal" (Breman 1996: 291). By 1996 ACTEA had linked 190 theological colleges and programmes in 30 countries. At present 85 institutions in 32 countries are in various stages of accreditation or as correspondent members. Not only has ACTEA been able to raise the standard of theological education in Africa, it has gained international recognition.

The accrediting process is vigorous and includes high standards for contextualization. They require concrete steps to be taken to ensure that the institution is led by Africans with a majority of staff being qualified Africans. They examine the curriculum to make sure that it is contextualized with culturally relevant courses. ACTEA standards require a vigorous Field Education Program so that students have hands-on experience using their learned skills in African church ministries.

Theological Education by Extension: TEE began in 1963 by the Presbyterian Evangelical Seminary in Guatemala as distance education specifically and exclusively for teaching theology. This innovative format of theological education was called TEE for the first time. Drs. Fred and Grace Holland became involved with TEE TEXT-Africa project in Anglophone Africa. Then in 1973 Dr. Paul White took up the project for Francophone Africa.

TEE is designed to train pastors, elders, and active lay people through programmed instructional materials in an extension ministry away from any theological institution. It enables older, married individuals the opportunity to gain theological and biblical training without the need to become resident in a traditional Bible School or seminary. The TEE books are written for Africa by Africans and missionaries. Weekly seminars are held where the ideas learned from the book are discussed and applied. "TEE has been described as 'the largest nongovernmental voluntary educational development in the world'" (Breman 1996: 319).

<u>Christian Learning Materials Center</u>: (Breman 1996: 307-317). Rev. Roger Coon had been appointed Coordinating Secretary of the Christian Education Commission in 1973. One of his first tasks was to travel throughout the Continent of Africa to consult with churches and seek cooperative planning for the development of Christian Education. After collaborating with Africans in dozens of countries and churches, he made this observation:

> *The church in Africa is an evangelizing church, but not a teaching and discipling church. These are observations supported by every Christian leader with whom I consulted throughout the continent. Christianity is often a veneer of sincere religious interest thinly veiling personal practices and unchanged cultural values that conflict with the teachings of Jesus. A Ministry of Education official...said, "The majority of the population identity themselves as Christian. But the roots do not go deep, the people are religious, religion is in everything they do. It is easy to simply replace one religion with another without it really changing the person. He is living the same, only having replaced one religion with another. Thus many nominal Christians who are eager to arrange for their children to be baptized are equally as involved in unethical professional practices as are non-Christians"* (Breman 1996: 308f).

In order to meet this desperate need for teaching God's Word to Christians, beginning in childhood, the Association of Evangelicals of Africa took a major step. In 1979 the executive committee of AEA "mandated the establishment of a Christian Education Curriculum Development and Publishing Company." A Planning Committee was appointed under the chairmanship of Rev. Isaac Simbiri, General Secretary of the Kenya Evangelical Fellowship.

The Christian Learning Materials Centre (CLMC) is "a pioneering African Christian educational facility to research and develop needed African written Bible teaching materials" (Breman 1996: 308f). It is a "semi-autonomous cooperative venture established by the AEAM [AEA]." Before the founding of CLMC, the Sunday School materials used in many evangelical churches came from overseas, albeit, adapted for African use. The aim of CLMC was to "supply evangelical churches with more suitable teaching materials written by Africans for African churches. The Christian learning materials were to be "culturally African, educationally effective, and thoroughly Biblical."

A few years after the first publications, the CLMC Sunday School materials were used by most of the English language Protestant churches in Kenya, including: Anglican, Baptist, Brethren, Pentecostal, Presbyterian, Wesleyan and Africa Inland Churches. They are now used in many other African countries (Breman 1996: 314).

Africa Bible Commentary: In 2006 a monumental task was accomplished, the publication of the *Africa Bible Commentary* (ABC), a one-volume commentary written by 70 African scholars (Adeyemo 2006). During the Second Pan Africa Christian Leadership Assembly in 1994, representatives of Protestant churches, both ecumenical and evangelical, identified a deficient knowledge of the Bible and faulty application of its teaching to be the primary weakness of the church in Africa. "The Bible needed to be interpreted and explained to the people in a familiar language, using colloquial metaphors, African thought-forms and nuances, and practical applications that fitted the African context" (Adeyemo 2006: viii). This dream was planted at that time.

Books are published by African theologians which end up in libraries of academic institutions and read by seminary students and professors, leaving the masses of Africans in the churches to languish. What is needed most is help offered to African people to understand the Bible better.

It was the Association of Evangelicals of Africa (AEA) that captured this vision and brought the *Africa Bible Commentary* into existence. The Executive Committee of the AEA and leaders of the SIM (Serving in Ministry) met on the NEGST campus in 2001, and agreed together to produce a one-volume Bible Commentary by enlisting 70 African scholars across the continent.

Tokunboh Adeyemo (Nigerian), the General Secretary of the AEA, became the General Editor. Samuel Ngewa (Kenyan), Professor of New Testament at NEGST, became the New Testament Editor, and Tewoldemedhin Habtu (Eritrean), a Professor at NEGST, became the Old Testament Editor.

The ABC is not an academic commentary that exegetes each verse. Rather it explains the biblical text section-by-section through the eyes of African scholars who "respect the integrity of the text and use African proverbs, metaphors and stories to make it speak to African believers in the villages and cities across the entire continent" (Adeyemo 2006: ix). This massive Bible Commentary of 1585 pages "does not speak of a Black Jesus. To do so would be a travesty of the Bible story and cheap scholarship. Instead, the ABC is true to the text and honest to its context both in the Bible days and in our day" (Adeyemo 2006: ix).

The Africa Bible Commentary Series: No sooner had the *Africa Bible Commentary* been published, the ABC Board decided that more was needed beyond a one-volume Bible Commentary. They determined to publish a whole series of commentaries on individual books of the Bible, using African scholars from both Anglophone and Francophone Africa who adhered to the statement of faith held by the Association of Evangelicals of Africa.

The Africa Bible Commentary Series is published in Nairobi, Kenya, by WordAlive (Hippo Books); in Bukura, Nigeria by Africa Christian Textbooks (ACTS); and published for the rest of the world by Zondervan.

This unique Bible Commentary is uniquely crafted with distinctive features. Each commentary is divided into preaching units that contain an exposition of the passage with contemporary applications. The purpose is to help pastors develop a series of messages based on the teaching of each book of the Bible. Referring to the Africa Bible Commentary, Dr. Douglas Carew commented, "A good and readable blend of excellent scholarship, heart-warming spirituality, and relevant application. It challenges African Christianity, and wider, to a necessary commitment of heart, mind and will." This reflects the heart of evangelicals and their approach to Scripture.

Dr. Samuel Ngewa, Professor of New Testament Studies at African International University, was chosen to be the Editor of the New Testament commentaries. He has published the first Bible commentaries in this series, one on *1 & 2 Timothy and Titus*, and a second on *Galatians.* Ngewa is a prolific writer who has also penned the commentary of five biblical books plus six articles in the *Africa Bible Commentary*. Independently, he has published *The Gospel of John: A Commentary for Pastors and Teachers.*

Africa Study Bible: This Bible found its origins in 2003 among African church leaders, Oasis International and Tyndale House Publishers. Dr. Danny McCain led an effort to evaluate the understanding of the Bible by English speaking church members in Jos, Nigeria, and the potential impact of having the Bible in clear, modern language using African vocabulary. Conversations were held with Dr. Tite Tienou from Burkina Faso and Senior Vice President of Education, Dean and professor of Theology of Missions at Trinity Evangelical Divinity School.

During an extensive tour of Africa in 2010 by Dr. Matthew Elliott, Oasis President, he "received a resoundingly positive response from seminary presidents, denominational leaders and academics across the continent. The consensus: it was essential that we create a study Bible to reflect the knowledge, culture and wisdom of Africa for the world, bringing insight to global Christianity" (Africa Study Bible: Internet).

Through much toil and effort the *Africa Study Bible* was published in 2017. African writers from 50 African countries (194 writers from Anglophone countries, 100 from Francophone countries, 11 from Portuguese-speaking countries and 11 from Arabic-speaking countries, including 69 female writers) provided the African application notes. In addition, supportive staff of editors, translators and administrative staff devoted 300 hours per week to accomplish this humongous task. Overseeing the project was the supervising editor, Dr. John Jusu (Sierra Leone), Academic Dean, School of Professional Studies at Africa International University (successor of NEGST). The African base of operations was at the Africa International University, Nairobi, Kenya, where the hundreds of African scholars throughout the continent were in contact through the internet. Through contact and consultation, the church leaders of many denominations of 100 million Africans have committed themselves to using the *Africa Study Bible* for discipleship.

The Bible translation used is the *New Living Translation,* copyrighted by Tyndale House Publishers. This application Bible includes 2,400 features with African proverbs and stories, application notes, African touch points where Scripture and the African way of life are considered and reconciled, and Learn features which provide key doctrinal understandings of God's Word.

Engagement of African Evangelical Women: An effort has been made to mobilize evangelical women to be engaged in growing and maturing the African Church through practical theologizing. The AEAM sponsored the "Pan African Christian Women Assembly" (PACWA) which convened in the Kenyatta International Conference Centre, Nairobi, Kenya, on August 5-12, 1989, with women attending from 36 African countries.

In the Preamble of the PACWA Covenant, the women declared, "We affirm our evangelical commitment to the authority of the Holy Scriptures in obedience to the Lordship of Jesus Christ" (Mbugua 1994: 145). These women asserted that their "time has come" to "stop the tide of liberalism and secularism with its resultant materialism." They asserted "the true dignity of women as found in Jesus Christ and contained in the Bible." They determined to "deliver Africa from moral decadence and ultimate collapse" and to "make disciples of African nations for Christ" (Mbugua 1994: 145).

Unlike their liberal counterparts, these evangelical women held tenaciously to biblical precepts. On the one hand, they resolved to become more like Christ through "the disciplines of personal Bible study, practicing the presence of God (prayer), fellowship in worship with other believers, and sharing in love by word and deed with society and keeping self from sin" (Mbugwa 1994: 146).

On the other hand, they addressed social issues as well. They affirmed that God is "just and fair to all of his creatures made in his image." He requires "justice, fairness, and good neighbourliness in all human relationships" whether in employment or in government. "Where God is biased," they proclaimed, "it is in favour of the oppressed, the widows, the orphans, the aliens, and the poor, the majority of whom are women." They went on to advocate equal treatment of men and women, and where women had been denied equal opportunity, "preferential treatment should be given to women" (Mbugwa 1994: 147).

Biblical and Theological Textbooks: For 30 years Wilbur O'Donovan taught in six theological institutions in Africa, qualifying him with familiarity with the African context. During five years he researched and wrote in consultation with 300 African Theological students and faculty members. With this background he published *Biblical Christianity in African Perspective* in 1996 in order to answer the real questions raised by African Christians (O'Donovan 1996). Dr. Haruun Ruun, Secretary General of the New Sudan Council of Churches commented: "This book is unique among the books I have read on the subject. It is pictorial, simply and precisely to the point. It is easy to read and understandable." Dr. Yusufu Turaki, of Nigeria wrote, "This book will sharpen a student's understanding of the issues, both doctrinal and practical that face African Christians today."

The 18 chapters are developed through a series of questions. The whole book progresses from one thought to another through questions. The book begins by describing the African worldview and then asks the question, "How do we build a theology that is biblical?" He concludes: "The need is not to mix the truth of the Bible with the teachings of other religions, but to state the biblical truth in ways that are true to African life and experience. In other words, theology must be truly Christian but also truly African in expression" (O'Donovan 1996: 5).

Throughout the textbook he writes simply and avoids controversial subjects that divide evangelicals. The book was written to instruct and strengthen believers in their faith, and not to engage in controversies that divide evangelicals.

Dr. Samuel Waje Kunhiyop, an ordained minister and former General Secretary of ECWA, Nigeria, Kunhiyop is a visiting Professor of Ethics at Brigham University, Karuu, Nigeria, and the author of *African Christian Theology.* Wilbur O'Donovan told his class of students that he hoped that his work would encourage "African authors to present the results of their own study in written form." In the words of Kunhiyop, "As a former student of Wilbur O'Donovan, I see this present book as a modest response to this desire" (Kunhiyop 2012: xiv).

Christian Theology written anywhere, in Kunhiyop's view, is "written to address questions that arise from their particular contexts. However," he continues, "it is critical to remember that an African Christian theology does not stand alone but is part of the larger context of the Christian story...An African Christian theology therefore needs to interact with truths that apply to all peoples, tribes and nations, such as in the subjects of revelation, sin, God, the spiritual world, the community of God and the end times" (Kunhiyop 2012: xv).

This textbook is scholarly with footnotes, an extensive bibliography and suggested further reading. The 250 pages cover all of systematic theology. It is filled with biblical references and frequent citing of African theological scholars. Unlike many theological textbooks from the West, which are pedantic and academic, this book is accessible, readable and interesting. The author is irenic in tone and gracious in his treatment of other theological positions.

Most importantly, Kunhiyop intermingles discussion of African issues with traditional topics of theology (Kunhiyop 2012: 191f). For example, when treating natural revelation, he cites both biblical teaching and its relationship with African Traditional Religion. He interacts with John Mbiti's assessment of ATR, but denies Mbiti's claim that African Religion is the same as the faith prescribed in the Scriptures" (Kunhiyop 2012: 21f). He devotes two pages on African views of the Supreme Being and eight pages on biblical teaching of God; 11 pages on Good Spirits (angels) and Evil Spirits (devil and demons).

Concerning Christ and salvation, he begins by saying, "Western theologies have often ignored the African context, and so African theologians have felt the need to express the Christian faith in a way that is deeply rooted in their own cultures and expressed in their own language" (Kunhiyop 2012: 18). He then enumerates several examples of African approaches to Christology followed by a critique. His evaluation begins by observing the "positive aspects" of their presentations and says, "It is good to use creativity when seeking to present Jesus in a way that makes sense to a particular community."

However, he points out the "problems with any study of theology that takes human culture rather than divine revelation as its starting point. A theology written 'from below' tends to emphasize how we relate to God rather than how God relates to us. The result is that many African Christologies make no attempt to deal with who Christ is but instead focus only what he does for us...they often contain sweeping generalizations rooted in anthropology rather than theology" (Kunhiyop 2012: 79). Kunhiyop concludes by saying, "Fundamentally, theology is making sense of the Word of God. The emphasis should be on understanding God from his perspective; thus his word should be the primary test of theology" (Kunhiyop 2012: 79).

Kunhiyop's 400 page textbook on *African Christian Ethics* is a magisterial book both in size and its relevance to Africa from a biblical perspective (Kunhiyop 2008). Both of his books are popular as textbooks.

Publishing and Promoting African Textbooks: "Africa Christian Textbooks" (ACTS), based in Nigeria with an outlet in Kenya, publishes evangelical textbooks for Africa. Currently, they themselves or in partnership with Langham Literature in the Hippo imprint, publish nearly three dozen textbooks authored wholly or in part by Africans. Langham Global Library also publishes African authored books on-demand. Numerous other evangelical publishers provide monographs or textbooks throughout the continent (Todd 2017: Email).

Bibliographical resources are available for theological institutions to learn of books relevant for Africa. *BookNotes* for Africa, edited by Paul Bowers, has a growing number of one-paragraph reviews for books related to African theological studies, presently numbering 1,400 books. Another helpful tool is Textbooks *for Theological Education in Africa: An Annotated Bibliography*, edited by Richard Starcher and Enosh Anguandia (Bowers 2017: Email).

Regrettably, most textbooks are not written by Africans. Authoring books is a gift which most people do not have, and is done mostly by introverts because writing requires much time, patience and perseverance. A large number of published works are derived from PhD dissertations which demanded diligence to obtain the degree. Once that requisite was completed, the writing dries up. The purpose of this book is to stimulate all believers in Jesus Christ who love and trust the Bible as God's inspired Word to tackle the difficult task of providing the African Church with practical and intellectually stimulating theological studies necessary for spiritual maturity.

Theological Publications: Here we mention a few of the many evangelicals who have published scholarly works over the years. **Tokunboh Adeyemo** wrote *Salvation in African Tradition* in which he expounded the biblical texts which undermine universalism. In addition to editing the *Africa Bible Commentary,* he wrote numerous other books and articles. **Tite Tienou** published *Theological Task of the Church in Africa* in 1982, and has written a variety of articles. **Yusufu Turaki**, ordained minister of ECWA, Nigeria, and Professor of Theology and Social Ethics in Jos ECWA Theological Seminary, Nigeria, is a prolific author and worldwide speaker. Among his publications are: *Christianity and African gods: A Method in Theology*, and *Tainted Legacy*. **James Kombo**, Deputy Vice Chancellor Academic Affairs and Professor of Systematic Theology, Daystar University, Kenya, is another prolific author and international lecturer. His doctoral thesis on the Trinity (Kombo 2000) formed the basis for later works, the most recent being, *Theological Models of the Doctrine of the Trinity: The Trinity, Diversity and Theological Hermeneutics (Global Perspectives)* (Kombo 2016). **Kwame Bediako** is a self-described Evangelical and founder of the Akrofi Christaller Memorial Centre for Mission Studies in Ghana. He has gained an international reputation as a stimulating author and speaker.

CONCLUSION

Scanning the history of African Theology reveals startling growth, from virtually no theological books by Africans in the early 1950s to a breath-taking explosion of books today.

Unfortunately, many of these books are based on faulty methodology. Their theology is built on the quick-sand of unbelieving western theologies. Only those theologies which are faithful to Scripture have lasting value.

The following chapter explores the kind of foundation needed to grow a dynamic, healthy African Church. Churches in the West are declining rapidly when fed the kind of theology that is based on human theorizing. Churches in the West that are growing are Bible based because the Word of God offers people the truth that meets the inner cravings of the human heart. The Holy Spirit who inspired the authors of the Bible is the life-giving, illuminating and energizing Person who grows the Church of Jesus Christ

3

FOUNDATION FOR AFRICAN THEOLOGY

The task of thinking through our Christian faith and applying divine truth to our cultural context is both desirable and necessary. But unless a house is built on solid foundations, it will crumble with the passage of time. The house to be built is a Christian theology in Africa. The foundation to be laid is our methodology whereby we develop Christian theology in Africa.

In this chapter we shall first examine the methodology of several African theologians. Then Guidelines will be suggested for those who desire to research issues that arise in particular African contexts.

A CRITIQUE OF PROPOSED METHODOLOGIES

Kwesi Abotsia Dickson

Kwesi Dickson (1929-2004) was a priest, theologian, author and professor at the University of Ghana, Legon. He also served as the seventh President of the Methodist Church in Ghana. Dickson was among the first African theologians who saw the critical need to develop an adequate methodology. In 1974 he made this accurate observation:

> *Admittedly, there has been a tendency, in talking of an African Theology, to look at the matter solely from the point of view of the contribution African life and thought can make, and hardly ever from the point of view of biblical revelation ... In other words, this quest for an African Theology could proceed on the basis of a faulty methodology, that is, by making a value judgement of certain facets of African life and thought and then seeking sanction from biblical revelation for its incorporation into the expression of the Christian Faith. It seems to us that the reverse is the only valid way to build up a Christian theology ... it would be inexcusable to fail to give biblical teaching pride of place in this quest* (Dickson 1974: 204).

One year later Dickson wrote an article entitled, "African Theology: Origin, Methodology and Content" (Dickson 1975). In this article he observes that the term, "African Theology," has been in use for the past decade, "but it is only now that the prerequisites for such theology are in the process of being defined" (1975: 41). He then mentions three areas where important developments could take place: the church's order of services, study of the Bible and the restatement of basic Christian doctrines.

But the article really fails to come to grips with the methodology by which African Theology is to be done. He does place great emphasis on the primacy of biblical revelation as one relates the Christian faith to African culture. "Indigenization," he says, is a term which makes "a separation between the central revelation of God in Christ, which revelation is unchanging and about which there can be no compromise, and the cultural incidentals of a Western nature which accompanied the Gospel to Africa; the latter must be either discarded or adapted to suit the African traditional culture ethos" (1985: 40).

Dickson shows that in the minds of many African theologians, biblical revelation does play an important role. "It is not accidental that the Ibadan consultation had for its theme 'Biblical Revelation and African Beliefs'" (Dickson 1974: 204). Elsewhere Dickson declares, "There is the need to make a serious study of the Bible, which, after all, is an indispensable source of theologizing since it reveals what God has done" (Torres 1978: 47).

But Dickson also raises our concern about his view of Scripture. He states that the study of the Bible has been "woefully neglected by the Church in Africa and... deserves urgent attention" (Dickson 1975: 42), according to Dickson. Yet he interprets this Bible from the critical point of view which rejects the absolute authority and unity of the Scriptures. "The many hermeneutical tools which scholars have defined over the years are indispensable," Dickson writes, "and in the departments of religious studies all over the continent care is taken to ensure that students are brought up to appreciate the modern critical methods of biblical study" (Dickson 1975: 42).

While evangelical biblical scholars use various hermeneutical tools for the interpretation of Scripture, these tools are all under the authority of the Word of God as we accept the Bible by faith. Faith in Jesus Christ is primary. And Jesus Christ had complete confidence in the Scriptures. Therefore, our faith in Christ compels us to hold to the same faith that He had in the Scriptures. We shall see later on in this book in greater detail what Jesus' attitude was toward the Scriptures. We can merely observe here that His confidence was absolute. "Truly I say to you," Jesus taught, "until heaven and earth pass away, not the smallest letter or stroke shall pass away from the Law, until all is accomplished" (Mt 5:18).

Dickson has apparently accepted the presupposition of the documentary hypothesis of the Old Testament (Dickson 1975: 43). In this western critical view of the Bible, Moses was not the author of the Pentateuch, the first five books of the Bible. Instead, the critics claim that an editor or several editors compiled the first five books of the Bible from various conflicting sources. In the same way, these critics believe, much of the Bible was compiled through the editing of many contradictory sources. The emphasis in the documentary hypothesis is the faulty, human effort to compile the Bible from various literary sources. By human reason the Scriptures are examined. Man determines what he thinks is true and what is in error.

This critical view of the Bible denies the unity of the Scriptures. The Holy Spirit is not the divine Author. Hence, there are many contradictions in the Bible. Therefore, we are not bound to accept what the Bible teaches. These critics for instance deny that Paul wrote the Pastoral Epistles (1 and 2 Timothy, Titus). Even though these letters claim to be written by the Apostle Paul and even though the Christian Church over the centuries has recognized them as canonical (that is, part of the inspired Word of God), critical scholars reject Pauline authorship because, in their opinion, Paul could not have written the letters as they stand.

With these assumptions Dickson opens himself up to serious distortion of what Scripture teaches. The unity of biblical revelation is rejected. When a theologian with these presuppositions takes biblical study seriously, he inevitably wanders from the historic faith of the Christian Church.

This is reflected in a paper Dickson presented in 1977 at the Pan African Conference of Third World Theologians held in Ghana. In his paper on the "Continuity and Discontinuity Between the Old Testament and African Life and

Thought" (Bares 1978: 39-52), he reflects on the Old Testament Scriptures. While he maintains that "the exclusivist attitude" in the Old Testament is predominant, another "tradition which, even if it was not the most publicised, was nevertheless striking for its rejection of an exclusivist attitude to the goyim" (Bares 1978a: 42).

Dickson here finds two conflicting theologies in the Bible. In most places, he says, you find "the exclusivist attitude," holding to an exclusive view of revelation and salvation through Israel alone. But Dickson believes that there is another teaching which rejects that "exclusivist attitude." Because of personal preferences he chooses the one over the other. Therefore, we conclude that in Dickson's opinion the Holy Spirit is not the One Divine Author of the Bible. Nor is there unity in what the Bible teaches but only conflicting theologies.

Such an approach allows one to pick and choose the "tradition" which is most acceptable and reasonable to the person reading the Bible. In this particular case Dickson assumes that the Most High God of whom Melchizedek was priest, was the heathen god, Baal, known in Phoenicia (1978: 42). Dickson concludes with von Rad, "such a positive, tolerant evaluation of a Canaanite cult outside Israel is unparalleled in the Old Testament" (1978: 44).

As evangelicals we cannot escape the inevitable loss and theological consequences of this unorthodox view of Scripture. Dickson notes that at one time the Old Testament was deemed to be very special. "The author of the Old Testament was held to be the Holy Spirit." Dickson acknowledges that, "This kind of attitude did affect the interpretation of the text in so far as it discouraged the raising of questions regarding the limitations of the authors" (Bares 1978a: 48).

This frank admission by Dickson must be understood and remembered. As we move along in our study of African Theology we must remember that the major differences between liberal theologians and evangelical theologians is over this very issue. Liberal theologians like Dickson do not believe in the same kind of Bible as evangelicals do. Their view of revelation is starkly different. For this reason their conclusions in African Theology will be radically different. And let us remember that the critical view of the Bible was not first developed in Africa. It was developed in the West and imported into Africa.

Dickson concludes,

> *In our time there is a diverse array of tools for studying the Old Testament (and indeed the Bible as a whole), and the influence of various other sciences has been recognized, such as sociology, psychology, and the phenomenology of religion, etc. the employment of these and other tools has resulted in a much broader understanding of the meaning and value of the Old Testament* (Bares 1978a: 48).

With this approach to the Scriptures, we need not be surprised by the differing perspectives in African Theology. As Dickson observes, the result is a "much broader understanding of the meaning and value of the Old Testament." The Old Testament (and for that matter, the New Testament) no more has the same weight of authority. We are no longer bound by that meaning and value of the Bible which the Christian Church once held due to the present day liberal belief in the nature of the Bible.

The fundamental reason for some radical opinions in African Theology these days is not that we are taking more seriously the African cultures and religion for the first time. The reason is the radically different view of Scriptures held by many of these theologians. And this radical view of the Scriptures does not have African roots. These theologians like Dickson learned their view of Scriptures from the liberals in western universities and seminaries, either directly or indirectly. Western liberal biblical scholarship has undermined the unity and authority of Scripture for these theologians. This leads to a broadening of theological options allowed.

As Daidanso writes, "Many of those who speak of African theology take a contrary course. Their tutors are the liberal theologians of Europe. So, under the cover of so-called African theology, is it not liberalism which is subtly finding its way in Africa?" (Daidanso 1983: 71).

Peter Kanyandago

Born in 1951 in Uganda, Rev. Peter Kanyandago is director of the School of Postgraduate Studies in Uganda Martyrs University where he is Professor of Ethics and Development Studies. He holds a Ph.D. in Canon Law from the Catholic University of Louvain, Belgium.

A careful study of all that has been written on African Theology reveals that frequent reference is made to the primary place of divine revelation in the Bible. And yet these authors reflect the same flaws as mentioned above in the writings of Dickson.

Kanyandago makes several commendable statements about the primacy of "the revealed Word." He has been concerned because he receives the impression when reading articles on African Theology "that traditional religions are a kind of another revelation." He then concludes, "However important these religions might be, I think the Christian cannot help subjecting them to the Word of God." This will necessitate "putting aside some of our traditional practices." The whole story of Christianity, whether in Europe, Asia or Africa, "is the story of conversion - turning around, transformation, altering..." (Kanyandago 1978: 343).

However, he ultimately undermines what he has said about the importance of the Word of God. He speaks of developing a methodology which puts "revelation and the African culture into a mutual criticism" (1978:343). A "mutual criticism"? African religion criticizing the Bible? In concluding his discussion on "the problem of methodology and the epistemological questions," he quotes with apparent approval the words of Maurier. "In my opinion the encounter that an African Theology sets up between the Word of God and African culture, should rather be a *reciprocal interpolation at equal terms*, putting in question in a mutual criticism the two partners..." [emphasis mine] (1978: 344).

This approach to African Theology will inevitably lead away from historic Christianity, for there is a serious loss of the supreme and final authority of Scripture. The theologian becomes the final authority who chooses what to believe and what to reject. The stark contrast between the theology taught by the early evangelists of Africa and what we frequently read of today is not the result of taking the African context more seriously. It is the result of a liberal view of Scripture.

Most of the churches of Africa were founded by evangelical Protestants or traditional Roman Catholics. But through the past 100 years, liberalism has infested most of the main line Protestant denominations overseas, beginning first with the seminaries and colleges. Roman Catholic schools have not escaped the Higher Critical view of Scripture. This low view of Scripture has gradually infiltrated many of the seminaries and theological colleges of Africa from whence this unbelief is filtering down to the local congregations.

Evangelicals have recognized the pitfalls of a low view of Scripture. The Seoul Declaration affirms:

> *We have found that some of the presuppositions, sources, and hermeneutics of theologies such as ethno-theologies, syncretistic theologies and liberation theologies are inadequate ... We unequivocally uphold the primacy and authority of the Scriptures. For us, to know is to do, to love is to obey. Evangelical Theology must root itself in a life of obedience to the Word of God and submission to the lordship of Jesus Christ* (1983: 9).

If there is any such thing as a legitimate Christian theology for Africa (and there surely is), then obviously, the African culture, worldview and religion must be seriously researched. The importance of such studies looms very large in all the literature on African Theology. The words of Nyamiti express what is said by virtually all other writers on African Christian Theology when he writes: "But the lion's share should be allotted to the African religions. Indeed, as regards African Theology, the African religions have a specially important role to play" (Nyamiti 1971: 18).

But the basic question in the methodology for developing an African Theology is the relationship between Scripture and traditional religion and culture. Is Scripture verbally inspired by God, the final authority for Christian faith, or are there other authorities?

We have seen that western missionaries confused their culture with the supra-cultural revelation of Scripture and unfortunately transported western forms of Christianity to Africa. This we lament. But unless we can establish a biblical relationship between Scripture and culture for African Theology, we shall be worse off. Culture will eat up God's revelation. The Word of God will only become an imagined word of God to men in particular historical situations. Though we may allege a certain primacy for the Bible, such claims are only cosmetic.

For evangelicals the Bible must have absolute authority. There can be no "reciprocal interpolation at equal terms" of the Word of God and African culture. What God teaches us in the Bible, and all that the Bible teaches, is God's Word. The Bible is our final authority of what Christians may believe and practice.

Pan-African Theological Conference

In 1977 the Pan-African Theological Conference, sponsored by the Association of Third World Theologians, was held in Accra, Ghana. About 90 delegates convened from Roman Catholic, Protestant and Orthodox Churches, mostly from Africa. Their Communique reflects this serious confusion in relating Scripture to culture.

On the one hand, they confess that "The Bible is the basic source of African Theology." "No theology can retain its Christian identity apart from the Scripture" (Pan-African Conference 1978: 3,5). On the other hand, they suggest other sources for theology. These include: the Christian heritage, African anthropology, African Traditional Religion, including traditional social relationships and contemporary forms of economic, political, social and cultural oppressions.

The basic question is: What is the relationship between the "primary witness of God's revelation in Jesus Christ" and these other sources? They speak of "a critical theology which comes from contact with the Bible, openness to the African realities, and dialogue with non-African theologies" (1978: 5). This suggests an equal interaction between all of these sources of theology with a mere "contact" with Scripture. The Bible is not said to be God's revelation to man but "the primary witness of God's revelation in Jesus Christ." This reflects a neo-orthodox view of revelation which rejects verbal, propositional revelation.

The study of African Traditional Religions is likewise important, they say, for ATR is "a major source for the study of the African experience of God." African religions can "enrich theology and spirituality" (1978:5). There is found here an unmistakable interchange, a dialogical relationship between the many sources of theology, without any recognition that the Bible is the final source of all authority which judges all else.

This Communique reflects the basic outlines of a methodology already being developed for African Theology. These delegates affirmed:

> *We believe that African theology must be understood in the context of African life and culture and the creative attempt of African peoples to shape a new future that is different from the colonial past and the neo-colonial present. The African situation requires a new theological methodology that is different from the dominant theologies of the West ... Our task as theologians is to create a theology that arises, out of, and is accountable to, African people* (1978: 6).

If African Theology is not first and foremost accountable to the Word of God, then it ceases to be a biblical theology. If African Theology is primarily accountable to African people, then it becomes an ethnic theology which severs connection with the Church Universal. The one Holy Catholic Church, of which all Christians are members, has One Head, even Jesus Christ. He has given us One Holy Spirit who indwells all believers. By His Spirit we are led to One Faith as we reflect upon God's special revelation which is the Bible. As soon as our theology ceases to be apostolic and catholic it ceases to be Christian. By apostolic we mean that our theology is rooted in the teaching of the apostles. By catholic we mean our theology proclaims universal Christian truth.

> *For Evangelical Christians, the revelation of God, the Word of God, is the absolute authority in matters of life and faith challenging men and women, habits, customs and cultures of men and of all nations, as well as political, administrative and religious institutions established among peoples. Evangelicals will therefore have a critical attitude toward their cultures, respecting in African habits everything which is not contrary to biblical faith and rejecting everything that is detrimental to the Word of God ...* (Daidanso 1983: 70).

Charles Nyamiti

Charles Nyamiti (born 1931), an ordained Roman Catholic priest from Tanzania, Professor Emeritus and a founding professor of the Catholic University of East Africa, he has written on methodology of African Theology (Nyamiti 1971). He speaks of various approaches or methods in the development of African Theology. The Pastoral Approach means that the development of theology should have pastoral motives of loving God and the Church. The "pastoral-minded theologian" will adapt theology for the help of his people so that "there will be no separation between theology and spirituality" (1971: 5).

The Apologetical Method in its negative aspect points out the insufficiency and defects of non-Christian religions. But the negative aspect of this method shows "that Christianity answers to, and surpasses, human needs and aspirations." The negative aspect is essential but it "tends to arouse polemic discussions and thus likely to hinder fruitful dialogue" (1971: 6). Therefore, the theologian should study the African and Christian themes to find parallels and differences and thereby show how Christianity fulfils the aspirations and needs of the African.

The Pedagogical Method seeks to expound Christian doctrine, solve problems and arrange theological textbooks. Nyamiti takes a typically Roman Catholic approach with great stress on philosophy in general and Thomas Aquinas in particular. When solving problems, you begin with the Bible, then consider the tradition of the church and then scrutinize the problem "by means of speculation, of which St. Thomas is recommended as the master" (1971: 13).

While Nyamiti is constrained by Roman Catholic official doctrine (cf. 1971: 1), he appears to have a similar problem as the Protestant scholars mentioned above, in addition to a uniquely Roman Catholic approach. Church tradition for a Roman Catholic determines the interpretation of Scriptures, for tradition is itself a form of revelation. Nyamiti says, "The African theology will have to search in the sources of revelation (Bible and Tradition) the kernel of Christian teaching ... beyond the cultural expressions through which it is conveyed" (1971: 22). In practice, then, church tradition for Roman Catholics is the binding authority as to what African theologians should believe. He defines African Theology as "the very self-same Catholic doctrine expressed and presented in accordance with the African mentality and needs" (1971: 1).

But it appears that Nyamiti also has a problem with the authority of Scriptures because of his critical approach to biblical origins. Instead of accepting the plain teaching of the Scriptures, he allows contemporary culture to determine what is really true or false.

According to Nyamiti, the fact that Paul taught the existence of spirits does not mean that we are bound to believe that spirits are objective entities. Saint Paul "does not simply dismiss the 'pagan' beliefs as erroneous, but he takes them at least as symbols useful for Christian demonology" (1971: 23). In other words, as we understand Nyamiti, even though Paul teaches the existence of personal spirit beings, he did this because he accommodated his preaching to the beliefs of the people. Therefore, Nyamiti apparently feels we are not bound to accept what Paul seems to teach.

Once again we are lost in the sea of theological speculation. Contemporary culture, ever changing and diverse, determines what is to be taken as mere "symbols useful for Christians," or what is literally true. If we preach the Gospel to people who believe in literal spirit beings, we may teach about spirits as a useful missiological approach, so as not to offend the people. But if the people to whom we preach do not believe in personal spirit beings, we may take this as merely useful symbolism. It would seem from Nyamiti's discussion that he does not necessarily believe in literal spirits as has been historically believed. This belief is born out of western rationalism. What is presented as African Theology is merely western rationalism in the guise of African Theology. It is neither African nor biblical.

Nevertheless, he concludes his book with a definitive statement on the primacy of Scripture that is commendable.

> *It is the African culture that has to be transformed to fit the Christian teaching, and not vice versa. It is here that the primary importance of the Bible should be duly taken into account. One should never lose sight of the fact that Sacred Scripture 'ought to be the soul of all theology.' Above all, the theologian should beware of making the Bible a mere instrument for confirming African conceptions and principles, instead of taking it as the starting point and criterion for judging the validity and limits of such conceptions and principles* (1971: 27).

John Mbiti

No study on African Theology would be complete without careful consideration given to John Mbiti, "the father" of African Christian Theology. He has been the most prolific Christian writer in Africa, having authored many substantial books and hundreds of published articles.

Sources for African Theology: Mbiti maintains that there are several sources which contribute toward African Theology, including African religions, African Independent Churches, major traditions of Christendom, biblical theology and the Bible.

From the writings of Mbiti we learn something of the great importance he places in African Traditional Religion and Philosophy. A major part of his scholarly effort has been the exposition of African Traditional Religion. He writes on "The Growing Respectability of African Traditional Religion" (1972b: 57). He gives lectures on the "Sources for the Study of African Traditional Religions" (1970b). He has written many books on African Traditional Religion, including: *African Religions and Philosophy* (1969); *Introduction to African Religion* (1975a); *African Concepts of God* (1970c); *The Prayers of African Religion* (1975b); *Akamba Stories* (1966). In many ways he has been in the forefront of those who both study and promote the positive investigation of African Traditional Religion which is to serve as the "valuable heritage" to which "Christianity should adapt."

> *The old nonsense of looking at African background as devilish, and fit only to be swept away by Euro-American civilization is or should be gone by now ... African religious background is not a rotten heap of superstitions, taboos and magic; it has a great deal of value in it. On this valuable heritage, Christianity should adapt itself and not be dependent exclusively on imported goods* (Mbiti 1972a: 147).

In Mbiti's opinion African Traditional Religion is a preparation for the Gospel and is fulfilled in Christianity. African Traditional Religion is placed on equal footing with the Old Testament as preparation for the coming of Christ.

> *When we turn to the New Testament, we find that African religiosity must here assume the listening posture, be at the receiving end, whereas in the area of the Old Testament a certain amount of give-and-take or mutual enlightenment can be carried out* (Mbiti 1972a: 172).

Mbiti does not assume that Traditional Religion is without rottenness. He calls on Christianity to "judge and save" African Traditional Religion. "We must give Christianity the opportunity and freedom," Mbiti pleads, "to remove deadness and rottenness from our traditional religiosity" (1972: 153). African Traditional

Religions are largely but not entirely compatible with Christianity. Traditional Religion can even bring "enrichment" for Christianity in Africa. But this is only after Christianity judges Traditional Religion.

One major source of African Theology according to Mbiti is the Bible. Unlike many African theologians who use little of the Bible in their writings, John Mbiti is among the forerunners who pleads for a greater emphasis on the Scripture.

Among all the papers presented at the 1966 consultation of African theologians in Ibadan, Nigeria (Dickson 1969), Mbiti's paper on Eschatology is the only one which sought to handle biblical revelation as it relates to African beliefs (Dickson 1969: 159-184). Mbiti laments, "Very few African theologians are putting their attention on Biblical studies ... Only here and there do we have the beginnings of Biblical theology among African scholars" (Mbiti 1976: 165).

Showing his concern for the development of genuinely biblical African Theology, he compiled a record of all published materials and presented them to the Pan-African Conference of Third World Theologians held in Accra, Ghana, in 1977. "The Biblical Basis for Present Trends in African Theology" is the title of his paper (Appiah-Kubi 1979: 83-94). This paper has been revised and updated in his more recent publication, *Bible and Theology in African Christianity* (1986: 46-63).

Mbiti's book on Eschatology is filled with Scripture references. Literally, hundreds of Bible references are scattered throughout the entire book, though he nowhere engages in any exegesis of the biblical text. In 1979 Mbiti lamented that "very little biblical material" could be found in any African Theology except his own essay on eschatology (Appiah- Kubi 1979: 85). Mbiti is quite correct. And the same generalization can be made of most writings which fall under the category of African Christian Theology today. Mbiti has at least tried to deal with the Scriptures.

> *Mbiti's concluding remarks show his great concern for biblical studies. Any viable theology must and should have a biblical basis, and African theology has begun to develop on this foundation. Edward Fashole-Luke is right in reminding us that the Bible is the basic and primary source for the development of 'African Christian Theologies'. Nothing can substitute for the Bible. However much African cultural-religious background may be close to the biblical world, we have to guard against references like 'hitherto unwritten African Old Testament' or sentiments that see a final revelation of God in the African religious heritage* (Appiah-Kubi 1979: 90).

Mbiti is to be commended for his admirable sentiments with which he concludes his paper:

> *As long as African theology keeps close to the Scriptures, it will remain relevant to the life of the church in Africa and it will have lasting links with the theology of the church universal. African theologians must give even more attention to the Bible than is sometimes the case. As long as we keep the Bible close to our minds and our hearts, our theology will be viable, relevant, and of lasting service to the church and glory to the Lord to whom be honour, dominion, and power unto the ages of ages. Amen* (Appiah-Kubi 1979: 91).

Further emphasizing the importance of the Bible in African Theology, Mbiti has devoted a whole book to the topic, *Bible and Theology in African Christianity* (1986). He affirms, "Nothing can substitute for the Bible" (1986: 59). In surveying the theological literature produced in Africa, he decries the weak emphasis on the Bible.

Generally, scholars have agreed that in the development of a relevant theology for Africa, both biblical revelation and African Traditional Religion are important. Contextualization of the Gospel necessitates serious study of both divine revelation in Scriptures and the African context, the lion's share of the latter being African Traditional Religion. Professor Mbiti has demonstrated genuine concern for both of these focal points.

Mbiti's book, *New Testament Eschatology in an African Background* (Mbiti 1971), reflects his general approach to African Theology. This 210 page New Testament study, in my opinion, is the most scholarly example of relating African traditional beliefs to a study of theology. No other African theologian has made such an extended research.

His first chapter is introductory, giving some historical and ethnographical data concerning the Akamba people, the coming of Christianity into Ukambani and the church planted there. Throughout the book he develops his topic of Eschatology in its various aspects.

The approach in each chapter is fivefold. First, he considers the Kamba traditional concepts related to the topic of eschatology in that chapter. Secondly, he considers the New Testament. Unfortunately, he does not make an inductive study of the Holy Scriptures. Instead, he examines the New Testament through secondary sources of various theologians.

Thirdly, he considers the teaching of "the main evangelizing agent among the Akamba, which is the Africa Inland Mission" (1971:3). Fourthly, he considers how the Akamba Christians understood this Christian teaching brought by the Africa Inland Mission. Finally, Mbiti renders his conclusions and deductions for each chapter.

Mbiti is an example of a Christian theologian who emphasizes the importance of biblical study and who tries to practice what he preaches. Regrettably, however, he did not study the Scriptures directly but through secondary sources of diverse theologians.

Liberal View of Theology: John Mbiti, however, approaches the Bible through the grid of liberal rationalism. The glasses which he uses to read the Bible are coloured by his liberal view of Scripture. Mbiti considers the Bible only a "human adviser." He writes, "As far as theology is concerned, let the Bible be our human adviser, and the Holy Spirit our divine adviser" (1986: 61).

The great divide between the evangelical and the liberal is their view of Scriptures. Since the evangelical accepts the absolute divine authority of the Bible by faith according to the testimony of Jesus Christ, therefore the Bible becomes the final authority for faith and conduct. But since Mbiti approaches the Scriptures with his liberal presuppositions, he therefore, arrives at liberal conclusions. His presuppositions have a profound bearing on his theologizing. His view of Scripture determines in a large measure his theological conclusions.

Unfortunately, Professor Mbiti does not engage in biblical exegesis. He does not wrestle with the meaning of our primary source of theology. Instead, as we have stated previously, he studies New Testament Scriptures, not inductively, but through the eyes of theologians who developed their theories of eschatology. He writes of Schweitzer and his "Consistent Eschatology," of Von Dobschutz and his "Transmuted Eschatology," of C.H. Dodd and his "Realized Eschatology," of R. Bultmann and his "Re-interpreted Eschatology," of J.A. Robinson and his "Inaugurated Eschatology," and of Oscar Cullmann. It is of great significance that at no time and in no place does he consider evangelical theologians.

In fact he treats the eschatology taught by the Africa Inland Mission and embraced by the Africa Inland Church as if it were some aberration of historic Christianity, some extreme, unbalanced view of Christian theology. The eschatology of the A.I.M. in its essence is that of historic Christianity and formerly embraced by all the missions which brought the Gospel to Africa. Belief in the second coming of Christ, future judgement and the final state of either heaven or hell, are found in all the creeds of Christendom, East and West, and from the beginning.

Byang Kato is correct when he objects to Mbiti's assertion that the Africa Inland Church is "without theological, doctrinal, historical, liturgical, or ministerial connections with other bodies of the Church universal." Kato contends:

> *His criticism is directed, however, against a line of interpretation of which evangelical missions are a part. The Africa Inland Mission (A.I.M.) follows the literal, though not literalistic, interpretation. They take the Word of God on its face value. The A.I.M. has simply passed on to the Africa Inland Church a well-established Protestant tradition* (1975: 80).

Indeed, it is Mbiti, not the Africa Inland Church, who has lost touch with the historic Christian teaching of eschatology. Though he never explicitly denies the existence of hell nor does he state categorically that every human being will be saved, he gives the general impression that he believes in universalism. Though he never denies that Christ will return again bodily as He went up to heaven, neither does he ever affirm the bodily return of Christ in the Second Advent.

Instead, he declares that "Jesus may have accepted current notions of Gehenna without necessarily endorsing them all" (1971: 66). Indeed, hell is reduced to a mere symbol by Mbiti, for he says, "If people are threatened with being cast into a lake of fire in the next life, the effectiveness of the symbol is largely lost and the Christian Gospel is reduced to negative threats which have no lasting impact upon those who receive or reject Christ" (1971: 70). Furthermore, he declares, "The New Testament is explicit that Jesus never promised us a heavenly utopia, but only His own self and His own companionship both in time and beyond, both in space and beyond" (1971: 89).

With his sweeping repudiation of the eschatological teaching of the A.I.M, and with the absence of any explicit affirmation by Mbiti that Jesus Christ will return bodily in the future to take His own people to heaven and consign the wicked to eternal damnation, we are compelled to ask several questions. Does Mbiti really believe that Jesus Christ will come in His resurrected body to earth again? Does he really believe that the hope of the Christian today is the blessed return of Christ as taught by the historic Christian Church? Does Mbiti believe that all those whom God has declared righteous by faith will spend eternity with Christ in a place called heaven? Does he believe that there is a hell, a place of eternal retribution for all those who reject the grace of God through Christ?

Instead of affirming the historic Christian truths about the end of this age, he speaks in another vein. "It is almost unthinkable that at the final Resurrection there should be portions of God's creation not involved in the process of presentation, not brought into the conscious presence of God" (1971: 172). He suggests that after death "there is almost certainly a spiritual transformation (or 'improvement'), a process of 'perfecting' the souls before the Parousia" (1971: 175). Though he admits this to be speculation, he is hopeful, and proceeds to declare: "We venture to speculate that the opportunity to hear or assimilate the effects of the Gospel is continued in the life beyond (cf. 1 Pe 3:19f), and that death is not a barrier to incorporation into Christ, since nothing can separate 'us' from the love of God (cf. Ro 8:38)" (1971: 175).

After death there may be a period of punishment, but Mbiti finds it "almost impossible to imagine that their punishment will last for all eternity in the same way that Redemption is for eternity" (1971: 179). To be "apart from Christ" for one day "is sufficiently tormenting to make the experience of the non-presence of God 'everlasting'." Furthermore, the love of the Father for His erring children "must ultimately win over even the most 'hopeless case' of sinners, and bring home the lost sheep to join the one great fold" (1971: 179). Everlasting punishment is therefore reduced by Mbiti to one day. Moreover, "God's love and presence will freely invade that soul (cf. Ro 8:35, 39) until – let us hope – the soul responds to the Father's embrace and kiss" (1971: 180). Thus the "second death" cannot be an absolute final reality in Mbiti's opinion (1971: 180).

For those in Christ there will be no physical resurrection of the body, Mbiti contends, "...for there is no explicit Scriptural warrant to support a materialistic view of the Resurrection body" (1971: 172). Furthermore, after some time beyond the grave we shall all lose our individuality so that we cannot recognize our friends as separate individuals. For we will be all in Christ and in one another. "The 'many' will be absorbed into the 'One'."

No doubt we should take seriously the concluding words of Mbiti when he confesses, "The details of what happens beyond the historical plane of human existence are neither for you nor for me to dogmatize about" (1971: 180). We all can say with Professor Mbiti as he states elsewhere, "...for I understand it only in part, since the mysteries of God are inexhaustible." But we lament his dogmatic repudiation of the eschatology of the historic Christian Church and his inability to embrace the biblical teaching of the end times. If he cannot dogmatically affirm truths concerning our human existence beyond the Parousia, then how can he dogmatically repudiate the eschatological teaching characteristic of the Christian Church for the past two millennia?

And we are distressed by his repeated dismissal of the futuristic aspect of the Christian hope. Any serious study of the New Testament discloses the importance of this future expectation of the believers. Paul on his missionary journeys never spent a long time in any city where he preached the Gospel. But the blessed hope of the second coming of Christ was apparently part of that Kerygma which he preached everywhere. The Christ Event was the heart of the Gospel, including Christ's birth, crucifixion, resurrection and second coming, even as we find in the Apostle's Creed.

For instance, he spent only a few months in Thessalonica. However, his two epistles make it quite clear that during that short time with them he had expounded concerning "the last things." Various expressions indicate that he had devoted much time teaching eschatological truth, the future events of the last days. Such expressions include: "*For you yourselves know full well...*" (1 Th 5:2); "*Do you not remember that while I was still with you, I was telling you these things*?" (2 Th 2:5).

On the one hand, Paul sought to give the Thessalonian Christians comfort in their future Christian hope because of the serious trials they were presently experiencing as believers. "But it is a false spirituality," Mbiti contends, "to escape into the Christian world of the hereafter at the expense of being a Christian in the here and now" (1971: 60). Though the Apostle Paul taught a lively hope in Christ in the here and now, he repeatedly and specifically held before the suffering Christians the future hope of the Lord's return. Whereas, the non-Christians have no hope (1 Th 4:13), the believers can look forward to the return of Christ when both the dead in Christ and the living shall be caught up to be with the Lord forever. Believers are to be encouraged by this future hope (5:11).

On the other hand, when Christ "is revealed from heaven with His mighty angels in flaming fire," he will render "retribution to those who do not know God and those who do not obey the gospel of our Lord Jesus. And these will pay the penalty of eternal destruction away from the presence of the Lord and from the glory of His power" (2 Th 1: 8, 9). Not only will God grant His children relief from their persecutors when He returns again, but He will repay the wicked opponents of the Gospel with affliction (1:6, 7).

Paul then exhorts the Thessalonian believers, "stand firm and hold to the traditions which you were taught, whether by word of mouth or by letter from us" (2 Th 2:15). This is precisely what the evangelicals seek to do by holding to the plain teaching of Scripture concerning these future events – the return of Christ, the resurrection of the body, the final judgement, and the final state of the just and the unjust. What troubles the evangelical is the tendency of many theologians today, including John Mbiti, to flirt with the notion of a universal salvation for all people and a denial of the future hope of the believers as historically understood by the Christian Church.

Mbiti pleads for relevant theology which will address the concerns of the Church in Africa which he enumerates as follows: "National Survival (Liberation, revolution, African culture, racism), Community survival (tribe, clan, age groups, drought, famine, pestilence, calamities), and Personal survival (health, healing, slums, housing, school, fees, clothes, witchcraft, magic, and sorcery)." Now we readily admit that African pastors, teachers and theologians ought to relate Scripture to these contemporary needs. That is vital. To ignore them is to dichotomize life into the earthly and heavenly concerns.

But the distressing fact is that in this article referred to above, Mbiti mentions no need to address the spiritual problems of man which are in fact the root cause for all forms of selfishness. If African Theology merely deals with those issues Mbiti mentions, this theology will also be impotent, for it will deal with the symptom and not the root cause. The fallacy of contemporary theology is the hope that we can humanize cultures by tackling the structures, without dealing with the basic spiritual problem of the human heart. Any social structure will become oppressive without the transformation of the human heart. God must change the heart of man through the new birth in order for there to be any improvement in relationships. God must sanctify His people by His Spirit and through His Word if men are to love one another in a warm hearted community. Mbiti complains that the church is "theologically provincial," but he fails to deal with the universal theological themes of the Scriptures. We need to "contextualize" Scripture, but we also need to let Scripture "de-contextualize" us. If we only pick and choose those crumbs that suit us, then we do not allow God to communicate "the whole counsel of the Word of God."

Illustration of Distorted Theology: "Time" plays an important part both in John Mbiti's analysis of traditional religion and in his theologizing. He has suggested that the African concept of time is "the key to our understanding of the basic religious and philosophical concepts. The concept of time may help to explain beliefs, attitudes, practices and general way of life of African peoples not only in the traditional set up but also in the modern situation" (Mbiti 1969: 16).

Not only is time "the key" to Mbiti's understanding of African Traditional Religion, but time is his chief theological concern in his major theological treatise, *New Testament Eschatology in an African Background* (1971). He contends that the African peoples traditionally have not thought much of the distant future. In fact, he argues that African languages (particularly the ones he has analysed) are incapable of communicating distant future beyond two years. In contrast to this African traditional phenomenon, the pioneering mission among his Kamba people taught an eschatology with the emphasis on the future. Hence, Mbiti contends that the A.I.M. did not faithfully contextualize the Gospel for a people whose language was incapable of expressing a distant future.

Since Mbiti constructs his ideas of the African concept of time on the Kamba concept of time and history (Mbiti 1971: 24-32), and since his theological views of eschatology relate to this traditional concept of time, it is quite illuminating to consider this in some detail, for it is a painful illustration of a distorted theology based on a distorted view of his own culture. Liberal theology is here being introduced into Africa in the guise of African Theology.

Mbiti begins by saying, "For the Akamba, time is not an academic concern; it is simply a composition of events that have occurred, these which are taking place now and those which will immediately occur" (Mbiti 1971: 24).

Time reckoning, therefore, is based on concrete events and not on numerical calendars. Numerical calendars with days, months and years are unknown to Africa. Instead, "phenomenon calendars" (Mbiti 1969: 19) are used which dates life on the basis of significant concrete events, such as a particular drought, pestilence, or earthquake. "Dating is done not in relation to an abstract scale, but in relation to particular events which are known to have occurred" (Parratt 1977: 119). Time is important at the point of the event and not at the mathematical moment.

A second major point of Mbiti is that "according to traditional concepts, time is a two-dimensional phenomenon, with a long past, a present and virtually no future" (1969: 17). "The future as we know it in the linear conception of Time is virtually non-existent in Akamba thinking. My findings from other African peoples have not yielded any radical difference" (1971: 24). The future is conceived of primarily as the rhythmic succession of events, the cycle of known and repeated occurrences. Annually, this relates to the planting season, rains and harvest and dry season, which are known and repeated cyclical events. In the life of individuals the future is thought of in terms of birth, marriage, bearing children and death. Thus the future is brief and incorporates what is normal and customary. "The *'sasa'* [Kiswahili for 'present'] 'swallows' up what in western or linear concept of time would be considered as the future" (Mbiti 1969: 22).

Mbiti claims to base his understanding of the Akamba and other African peoples on the "analyses of myths and language." Most African peoples have myths of the past, myths of creation, the origin of man, the coming of death. "The significant point for our purposes here," Mbiti declares, "is that there are no myths about the future, as far as I have been able to gather from all the available sources that record African myths and stories" (1971: 25). Therefore, it would appear "that the future dimension of Time has not been formulated and assimilated into the mythology of African thinking and conception of the universe" (1971: 25).

Linguistically, Mbiti has analyzed the tense patterns of eight East African languages, including Kikamba. Of the nine tenses in Kikamba, only three refer to the future, "an extremely limited range of the future stretching to about six months, and in any case not beyond two years from NOW" (1971: 27). Mbiti makes some amazing categorical statements about the impossibility of Kikamba expressing distant future.

> *People cannot articulate what is in the distant future; they cannot speak about it and cannot, therefore, form myths about it. The Kikamba language is incapable of sustaining such a reality. Only what is in the rhythm of natural phenomena (day and night. rain and dry seasons, birth, marriage and death etc.) can be thought about and expected to take place as it has always been* (1971: 27).

Therefore, *zamani*, (Kiswahili for "past"), is the focus of traditional concern. The forefathers who once lived in the present have slipped back into the past. From them the living receive direction and guidance. Those people living now in the present are destined someday to slip into the world of the spirits, slip into *zamani* (past) and continue to give guidance and direction to those in the present.

There is no African traditional concept of an eschatological future or golden age. What the people know now will always be. There is no anticipation of the cataclysmic end of the world or some future judgement. What will be is what has always been. Mbiti acknowledges, however, that "a future dimension of Time is being born in Akamba thinking and life. This is partly due to the Christian concept of Eschatology, and partly to a western type education..." (1971: 31).

Zamani has its own "past," "present," and "future." Even as a person goes through a process of becoming human, (passing through the various rites of passage in life), even so "death is a process which removes a person gradually from the '*sasa*' period to the '*zamani*'" (1969: 25). When the living die they enter the recent past when the living-dead are remembered. But gradually they slip further and further into *zamani*.

After five generations no one can remember them by name. At that time they lose their "personal immortality" and enjoy a mere "collective immortality" when they are mere "its," unknown by name. When the living-dead cease to be remembered by name, they are more greatly feared by the living.

Mbiti concludes, that "the traditional concept of time is intimately bound up with the entire life of the people, and our understanding of it may help to pave the way for understanding the thinking, attitude and actions of the people" (1968: 28).

Scholarly Appraisal of Mbiti's View of Time: Mbiti's interpretation of the African's concept of time, particularly his assertion that the distant future is non-existent and meaningless, has stirred up much criticism and outright repudiation. Some condemn the idea as "nonsense."

Although Mbiti claims to base his conclusions on eight East African languages, including Luganda (Mbiti 1971: 26), Kato reports the conversation he had with a Harvard Ph. D. Buganda by the name of Balintuma Kalibala who

> *strongly rejected the notion that Africans cannot conceive of the future. When I asked if Buganda of Uganda are among the 'other African societies' who share this supposed Akamba belief, Kalibala replied, 'This is absurd. The African theologian who believes that kind of thing is following what Europeans have taught him. He has not been home to find out things for himself.' He then added, 'we absolutely believe in the future'* (Kato 1975: 61).

Another Buganda, Dr. A. Lugira of the Makerere University said, "Professor Mbiti is giving his own opinion; it is academic. His basis is Akamba, and that should be limited there. My people, Buganda, do have a future concept of time" (Kato 1975: 62).

Another critic comments,

> *While it is correct to observe, as others have, that in Africa "there is no concept of history moving 'forward' towards a definite future climax", it is clearly distorting things to represent the African concept of time as the mirror opposite of the Western notion, so that "history moves backward", from the present, ending up on the past, which is a permanent "graveyard of time". This is patently absurd* (Ray 1972a: 83).

Other scholars, however, have been more generous toward Mbiti. "Dr. Mbiti has grown up in the culture of which he is writing," comments Newell Booth. "He could be wrong, or he could have expressed his views poorly but it is unlikely that what he says is 'patently absurd'" (Booth 1975: 82).

John Parratt gives a thoughtful assessment of the whole issue:

> *It may be said at once, that the idea of the future only becomes meaningful on a linear view of time – time conceived in terms of a straight line, progressing from one point to the next towards an ultimate end. This view of time is not found in Eastern religions, is absent from ancient Greek science and represents a fairly late development even in European thought. It is furthermore not characteristic of primitive thought generally. It would be surprising therefore if it were found to be typical of African thought* (Parratt 1977: 118).

The linear concept of time is traced by biblical scholarship to "the Judaeo-Christian tradition." Cullmann points out that the Christian teaching tended to be "eschatological," moving to a *telos.*

> *The linear concept of time proves to be as much an alien imposition upon African thought as it was upon the ancient world. In traditional Africa time is neither conceived of in a linear fashion, nor does it move towards an eschatological telos. In so far as the linear method of time reckoning is employed it represents a foreign element, which may be regarded as part of the legacy of Western Christianity or of colonial influence* (Parratt 1977: 123).

In conclusion Parratt concurs with Mbiti that the traditional African concept of time was not linear and that African societies "are predominantly backward-looking" (Parratt 1977: 123).

A Second Look at Mbiti's Theology of Time:[1] Through field research we conclude that several of Mbiti's concepts are valid.

However, Mbiti has in fact been "inclined to overstate the case," when he writes, "the people cannot articulate what is in the distant future." This judgement is based on the persistent and vigorous reaction of the Kamba themselves when discussing this topic over the years.

The fact is that the traditional Kamba were capable of speaking of the future and in fact did so. No Kikamba grammar affirms what Mbiti here affirms. The indefinite future tense is formed the same way as the indefinite past. Usage of the language by the people determines the meaning. The Kamba manifest by the usage of their language that they do conceive of the distant future. Those Kamba in my acquaintance categorically assert that it is absurd to say that the Kikamba language is incapable of conveying a distant future.

One source of evidence omitted by Mbiti is the existence of traditional prophets. Kamba prophets were famous for their ability to predict unusual and distant events. Syokimau, for instance, prophesied that the white men would come, that there would be a snake stretching from Mombasa to Lake Victoria, and that people would carry fire in their pockets. The snake turned out to be the Uganda railroad and the fire in the pockets referred to the matches. Prophets such as Syokimau did predict unusual events in the indefinite future.

Today the Christian Gospel has liberated the Akamba so that they can exercise their full potential in dealing with the future creatively.

The Gospel has provided a new concept of time, moving forward toward a goal, instead of looking backward to traditions. This has occurred repeatedly throughout history. Cullmann notes that the New Testament concept of time was the opposite of the Greek view of time.

> *We must start from this fundamental perception, that the symbol of time for Primitive Christianity as well as for Biblical Judaism and the Iranian religion is the LINE, while in Hellenism it is the CIRCLE. Because in Greek thought time, if not conceived as a progressing line with beginning and end, but rather a circle, the fact that man is bound to time must here be experienced as an enslavement, as a curse. Time moves about in the eternal circular course in which everything keeps recurring* (Cullmann 1964: 50).

Traditional Africans were very much like traditional Greeks before the coming of the Gospel in being cyclically oriented and backward looking. Christianity has given a new perspective on time. Even secular western culture which has disowned its Christian origins has retained the linear concept of time.

We find that the traditional Kamba concept of time is fast eroding. As Christians set an example of planning for the future, as schools and government encourage plans for development, so the older traditions are gradually breaking down.

We conclude this critical appraisal of John Mbiti by observing that he has made two fundamental errors: first, is his assessment of the traditional concept

---

[1] A substantial part of the Kikamba linguistic analysis of "time" was made by a Kamba, Pastor Muema Joel, a former student at Scott Theological College, during a class research project. Contributing were other Kamba from Kitui, including Mwikali, Mutunga, Ngwalu, Kingoku and Thitu. Other Kamba were also consulted.

of time, and the second is his theological understanding of the Scriptures. He has criticized mission Christianity among his people because he alleges they did not contextualize the Gospel to suit the mentality of the Akamba. The A.I.M. was in error, Mbiti states, for stressing the futuristic aspects of eschatology – the second coming of Christ as historically taught by the Christian Church. Eschatological teaching concerning the Second Advent should have been more oriented to the present, Mbiti contends, because the Akamba were *incapable* of conceiving any future beyond two years.

These twin errors of Mbiti's – an ethnological and theological error – have been eulogized by some as a refreshing example of contextualizing by Africans today. However, a careful study has revealed that Mbiti's understanding of biblical eschatology and his perception of African belief in time have been distorted. How tragic!

Mbiti unintentionally demeans the African by stating that they are "incapable" of understanding and embracing the biblical teaching of eschatology. However, history has demonstrated that the Kamba and other Africans are not only capable of understanding the distant future as outlined by Scripture, but have in fact embraced the future hope of Christ's return and our home in heaven.

If the African Christian Church is to remain evangelical in her convictions, there must be greater faithfulness to the Word of God. We must allow Scripture to "de-contextualize" us so that we can be liberated to be what God has created us to be. And we ought not to distort African traditions to suit our theologically liberalizing tendencies. Neither should we demean Africans by suggesting that they are unable to think outside their traditional worldviews.

Byang Kato

Among all the African theologians about whom we have written thus far, the late Byang Kato (1936-1975) is the one who has addressed the theological pitfalls in Africa the most forthrightly. On the one hand, Kato taught the need for respect of the African traditional heritage. He believed that evangelicals should contextualize the Gospel. On the other hand, he warned evangelicals of liberal theology being introduced under the cloak of African Theology.

Kato recognized the inadequacy of former judgements made of African Traditional Religion (1975: 18-24). He also accepted the need for cultural authenticity, for he says, "The search for authenticity through culture remains a desirable element in many African societies. The attitude of Christians toward cultural renaissance need not be negative" (1976: 146).

But Byang Kato was greatly exercised by the fact that he perceived African Theology turning more to African Traditional Religion as a source of theology, than to the Scriptures. Kato lamented, "Theology in Africa is increasingly turning to African traditional religions rather than to the Bible as its absolute source" (Kato 1976: 147). He regretted that many theologians were spending most of their time defending African Traditional Religions and practices which are "incompatible with biblical teaching" (1976: 146). "In the African evangelicals' effort to express Christianity in the context of the African, the Bible must remain the absolute source. The Bible is God's written Word addressed to Africans - and to all peoples - within their cultural background" (1976: 148).

It is significant that Kato made a statement which is almost a carbon copy of the statement made by Mbiti. "The noble desire to indigenize Christianity in Africa must not be forsaken. An indigenous theology is a necessity. But one must not betray Scriptural principles of God and His dealing with man at the altar of any regional theology" (Kato 1975: 16). Kato, like Mbiti, recognized the need to develop a more relevant theology for Africa. Kato, like Mbiti, stressed the need to make the Bible our primary source.

Why then do they differ in their outcome? Kato makes many critical assessments of John Mbiti and Bolaji Idowu, devoting three chapters to Mbiti and two chapters to Idowu, a total of 70 pages out of a total of 184 in the book. Mbiti speaks of Kato launching "a most bitter attack on myself, Professor E.B. Idowu and ecumenism" (Appiah-Kubi 1979: 85). If both are concerned about the two poles inherent in African Theology, the Bible as the primary source and the context of African religion and culture, why should they clash in such a fundamental way? Did Kato simply misunderstand Mbiti, as Professor Mbiti claims? (1986: 48).

We readily admit that the late Byang Kato was a fledgling young theologian who made some errors when interpreting several of the African theologians (cf. Bowers 1980). However, his fundamental concern for the spread of syncretistic liberal theology in Africa, and in particular, the creeping universalism within some theological circles, was correct. His warning of the liberal pitfalls in African Theology is most relevant for evangelicals even today.

But the question remains. If Kato like Mbiti was concerned about the primacy of Scripture in all theologizing, and if Kato like Mbiti was concerned about an authentic and relevant theology in Africa which utilized African thought patterns, then why did Kato clash with Mbiti in such a forthright manner?

The answer is quite plain. Byang Kato approached the Scriptures with full confidence in its unity and authority because the Holy Spirit is the Divine Author. Believing in the plenary, verbal inspiration of Scripture, Kato did not doubt the full authority of Scripture. There are no conflicting, variant traditions in the Bible from which one can pick and choose as he pleases. The Bible is not merely a witness or testimony of the first Christian community. Nor is it the means of revelation. Kato interpreted Scripture as the inerrant Word of God, using the grammatical-historical hermeneutical principles which are fundamental for all biblical hermeneutics. This does not guarantee agreement on everything by evangelicals as can be readily demonstrated. But despite the many differences, there is marked unity on all the "fundamentals" of the faith. And this is due to the fact that evangelicals take seriously the plain teaching of Scripture.

Kato affirms:

> *...the search for an African personality should not lead Africans to a compromising position. This is not to suggest a moratorium on further research on African thought patterns. But in the African evangelical effort to express Christianity in the context of Africa, the Bible must remain the absolute source. The Bible is God's written Word addressed to Africans - and to all peoples – within their cultural background* (1985: 43).

In contrast, Mbiti approaches Scripture as "a human advisor" (Appiah-Kubi 1979: 91). We ask, in what sense is the Bible only our human advisor? In what sense does the Holy Spirit advise us apart from and contrary to the plain teaching of Scripture? True, the 66 books of the Bible were written by prophets and apostles in such a way that their personalities were fully utilized. In no sense was Scripture dictated by the Holy Spirit. Writing styles of the various human authors all reflect their personalities, educational background, personal experiences and unique historical situations.

Nevertheless, the Scripture affirms that these human authors were superintended by the Holy Spirit in such a way that everything they taught is true. These human instruments "were moved by the Holy Spirit," "they spoke from God," "no prophecy was ever made by an act of human will" (2 Pe 1:21).

Kato was biblical and historically correct to be concerned with the spread of implicit and explicit universalism on the continent of Africa. In addition to universalism being in theological vogue throughout the west, we have additional factors here in Africa. "An emotional touch," as Kato said, "out of genuine love for the ancestors who die without the knowledge of the way of salvation, is a big attraction to universalism" (Kato 1975: 13).

We cannot pretend that there is no problem. We ought not to be blind to the facts. Loss of biblical authority in ecumenical circles has led to a departure from the historic Christian faith. Tokumboh Adeyemo, the former General Secretary of the Association of Evangelicals of Africa and Madagascar, declared:

> *Concentrated efforts are being made in our universities and other places of higher learning to produce theology for our churches, but the output so far cannot be truly called 'Christian.' The proponents of this African theology, however, not only use Christian terminology, but claim to be Christians ... In the African evangelicals' effort to express Christianity in the context of the African, the Bible must remain the absolute source* (Adeyemo 1979b: 16).

It seems regrettable that we must engage in polemics. How much better would it be if we could all live and let live. Division in the Christian Church is tragic. Would that we could agree with Mbiti when he pleads, "There is enough room for each one of us to make a scholarly contribution without resorting to groundless attacks on others, even if one may hold different opinions or interpretations of the Scriptures" (1986: 49). Within the fold of orthodoxy there should be room for different opinions without groundless attacks on others.

Yet liberal Christianity is another religion, not the historic Christian faith. When the foundation of Christian authority is emaciated through a low view of Scripture, when the fundamental elements of the Gospel are altered by accommodation to rationalism, we are compelled to speak out in fidelity to Jesus Christ our Lord and Saviour. Evangelicals seek to follow the admonition of Jude, the servant and brother of Jesus Christ who appealed to his readers, "that you contend earnestly for the faith which was once for all delivered to the saints" (Jude 1: 3). And this is what the late Byang Kato has tried to do together with countless other evangelicals throughout the continent.

GUIDELINES FOR DEVELOPING AFRICAN BIBLICAL THEOLOGY

Anyone who has observed both the erection of a large building and the demolition of another will recall the striking contrast. The foundation takes an extraordinary amount of time and effort. The building's destruction, however, occurs quickly with a loud crash.

We have taken some time in the painful examination of attempts by good people to construct an African Theology. We have sought to disclose the faulty foundation upon which they have begun the task. With a low view of Scripture, no theology will stand the test of time. Like so much of the experimental theologies of the West these days, they last a few short years and then are bypassed for newer, "more relevant theology."

In the first section of this chapter we have sought to point out the unbiblical presuppositions which help shape much of the methodology for African Theology. In this sense our purpose has been negative.

The major question for evangelicals is this: "How shall we develop African Biblical Theology?" Having traced the historical development, we are conscious that the foundational task for all theological reflection is the development of methodology that is both consistent with Scripture and workable in our African context. A faulty methodology will lead to a faulty theology even as a poor foundation results in a poorly constructed building.

In this second section our purpose is positive, to propose guidelines for the development of an evangelical theology in Africa. To build an evangelical theology is more difficult than the demolition of liberal theology. But as evangelicals we must not be content with critical judgements. We must eagerly and energetically construct an evangelical theology for our African context.

We have seen that for African Theology to have any meaning, it must be done mainly by African Christians who are rooted in African culture. Given the past history of Africa, any other thought would be dubious. Many Africans today have grown up in Christian homes, removed from traditional religion. After spending years overseas in their studies they have become bi-cultural and westernized in their orientation. Evangelical Africans who are in basic touch with their African context are the main ones who can build a biblical theology in the African context.

Yet we all learn from one another. As Kanyandago has said, "Being African is not a necessary condition for doing African Theology otherwise we risk to define it in terms of race and colour" (Kanyandago 1978: 342; cf. Dickson 1974: 204). The Third World Theologians affirmed in the Seoul Declaration,

> *We give thanks to our sovereign God who has preserved and renewed the church during the past nineteen centuries. We express our indebtedness to the creeds of the Early Church, the confessions of the European Reformation, and the spiritual awakening of the revival movements in modern times. We recognize the contributions western churches and missionary agencies in the birth and growth in many parts of the Third World* (Seoul Declaration 1983: 8).

It is within this context of mutuality that we propose the following guidelines in the attempt to develop an evangelical theology in the African context.

Reference has been made in various articles and books to the importance of guidelines but nothing much has been detailed. Imasogie has written a book of 92 pages entitled, *Guidelines for Christian Theology in Africa* (1983). But regrettably, he has devoted only six pages in the book to actual "Proposed Guidelines." And these pages say nothing of methodology. They simply recommend three motifs for Christian theology in Africa.

For an evangelical, the development of guidelines for methodology is most crucial. How do we develop theology in any context? What troubles evangelicals is not that African Christians are reflecting on God's Word, but that some have an unorthodox view of Scripture and interpret the Bible in such a way that they do not do justice to the biblical message. As Dickson affirmed in 1974, "African Theology could proceed on the basis of a faulty methodology" (Dickson 1974).

Following is a proposed definition for the process of contextualizing Christian theology together with an expansion of each concept. This is an attempt toward developing a methodology of contextualizing that will make theology both relevant to the context and faithful to the Scriptures.

Contextualizing theology is that 8) dynamic process whereby (1) the people of God, (6) living in community and interacting with believers throughout time and space, (4) under the illuminating guidance of the Holy Spirit, (9) proclaim (7) in their own language and thought forms, (5) the Word that God has spoken to them (3) in their context (2) through the study of the Scriptures.

1. Contextualizing is done by the People of God.

Unregenerate men and women cannot do theology. Nor can individual believers in isolation from the believing community do theology. The study of Scripture and the understanding of the will of God can only be done properly by those who have entered a covenant relationship with the living God through personal faith in Jesus Christ.

Bruce Nicholls speaks of "starting from within the circle of faith-commitment" (Nicholls 1979a: 55). Nominal Christians cannot make effective and faithful theologians for the Word of God must be grasped by faith and not merely by the intellect. Christian theologizing is far more than an academic exercise. Without genuinely saving faith we can neither believe that God is nor understand the spiritual insights in the Bible.

We live in a day when professing Christians do not see any relevance in prayer, worship and evangelism as it has been understood historically by the Christian Church. Bishop John Robinson in his book, *Honest to God*, confessed that he and many other seminarians did not see any relevance in the churchly discipline of prayer. Rev. James Cone rejects the value of prayer during this time of black revolution (Cone 1970: 234). The problem with many theologians is that they either do not have a living faith in Jesus Christ, or they do not approach life from within "the circle of faith-commitment."

> *The contextualizing of biblical theology in a changing world demands a rethinking of the whole process of doing theology. But the Bible itself insists that the starting point must be from within the circle of faith-commitment to God's self-revelation in Christ. With the weakening of assurance of the knowledge of the content of the Christian faith, many theologians and communicators are, in practice, making the cultural context the starting point* (Nicholls 1979a: 55).

When we speak of the "People of God," we do not mean the elite who know the original languages of the Bible and have graduate degrees in theology and philosophy. The "people of God" are not restricted to the professors of theology in the universities and theological colleges. The people of God are doing theology at every imaginable level: Christians reading their Bible and applying God's truth to their own lives; lay persons who study Scripture in preparation for teaching, witnessing and preaching; evangelists who study Scripture in order to proclaim the Gospel and bring men and women to faith in Christ; pastors, both ordained and non-ordained, official clergy and lay clergy, who study the Bible in order to preach the Word of God relevantly to the people on Sundays; men with a prophetic ministry who study Scripture in order to call society back to the ways of the living God, ways of justice, and righteousness; teachers who study Scripture in order to instruct students preparing for some greater Christian ministry; scholars who study Scripture in order to write books and articles both at the popular and professional level. The People of God at every level are doing and ought to do theological reflection.

Theological errors causing the most damage to the Christian church usually come from the top and filter down. What is needed in developing African Biblical Theology is the involvement of all Christians in the task of studying the Scriptures. When we listen to the biblical insights of lay people, we are listening to genuinely contextualized theology. Hassing calls this "*theologia in loco*, theology at the grass roots." "Only as the grass roots get involved will Christian answers to African questions be forthcoming" (Hassing 1971: 514). Therefore, the actual research involved in developing African Biblical Theology must embrace the grass roots level – not to determine our beliefs by what the majority of people think, like a Gallop Poll, but to gain genuine insight into what the genuine needs and solutions are in the African context according to the Scriptures.

2. Contextualization is Through the Study of Scripture.

If the starting point for those doing theology is in "the circle of faith-commitment," the focal point is the study of Scripture which has priority over everything else.

Theologians, who outline the various sources of theology, always acknowledge that the Scripture forms a primary source. But in practice the Bible is not normative. For this reason it seems best for evangelicals to acknowledge only one source of biblical theology, namely, the written Word of God. This must be understood through the illumination of the Holy Spirit and in the context of the reader. But the one source of theology can never be confused with or in some way be comparable to the context. Scripture, therefore, becomes the one source for evangelical theology and that one source is normative.

The problem we are dealing with is the relationship between the Bible and context. Karl Barth waged a vigorous war against the old modernists whose "natural theology" ate up "grace" as revealed in Scripture. There is real danger that our cultural heritage will effectively cancel out what God clearly teaches in the Bible. This has been a problem in the past and will continue to be so.

The problem throughout history is that men with good intentions seek to accommodate the Christian faith so as to make it more relevant and acceptable. Today western theologians such as Bultmann, Tillich, John T. Robinson and others seek to make Christianity acceptable to secular man. But in their adjustments to western culture, they have surrendered the heart of the Christian faith. As Donald McGavran has written, these adjustments must be rejected "on the grounds that instead of revelation judging culture, in such adjustments the culture has weighed revelation, found it wanting and folded it into a syncretistic form agreeable to modern man" (Yamaori 1975: 45).

The tragedy is that the rationalism of the West has now seeped into the African Church through western scholarship. The western rationalists have provided the "theological" rationale to accommodate the Word of God to the African culture. With the loss of divine authority in Scripture, we are left with no sure standard of truth.

Bishop Desmond Tutu quotes with approval Maurice Wiles, a western theologian, who said, "There are no fixed criteria for the determination of theological truth and error. We ought therefore to be ready to tolerate a considerable measure even of what seems to us to be error, for we cannot be certain that it is we who are right" (Tutu 1975: 31). When the Scriptures become a mere witness to the testimony of the people of God, when the words of the Bible in the original language are no longer the very Word of God, then Christians are left to their own subjective opinion as to what is true or false, what we can accept or reject.

Fortunately, there is a growing number of African theologians who are writing and speaking from the evangelical perspective. Tokumboh Adeyemo calls on evangelical Africans to make a total, unconditional and exclusive commitment to the authority of the Bible. He believes that the theological battle in Africa will be won or lost in the areas of the truths concerning inspiration, infallibility, inerrancy and absolute authority of Scripture (Adeyemo 1979b: 16,17). The future vitality of the Christian Church in Africa depends on such commitment by evangelical theologians. Adeyemo has written forthrightly as an evangelical on the question, *Salvation in African Tradition* (1979a).

Having resolved by faith that the Bible is indeed the infallible Word of God, we are then faced with the method of interpretation. Hermeneutics includes both the subjective and objective elements. The objective element involves the "scientific" approach of the grammatical-historical method of exegesis in which we seek to know the meaning of the text as the original author intended. Interpreting Scripture requires lexicons, grammar books and a careful examination of the literary context of the biblical passage being studied. Knowledge of the historical and geographical context sheds light. Confident of the unity of Scripture due to its divine inspiration, comparing Scripture with Scripture brings clarity.

The subjective element involves the existential involvement of the student in the understanding and appropriation of the text to one's life. This is frequently called the "hermeneutical circle" (Padilla 1979). Nicholls speaks of it as "the objective-subjective principle of distancing from and identification with the text" (Nicholls 1979a: 49).

There is in this a two-way process of encounter. Nicholls seeks to maintain a "balance between the objective authority of the Word of God and the subjective experience of the interpretation." On the one hand, we need to distance ourselves from the text by critical study of the Bible. "The task of exegesis is the recovery of the *sensus literalis*, the literal or natural meaning of the text, involving the right use of the linguistic tools and historical method, traditionally known as the 'grammatical-historical' method" (Nicholls 1978: 49). This he distinguishes from the more speculative historical critical method which operates on the documentary hypothesis of Scripture. Instead of us refashioning Scripture, we need to allow the Scripture to refashion our own pre-understanding, "recognizing its objective authority and its internal harmony" (Nicholls 1979a: 49).

On the other hand we need to identify with the text. This is "the fusion of the horizons" as the Holy Spirit illumines our hearts. Although the neo orthodox accuse the evangelicals of stressing the cold, factual, propositional doctrines of the Bible, this is factually untrue.

We believe the essential teachings of the Bible are clearly taught, a principle commonly spoken of as the principle of perspicuity. As believers meditate upon Scripture, the Holy Spirit illuminates the heart. As we approach God in the Scriptures through prayer, God speaks to us regarding our responsibilities in our context. This is the subjective aspect of the hermeneutical principle.

3. The Context of the People of God.

By "context" we refer to the whole environment in which the people of God live, including the social, economic, educational, religious, philosophical and political; in brief, man's culture. Culture is not static and therefore, God must address each generation in each culture through His Word.

The emphasis in contextualized theology is taking the context of the present day student of the Bible more seriously. We know that God speaks to us in terms of our concrete, living situations. If we do not understand the Bible as it applies to our own context, we have not truly understood the Bible for ourselves. Thus there is an interplay between the Bible and our context.

"The Willowbank Report" on Gospel and Culture, sponsored by the Lausanne Committee for World Evangelization, explains the contextual approach.

> *It is the need for this dynamic interplay between text and interpreters which we wish to emphasize. Today's readers cannot come to the text in a personal vacuum, and should not try to. Instead, they should come with an awareness of concerns stemming from their cultural background, personal situation, and responsibility to others. These concerns will influence the questions which are put to the Scriptures. What is received back, however, will not be answers only, but more questions. As we address Scripture, Scripture addresses us. We find that our culturally conditioned presuppositions are being challenged and our questions corrected. In fact, we are compelled to reformulate our previous questions and to ask fresh ones. So the living interaction proceeds* (Lausanne 1978: 11).

Thus our knowledge of God and His will for our lives is deepened as we grow in our understanding of His Word related to our context. "Out of the context in which his word was originally given, we hear God speaking to us in our contemporary context, and we find it a transforming experience. This process is a kind of upward spiral in which Scripture remains always central and normative" (Lausanne 1978: 11).

Culture is related to theology in several ways. First, culture forms the grid (or the glasses) through which man perceives the revelation of God. Communication is not simply one way, from God to man. People immersed in culture have certain perspectives and viewpoints. They see things in a particular manner.

> *Whenever an interpreter approaches a particular biblical text he can only approach it from his own perspective ... Thus the interpretative process involves a hermeneutical circle in which the interpreter and the text are mutually engaged and that the interpretation inevitably bears the marks of its historical context* (Stott 1979: 89).

This means that culture both hinders and helps man in his understanding of God's revelation. It hinders him because his pre-understanding may deflect from or obscure his perception of what God has really said. It may help him in that "every situation makes possible a certain approach to Scripture which brings to light aspects of the message which in other situations remains less visible or even hidden" (Stott 1979: 90).

Culture provides the language in which Scripture is translated and by which the Gospel is understood. Vocabulary, syntax, figures of speech, analogies, patterns of logic and arrangement, religious and philosophical concepts and functions, all form together the medium by which a theology is conceptualized and communicated. Thus we have already seen that Bible translation is in itself a form of theologizing. Choices must be made as to the meaning of the original text. This is interpretation. Choices must be made in the way the original text is to be communicated. This is interaction with the culture. Since language is a near perfect mirror image of any given culture, the choice of language to be used in translation of the Bible involves an interaction between Gospel and Culture, between the Word of God and the worldview of the people.

Context, man's culture, provides redemptive analogies by which men are able to understand the revelation of God. Don Richardson in *Peace Child* has demonstrated this. These analogies may be found in legends and records of the past. Or they may be found in contemporary beliefs and practices. But they are cultural road ways which lead people to an understanding of the Gospel. Thus culture can form bridges, points of contact, by which Jesus Christ is made known and real to people.

Context also poses questions for which each culture seeks an answer. The particular problems and emphases in a given culture may be significantly different from another culture. Since theology is meant to be the application of God's Word to people in their needs, theology should be practical. This is the reason that aspects of theology written in the west are inadequate for Africa today.

We can say beyond dispute that God has spoken to human beings in certain cultures and has accommodated Himself to the limitations of their experience. This can be seen in the Scriptures as God disclosed Himself progressively over the years to the children of Israel, then to the apostolic church in Hellenistic culture.

There can be no question that we are all culturally conditioned in the sense that we are profoundly affected by the culture in which we have been enculturated. But the question is, to what extent is the revelation of God free to break through to every human being? Is God able to disclose all that He has said in Scripture to every person in every culture? When God discloses Himself to someone, is this only an existential encounter, an experience without cognitive content? Does God reveal propositional truth and is this verbal truth transferable and comprehensible by all people in all cultures? Are we today able to grasp the original intention of the authors who wrote to people living in a totally different context from ours?

In brief, the question is this: Could God reveal himself and his will to the prophets and apostles of old, and in turn, could God's propositional revelation be understand by us today in our diverse cultures?

Biblically, we cannot separate the mighty acts of God in history from the interpretation and meaning of those events. Scripture not only records the revelatory events but the inspired meaning of those events. And God sovereignly chose the Semitic Hebrew culture through which to disclose His eternal will for all mankind. As Nicholls affirms:

> *In divine wisdom God chose Abram out of a Mesopotamian culture and through his descendants formed a carrier culture that reflected the interaction of the supra-cultural content and the cultural form. Thus there is a uniqueness about the Hebrew culture of the Bible. It is not just a culture alongside any other culture, but it becomes a unique culture that carried the marks of the divine-human interaction. In the providence of God this culture was able to faithfully carry the uniqueness of the divine message of creation, sin, redemption and supremely the Incarnation and resurrection of the divine Son* (Nicholls 1979a: 46).

Thus God providentially prepared a culture through which He could reveal His will for all peoples without distorting that message. The Hebrew culture became the carrier culture which was uniquely capable of receiving divine revelation without undue bias or distortion.

To what extent does our own culture distort and distend our ability to comprehend divine revelation? While culture forms the grid by which we perceive the Scriptures, that cultural grid is not so opaque that we cannot perceive the fundamental teachings of Scripture. Some suggest that all theologies are the result of cultural conditioning so that the basic explanation for the conflicting theologies in the Christian Church today is the differing cultural contexts out of which those theologies arose.

But this is a simplistic explanation. No doubt cultural dissimilation did play a part on occasions. For instance, the Reformation succeeded best among the Germanic and non-Latins who were rebelling against Roman control. Luther's own personal experience led him to find "salvation by grace through faith alone" to be the key to Christian theology. And the non-Latins in western and northern Europe embraced Reformational teaching.

But cultural dissimilation does not provide an adequate explanation for the differing theologies. Salvation by grace alone, through faith alone, in Christ alone, is a biblical truth, amply demonstrated from the study of the Bible. And it was seriously compromised by the teachings of the Roman Church. This biblical truth has been embraced by peoples of all cultures, not by imperial decree, but by faith through the study of the Bible. Such an explanation of cultural dissimulation for differing theologies ultimately leads to agnosticism, for any theology can be justified as a response to divine revelation in a given culture. Nor does it explain the fact that Christians from every culture in the world today were able to assent to the Lausanne Covenant freely, and not by coercion.

Culture provides the seasoning of the food but does not change the nature of the food. We are not totally conditioned by our environment, though we are obviously influenced by it. Culture may create different emphases in theology, but will not create conflicting theologies nor change the basic thrust of Scripture.

Culture then becomes the tool by which we communicate God's Word to others. Our cultural context is the medium through which God communicates and by which we respond. But culture does not change the content or meaning of theology. Context is a servant and not the master.

4. Contextualization is by the Illuminating Guidance of the Holy Spirit.

Doing theology in context is not possible without the Holy Spirit, nor is it possible by the Spirit alone. The Holy Spirit illuminates the Word, quickens the mind and empowers for living. A true response to Scripture is therefore, not possible apart from the work of the Holy Spirit. But the Spirit only works in the minds of believers primarily through the Scriptures.

The Holy Spirit was sent by the risen Lord to lead his disciples into all truth, truth which was tied to the words of Christ (Jn 16:13). The Holy Spirit does not speak on his own, "but whatever He hears, He will speak." The same Spirit who inspired the written Word of God (2 Ti 3:16) is the one who illuminates that Word (1 Co 2). Thus Scripture is the yardstick to judge whether or not an alleged insight by the Holy Spirit has divine origin or not.

5. Contextualization is by the Word that God has Spoken.

The "word that God has spoken" is here distinguished from the written Word of God, for it refers to that which God speaks to us through Scripture derived by the illumination of the Holy Spirit. This presupposes only a partial understanding of the total revelation. Theology contains insights that are gained through the study of the Bible. But these insights are fragmentary. This necessitates a continual return to the Word of God for correction, clarification and confirmation. The written Word of God must always judge the "word that God has spoken." For we are frequently led to conclusions which we erroneously credit to the Spirit.

This principle recognizes two factors: that God speaks differently, though not conflictingly, to different people living in different contexts, and that which people profess to hear spoken to them must ever be subjected to the written Word of God.

This principle is admirably demonstrated by Andersson's study of the Lutheran church founded in Congo, Brazzaville (Andersson 1968). Andersson, a Lutheran missionary, desired to know whether the Lutheran Christians in the Congo understood the truth of justification by faith alone. Or did they depend on a salvation by works?

Andersson discovered that the Africans understood the words quite well but interpreted them differently, adapting them to their own traditional worldview.

Instead of being concerned about a merciful God, these Africans were concerned about a powerful God who can secure happiness on earth. The African Christian interpreted salvation in terms of good health, a long life, abundant possessions and many children. "For them salvation was not salvation of the soul, but something which made life secure here below, namely bodily health, happiness in this life, prosperity, success in all undertakings" (Andersson 1968: 149).

These Christians heard the Gospel through their own cultural grid. They saw God as the powerful One who could help them in their present needs. Surely, the Bible has much to say on this subject. They heard this word because of their cultural grid.

But every word of God spoken to us existentially must be continually subjected to the authority of the written Word of God. These African Christians needed to hear that Jesus Christ is Lord who has power over all spirits. This is a biblical truth desperately needed in their context. But they also needed to hear the Word of God that salvation is by grace through faith alone, even though this concept was foreign to their culture and strange to their ears.

Therefore, we agree with those missiologists who declare that each culture forms a grid which enables people to see certain truths not so clearly understood by people in other cultures.

But we as evangelicals also insist that while culture enables men to grasp certain truths, it also blinds them from seeing other truths. And the Holy Spirit must enlighten everyone in all cultures concerning God's whole truth. The whole Bible is intended for every man. "All Scripture ... is profitable."

Therefore, we need to return repeatedly and humbly to the Scriptures to compare our understanding of what God has spoken with the written Word of God.

6. Contextualization is Done by the Living Community, Interacting with Believers throughout Time and Space.

Contextualizing theology is not done in the ivory tower of a classroom or library. It is not primarily an academic exercise by individuals. As the community sits together with the Word of God, there is a growing understanding of what God is saying to them in their time and space.

Koyama in his book, *Water Buffalo Theology* (1976), is a good example of how <u>not</u> to do theology in context. While it provides interesting reading and certainly reflects a desire to relate to the culture where he serves, it has three serious defects. First, he only plays with Scripture, without seriously grappling with the Word of God. What is needed is exegesis of the Scripture. Secondly, it is not "Buffalo" Theology, but rather a westernized version with all sorts of ideologies learned from the West creeping into it. Ralph Covell asks this question, "Is this a product of his Asian mind, or of his ten years of American training? ... I question whether this is really 'water buffalo theology.' Its very sophistication seems more appropriate for the University classroom" (Covell 1977: 56). Thirdly, he fails to distinguish between natural theology and biblical theology.

Truly contextualized theology cannot be done by theologians in Geneva or Rome. Nor can it be done by men whose minds are immersed with western categories of thought and western ideologies. This means that mature African Biblical Theology cannot evolve within a generation, though steps can be continually taken.

Each of us is sorely limited. We are finite human beings who learn slowly. Solomon observed years ago, "There is nothing new under the sun." Candid confession will reveal that original thought is slow in coming and rare as precious stones. We have all been profoundly influenced by those who have taught us. And since most of our teachers have had western origins, we cannot escape our western influence. African Biblical Theology will come. But mature theological reflection that is both truly biblical and authentically African will take time.

To recognize this fact will enable us to resolve several problems. Knowing that the development of African Biblical Theology is an enormous project that entails generations, we need not become frustrated at the slow pace. Furthermore, we ought not to pretend that some theological contribution we may make is so original or so authentically African. Progress in theological reflection is measured by small steps, not light years.

And contrary to opinion and despite what we have already said, theology is spontaneously being contextualized in Africa through Christian hymns written to traditional melodies and rhythms, through sermons preached in churches and schools by the African believers, and through the interaction of Christians with the Word of God in their context. Wherever you have the Bible translated in the vernacular languages, you have the basis for a contextualized theology. Theology is essentially translation of the truth of God into the language of the people.

The whole issue of theology being a community affair, as they interact with believers throughout time and space, is an extremely important matter. We need to interact with Christian thought worldwide and through the 2,000 years of Christianity. This point has been placed nearer the end of the Guidelines for a purpose. If Scripture is to be normative, then it must not be obscured by theological traditions.

But African Biblical Theology should not be provincial or narrow. Otherwise it becomes sectarian and ethnic. All Christian theology should be rightly related to the historic Christian affirmations of the Faith, the basic doctrines of the historic Christian Church. Peter Berger contends, "The fundamental questions of theology have been passionately considered for at least 2,000 years. It is ... insufferable arrogance to think that one can begin theology in sovereign disregard of this history" (Fleming 1980: 56). While evangelicals do not regard tradition, including theological affirmations of the church, on the same par with Scripture, we would be blind to ignore the past and fail to interact with the past.

The context adds the pepper and salt but it does not alter the content in such a way as to create a conflicting theology. The beauty of the Christian faith is that in spite of the hundreds of denominations and differing theological emphases, those who are truly evangelical in their faith can all ascribe to the Nicene Creed and the Lausanne Covenant. There is something more that unites us than an administrative structure. We believe in one Holy Catholic Church which is united by the apostolic faith. Jesus Christ as He is revealed in Scripture, and the essential elements of the Gospel revealed in the Word of God, are the bond that brings us together. For any theology to sever that bond would be a disaster and proof of its unsound presuppositions.

7. Contextualization is in Their Own Language and Thought Forms.

Contextualization is pre-eminently rooted in the vernacular translation of the Word of God. That translation must be both faithful to the biblical text in Hebrew and Greek and it must convey the message with the same meaning and impact as it conveyed to the original hearers. Without translation of Scripture, you can have no contextualized theology. Therefore, translation is crucial.

Once Scripture is translated into the vernacular, theological reflection by the people is then possible, free to draw upon figures of speech, analogies, patterns of logic and arrangement, religious and philosophical concepts. Theology is proven to be contextualized by the response it evokes from the people. If the truth of Scripture is communicated by a medium which seems foreign, then it is not contextualized. If the message pierces the heart and seems like their own, then it is contextualized.

8. Contextualization is a Dynamic Process.

"The Word of God is living and active. Sharper than any double-edged sword, it penetrates even to dividing soul and spirit, joints and marrow; it judges the thoughts and attitudes of the heart" (Heb 4: 12).

The Word of God is living because of the active work of the Holy Spirit in bringing it alive to the people of God as they read it. As men respond to the Word, there is growth in understanding. The ultimate purpose in divine revelation is not mere information but transformation of life as people know

God. Propositional truth is imparted through biblical revelation, but the ultimate purpose is to change lives and bring men into a living knowledge of Jesus Christ. Theology therefore, ought not to settle for better understanding of revelation. As the living Word interacts with the believer there is growth and development in greater commitment to God and obedience to His Word. "This radical reorientation of the whole life is the core intention of the Christian Gospel, with the informational content as instrumental and the behavioural changes as logical entailment" (Taber 1979: 112).

But the dynamic nature of the Word of God means that we also come into better understanding of the will of God. The picture Paul paints in Ephesians 4 is that of being built up "until we all reach unity in the faith and in the knowledge of the Son of God and become mature, attaining to the whole measure of the fullness of Christ." The goal of theology is unity. And since theology is a dynamic process through contact with the living Word of God, interacting with an ever changing culture, ever in dialogue with the people of God living in community throughout time and space, this theology can move toward that goal established by the Apostle Paul, namely, "unity of the faith."

"Dynamic process," therefore, does not mean shifting and changing. Nor does it imply theologies that differ in their essential content. By this we mean a living relationship with Jesus Christ and His Word, so that our behaviour becomes more and more like Christ, so that our understanding of God and His will becomes increasingly clearer to us. "Unity of faith" is the accent of the Apostle Paul which is in contrast to the contemporary emphasis on diversity. This is not a unity forced on a people. Nor is it uniformity in every detail of theological understanding. But it is a recognition that God is One, that He has spoken in Scripture which is marked by harmony and unity, and that as the Holy Spirit leads His people into the study of Scripture there is growth, both in life and understanding.

9. Contextualization is for Proclamation.

Proclamation implies mission. Theology ought not to be an academic discipline unrelated to life and mission. Theology is the reflection on the Word of God so that correct behaviour results. The motive of contextualization is obedience to the mission of the Church. The primary concern of the apostolic Church was not to do theology but to proclaim the Gospel faithfully to the nations in obedience to Jesus Christ. Paul was a task theologian, not a systematic theologian. But all proclamation is theological, although some preaching is better theology than others.

Proclamation is inextricably connected with the knowledge of God's Word. "How, then, can they call on the one they have not believed in? And how can they believe in the one whom they have not heard? And how can they hear without someone preaching to them?" (Ro 9:14).

Our goal as theologians, then, in seeking to contextualize our theology, is to preach the Word of God more effectively and more faithfully. The best theologians are "task theologians" who are reflecting upon the Word as they seek to proclaim the Gospel in mission.

4

HISTORICAL PANORAMA OF THE CHURCH'S VIEW OF SCRIPTURE

We have seen in the last chapter that virtually all those doing African Theology agree on a multiple of issues, except one. They fundamentally disagree on the nature and role of Scripture in the development of African Theology.

Though this chapter may seem like a diversion in a book devoted to African Theology, it seems wise to take a step back and see what the Christian Church has thought about the Bible throughout her history. It may well be that most of those writing African theologies are not aware of the historic stance of the Christian Church on Scripture, and the reasons for the revolutionary changes that have taken place in western nations during the past two centuries in the area of philosophy, theology and virtually all sciences.

What follows is a bird's eye view, a summation of what should be a whole book. It is hoped that this brief, simplified sketch will shed light on the sources from which many African theologians are drawing their presuppositions and preunderstanding which underlie their theologizing.

ORTHODOX STANCE IN CHURCH HISTORY

We begin with the claims of Scripture and specifically with the claims of Jesus Christ, the Lord and Saviour of the Christian Church.

The Claims of Scripture

The Holy Writings of the Christian Church, found in the Canon of 66 books in the Old Testament and New Testament, are marked by the divine and human elements.

On the one hand there is abundant evidence that the Bible is a human production, not a document dictated by God or his angels. The individual personalities, backgrounds, writing styles and interests are plain for all to see. Luke, the author of both the Gospel by his name and the book of Acts, "carefully investigated everything" from both "eyewitnesses and servants of the word" (Lk 1:1-4). As a medical doctor his medical interests and vocabulary are evident.

On the other hand the prophets and apostles who wrote the Scriptures claimed to be proclaiming the Word of God under the inspiration of the Holy Spirit. The Old Testament prophets repeatedly declared, "Thus saith the Lord," and "the Word of the Lord came, saying."

The apostle Peter affirmed:

> *...no prophecy of Scripture came about by the prophet's own interpretation. For prophecy never had its origin in the will of man but men spoke from God as <u>they were carried along by the Holy Spirit</u>* (2 Pe 1:20-21).

The Greek words translated, *carried along*, convey a forceful role of the Holy Spirit in the inspiration of God's Word. The Spirit of God had full control of the prophets who wrote the Scriptures. They were impelled and driven along by the Holy Spirit.

The reason why the Scriptures are authoritative is that the Scriptures were "breathed-out" by the Holy Spirit. When writing to his son in the faith, the apostle Paul addressed Timothy by saying:

> *...from infancy you have known the holy Scriptures, which are able to make you wise for salvation through faith in Christ Jesus. All Scripture is God-breathed and is useful for teaching, rebuking, correcting and training in righteousness, so that the man of God may be thoroughly equipped for every good work* (2 Ti 3:15-17).

The Bible was not so much *inspired* (breathed-into) as it was *breathed-out* by God through the Holy Spirit. Therefore, *all* Scripture is profitable. Nothing is irrelevant or insignificant. The whole of Scripture is God's Word.

The New Testament writers have taken their cue from their own Lord and Saviour. For it was Jesus Christ who taught:

> *Do not think I have come to abolish the Law or the Prophets; I have not come to abolish them but to fulfil them. I tell you the truth, until heaven and earth disappear, not the smallest letter, not the least stroke of a pen, will by any means disappear from the Law until everything is accomplished* (Mt 5:12-18).

Jesus unambiguously affirmed the full authority of the Scriptures. "The smallest letter" was no doubt the *yod* in the Hebrew Bible, or the *iota* in the Greek alphabet. The "least stroke of a pen" was probably the tiny stroke or part of a letter used to differentiate Hebrew letters.

Jesus here taught that the Scriptures were authoritative down to the smallest word or letter. Nothing can be dismissed as irrelevant or unimportant. Nothing is in error. The Scriptures were *verbally inspired*.

When disputing with the Jews, Jesus quoted the Scripture and then said, "Scripture cannot be set aside or cancelled or broken or annulled" (Jn 10:35 *Amplified*). Jesus had complete confidence in the Word of God.

During his high priestly prayer when speaking to his heavenly Father, he said, *"Sanctify them [the apostles] in the truth; your word is truth"* (Jn 17:17). Since God cannot lie, his Word is truth; and since the sacred writings of the Hebrew prophets and Christ's apostles were breathed out by God, what they wrote is God's Word. It does not *contain* truth. God's Word *is* truth.

The Scriptures are the written Word of God. Jesus Christ is the living Word of God, the final Word from God (Heb 1:1-4). We know nothing of the living Word, however, apart from the trustworthy account of the written Word of God. In Jesus Christ we find the analogy for the authorship of the Scriptures. The confession of the Christian Church is unanimous – Jesus Christ is fully human and fully God.

In the same way, the Bible is fully human (a human production with human beings using their own personalities, abilities and intellect) while being fully divine – God's inspired, inerrant Word – because the Sacred Writings were "breathed-out" by God himself as the authors were "carried along by the Holy Spirit." This is not dictation for that would mitigate the human element. But human authorship does not necessitate mistakes any more than the humanity of Adam and Eve would mean that they were sinners upon their creation.

The Teachings of the Historic Church

On the basis of these truths stated above, the historic Christian church has valued and cherished the Bible, the Canon of 66 books, as the authoritative, infallible and inerrant Word of God.

The apostolic fathers recognized the absolute authority of the Old Testament which they interpreted in light of Jesus Christ. Full confidence was accorded the words of Christ and the teachings of the apostles. According to Theodor Zahn, "The possibility that an Apostle could have erred in the doctrine and instructions which he directed to the congregations had obviously no place in the circuit of ideas in the Post-apostolic Age" (Neve 1946: 41).

Tertullian from Carthage, North Africa, in the 2nd century, described the individual Old Testament texts as "the commandments of God," and the canon as the Scripture of the Holy Ghost (Lewis 1996: 136). Irenaeus, bishop in Gaul (modern day France) in the Western Roman Empire in the 3rd century wrote, "The Scriptures are indeed perfect, since they were spoken by the Word of God (i.e. Christ) and His Spirit," thus affirming the infallible, verbal inspiration of Scriptures (Lewis 1996: 136).

Gregory of Nazianzus, the Archbishop of Constantinople in the Eastern Roman Empire in the 4th century, argued on the basis of Jesus' teaching that "the smallest stroke of Scripture derives from the Holy Spirit, and that even the slightest nuance of the inspired writer is not in vain" (Lewis 1996: 135).

Jerome, the venerable translator of the Latin Vulgate Bible in the 4th century, "upheld verbal, plenary inspiration" of the Scriptures (Lewis 1996: 135).

Saint Augustine, Bishop of Hippo in North Africa, and perhaps the most influential theologian of the early Christian Church, held to the complete dependability of the Bible. He said: "I have learned to yield this respect and honour only to the canonical books of Scripture: of these alone do I most firmly believe that the authors were completely free from error" (Erickson 1998: 251).

These are the testimonies of the early Christian Church. The Catholic Church during the medieval age did not alter their view of Scriptures although they diluted its influence which we shall consider later.

All the major Protestant Reformers held to the infallible and unerring authority of Scripture.

Martin Luther said, "*The Scriptures have never erred...The Scriptures cannot err...It is certain that Scripture would not contradict itself; it only appears so to the senseless and obdurate hypocrites*" (Erickson 1998: 252).

Through John Calvin's influence the Westminster Confession of 1646 stated, "The Supreme Judge, by which all controversies of religion are to be determined...can be no other but the Holy Spirit speaking in the Scripture." Furthermore, "The infallible rule of interpretation of Scripture is the Scripture itself" (Leith 1977: 196).

An examination of the creeds for all the major branches of Protestantism shows that they all upheld a high view of Scripture whether Lutheran or Reformed, Baptist, Methodist or Anglican. They are unanimous in their affirmation of the trustworthiness of the Bible. For example the Baptist New Hampshire Confession states, "...that it has God for its author, salvation for its end, and truth, without any mixture of error, for its matter" (Leith 1977: 335).

Because no controversy over the authority of Scripture had erupted among the Protestants, less attention was paid to that doctrine immediately after the Reformation. But when liberals began undermining the authority of Scripture in the late 19th century, conservative theologians wrote extensively on the subject.

Archibald Alexander, Charles Hodge, A.A. Hodge and B.B. Warfield in Princeton University wrote voluminously, defending the full inerrancy and infallibility of Scripture (Feinberg 2001: 158).

In the opinion of Dr. J. Oliver Buswell, the historic view of the Christian Church concerning Scriptures was accurately summarized in the declaration of the General Assembly of the Presbyterian Church in the United States of America originally adopted in 1910, repeated in 1916 and again in 1923:

> *It is essential to the Word of God, and to our standards, that the Holy Spirit did so move, guide, and inspire the writers of the sacred Scriptures as to keep them from error* (Buswell 1979: 192).

However, during the past one-thousand years humanistic ideas creeped into the Church during two waves. The first wave occurred during the medieval period.

Competing Authority during Medieval Age

Throughout history good intentions have often had unintended consequences. The Bishops and Councils of the Christian Church sought to counteract errant beliefs through church authority. The pope, bishops and councils exerted their authority by issuing edicts and rulings in order to maintain order and orthodoxy within the expanding Catholic Church. In time these official decisions became traditions that were embraced as an authority on par with the Scriptures. Church traditions were considered normative when interpreting Scripture. This development relegated Scripture to a secondary role because the interpretation of Scripture by church tradition was final. In practice the Church embraced a second authority in addition to the Scriptures, namely, tradition.

For example, the seventh ecumenical Council held in Nicaea in AD 787 dealt with the image controversy. The question was whether the Church should continue using "the venerable and holy images" of Christ, images of the "spotless Lady, the Mother of God," and images of the "honourable Angels," all the Saints and "all pious people." Their authority was church tradition, stating,

> *We, therefore, following the royal pathway and the divinely inspired authority of our Holy Fathers and the traditions of the Catholic Church (for, as we all know, the Holy Spirit indwells her), define with all certitude and accuracy...* (Leith 1977: 55).

Humanistic ideas from pagan culture stealthily creeped into the Church and as these beliefs and practices were officially endorsed by the bishops and councils, they became part of Church Tradition, and hence, the orthodoxy of Christianity.

Prior to Constantine the Great, the Roman Emperor, Christians were a persecuted minority. But when Constantine issued the Edict of Milan in AD 313, decreeing tolerance for Christianity, he began the process of Christianizing the Roman Empire. The final step was taken by Emperor Theodosius I in AD 380 when he issued the Edict of Thessalonica that made Nicene Christianity the sole state religion.

As a result the "little flock" of Christian believers multiplied and spread rapidly. Being baptized as a Christian had become socially acceptable and even prestigious. By AD 500 the large majority of the population of the Roman Empire was professing Christian. These included the northern German "barbarians" like the Goths, Visigoths, Ostrogoths, Vandals and Franks. (They were called "barbarian" because they did not speak Latin or embrace the Graeco-Roman culture.)

Flooded with converts, the Church was unable to properly teach and instruct. The newly baptized believers brought into the church diverse pagan ideas. The Church decided to accommodate and "Christianize" these beliefs and practices. In this way humanistic beliefs and practices were embraced by the Church, and whenever bishops or councils made official statements concerning these practices, they became authoritative traditions.

"The pagan custom of raising men to the rank of gods or demigods, against which the Christian apologists so vigorously protested, crept into the Church in the honours paid to the apostles, martyrs and angels" (Latourette 1937: Volume 1, 319). Some Christian leaders actually rejoiced in the fact that martyrs were substituted for the pagan gods and given their glory. Pagan divinities continued in the Christian church with a thin veneer of a Christian name.

When churches were built on the sites of pagan temples, the old associations continued. "The cult of the Virgin Diana may have contributed to the worship of the Virgin Mary and more than a coincidence may possibly be seen in the fact that one of the earliest churches in honour of Mary rose at Ephesus on the site of the famous Temple of Diana, and that in the same city in 431, a synod was held which first officially designated Mary the Mother of God" (Latourette 1937: Volume 1, 320).

The ancient Lares in Italy (gods of the Roman households) were replaced by the Virgin, or the saints, or figures of the child Jesus. In Sicily, the Virgin took possession of the sanctuaries of Ceres and Venus and the pagan rites associated with them were perpetuated in honour of Mary. One pagan temple of Quirinus became the Church of St. Quirino. Thus a pagan god was canonized (Latourette 1937: Volume 1, 321).

In this way the medieval church embraced practices, adapted from the pagan religious heritage of the new converts, such as praying to the dead saints, praying for dead believers in purgatory, praying to Mary, paying money (indulgences) to the church coffers for the forgiveness of sins, and requiring deeds of penance for the remission of sins. None of these beliefs or practices were taught in the Scriptures, but they were held as true because of church tradition.

Thomas Aquinas (1225-1274), a Dominican friar, became the most influential theologian during the medieval age. Aquinas is held in high esteem today and his views are still prominent in the Roman Catholic Church. However, his understanding of the original sin of Adam and Eve was flawed and this has brought havoc to Christian thought. Aquinas taught that Adam's Fall corrupted only part of human nature, but not the intellect.

This meant that people could rely on the intellect and reasoning to find truth apart from special revelation. People were free to mix the teachings of the Bible with the teachings of non-Christians, including the pagan Greek philosophers. Gradually, philosophy was separated from biblical revelation. Philosophers began to act independently of Scripture. Human beings became autonomous creatures who could search for truth in other cultures, philosophies and religions, apart from divine revelation in Scripture.

Through these teachings, the synthesis between biblical teaching and pagan philosophies accelerated. Syncretism had been a problem during the medieval period with such accretions as prayers to and for the dead, the cult of Mary, purgatory, and works righteousness. Human beings were thought able to turn to God themselves by meriting the merit of Christ, a mixture of Christian thought with ancient pagan thought. Thomas Aquinas gave scholarly justification for the autonomy of man in his search for truth. Humanism had been enshrined in church doctrine.

Because the Christian Church had given traditions authority equal to, and in effect, above the authority of Scripture, Martin Luther and a host of other reformers arose in protest. They had no desire to leave the Roman Catholic Church. Instead, they wanted to reform it by returning to the Scriptures. *Sola Scriptura* (Scripture Alone) became the rallying cry for the Protestant Reformation.

The words of Martin Luther at the Diet of Worms in 1521 lay down the cardinal issue that led to the Protestant Reformation. There cannot be two authorities for faith, Scripture and Tradition. Scripture alone is our final authority.

> *Unless I am convicted of error by the testimony of Scripture or (since I put no trust in the unsupported authority of Pope or of councils, since it is plain that they have often erred and often contradicted themselves) by manifest reasoning, I stand convicted by the Scriptures to which I have appealed, and my conscience is taken captive by God's Word, I cannot and will not recant anything, for to act against our conscience is neither safe for us, nor open to us. On this I take my stand. I can do no other. God help me. Amen* (Bettenson 1947: 282f).

Despite the protesting of the Protestant Reformers, indeed, because of them, the Roman Catholic Council of Trent in 1563 decreed that the very issue which gave rise to Protestantism should be canonized. The Christian Church, according to the protesting Reformers, should have doctrines based only on one authority, namely, the Holy Scriptures. Tradition, as valuable and helpful as it may be, must always be subject to the teaching of the Word of God. But the Roman Church at the Council of Trent decreed:

> *...to check the unbridled spirits, it decrees that no one relying on his own judgement shall, in matters of faith and morals pertaining to the edification of Christian doctrine, distorting the Holy Scriptures in accordance with his own conceptions, presume to interpret them contrary to that sense which holy mother Church, to whom it belongs to judge of their true sense and interpretation, has held and holds, or even contrary to the unanimous teaching of the Fathers, even though such interpretations should never at any time be published* (Leith 1977: 403).

HUMANISTIC UNBELIEF UNDERMINES BIBLICAL AUTHORITY

For Protestants, the troubling issue of Church Tradition in the Roman Church, which overshadowed the authority of Scripture, has been resolved. *Sola Scriptura* (Scripture alone) was their guiding mantra during the Reformation in the 16th century.

But an even more devastating attack against the authority of Scripture came in modern times which has infected both Protestants and Roman Catholics.

The Renaissance

During the medieval period, Europe was the cradle of Christendom. The Church and the State worked hand in hand. Everyone was a professing Christian and paid allegiance to the Pope. They all embraced the same worldview.

During the late medieval period, the 14th, 15th and early 16th centuries, a cultural, intellectual and religious awakening occurred throughout Europe known as the Renaissance. The population rebounded after the devastating black plague, the economy flourished, towns and cities sprouted, universities were founded, and a rebirth took place. The Renaissance had dawned.

The Renaissance aroused enthusiasm for Greek and Roman classics. Instead of focusing on Christian dogma and the Church's authority, the Renaissance witnessed, what its proponents believed, the "rebirth" of man by harkening back to the pre-Christian era of Greek and Roman culture. During the Renaissance the humanists remained nominally Christian, but were enticed by Geek and Roman culture.

The Renaissance brought many positive features. Culture was stimulated. The arts and architecture became vibrant and creative. The return to the classics, especially the Greek language, paved the way for the Reformation.

The Latin Vulgate Bible was the official Bible during the medieval age, a language which the common man could not understand. Desiderius Erasmus (c. 1466) was a humanist in the Renaissance tradition who defended the translation of the Bible from Greek into vernacular languages. Through his masterful translation of the Greek New Testament, the minds of the Reformers were stimulated to understand the Gospel through the language used in the New Testament.

Harbingers of the Protestant Reformation sprouted. John Wycliffe (c. 1320-1384) in England, and John Huss (1369-1415) in Bohemia, (the predecessor of the modern Czech Republic), both stressed the Bible as the supreme authority above church traditions.

While the Renaissance produced many admirable advances in knowledge, architecture and the arts, it had a downside with unintended consequences. God was no longer the centre of the universe, man was. Man reasoned and acted with autonomy, independent of God. Instead of depending on God's revelation for guidance and wisdom, man thought he was able to shape his own worldview through human reason alone. By detaching man's thinking from God's revelation, the Renaissance promoted the development of humanism in which man was the centre of the universe who held his destiny in his own hands.

In his own way, Thomas Aquinas (1225-1274) played a significant role in this development. His epic theological achievements syncretized philosophy with theology. Placing great confidence in man's natural ability to reason, and being enchanted with Greek and Roman philosophers, he utilized the philosophical ideas of Aristotle in particular. The Bible ceased being the supreme rule of faith and conduct. Autonomous reason played a determinative role. Philosophical ideas competed with Scripture for acceptance.

Francis Schaeffer refers to a fresco painted in 1365 by Andrea da Firenze which illustrates what was taking place in Catholic theology under the influence of Aquinas. Thomas Aquinas is seated on a throne in the centre of the fresco. On the lower level of the picture are Aristotle, Cicero, Ptolemy, Euclid, and Pythagoras – all Greek philosophers. And on the same level are Saint Augustine and other Christian thinkers. Roman Catholic theologians were now able to create Christian theology from both past Christian thinkers and pagan philosophy (Schaeffer 1976: 52).

Like yeast that slowly works its way through the dough, humanism, with its view of autonomous mankind, began penetrating the worldview of western culture until it sprouted in full bloom during the period commonly called the Enlightenment.

The Enlightenment

The worldview of western civilization in philosophy, theology and science was radically reoriented during the Enlightenment, dated during the "long 18th century" (1685-1815). Commonly known as the Age of Reason, philosophers turned away from Scripture and church authority to reason as the ultimate source of knowledge.

What is the Enlightenment? Immanuel Kant answered the question in 1784:

> *Kant replied that enlightenment was humanity's coming of age. It was the emergence from the immaturity that caused human beings to rely on such external authorities as the Bible, the church, and the state to tell them what to think and do. No generation should be bound by the creeds and customs of bygone ages. To be so bound was an offense against human nature, whose destiny lies in progress* (Brown 2001: 377).

The floodgate of unbelief had been thrown wide open. Voltaire (1694-1778), often considered "the Father of the Enlightenment," led the unrelenting attack against the Catholic Church in France. All creeds were dismissed. Like the Deists in England, Voltaire claimed that true religion was the religion of reason and nature. Christianity was perverted by "priest craft." He rejected the traditional proofs of Christianity, denying Old Testament prophecies and rejecting all miracles recorded in Scripture (Brown 2001: 378f).

This led to the quest for the historical Jesus. Interpreting everything naturalistically and rejecting everything supernatural, they began to reinterpret the Gospel's account of the life of Christ whom they saw as a simple Galilean preacher with moral teaching. Hermann Reimarus (1694-1768) believed Christianity was built on fraud with baseless claims of miracles and the resurrection. Scholars began the fruitless task of disentangling the historical from the mythical in the Gospels.

The rationalistic approach of the Enlightenment contained the seeds of its own demise. By eliminating mankind created in the image of God, men and women were increasingly viewed as a biological machines, mechanistically governed without free will. By dismissing all authority and approaching the philosophical venture with sheer scepticism, David Hume (1711-1776) turned scepticism against itself. How can we trust reason? Confidence in our ability to reason was questioned. The rationalistic endeavour to find truth and ultimate reality became arid and barren, leading to a revolt against reason.

Romanticism

Reacting against the rationalism of the Enlightenment, there developed a movement that stressed "emotionalism, sensualism, fantasy and imagination over rational order and control. Reality is found not by rational thought but through feeling, immediate experience, spiritual illumination, brooding and listening to the inner voices" (Pierard 2001: 1040).

Jean-Jacques Rousseau (1712-1778) played down reason and saw the restraints of civilization as evils: 'Man was born free," he said, "but everywhere he is in chains!'" For Rousseau "primitive man" was "the noble savage," superior to the civilized man. He wrote, "If man is good by nature, as I believe to have shown him to be, it follows that he stays like that as long as nothing foreign to him corrupts him" (Schaefffer 2976: 154-155).

Inspired by both the rationalistic unbelief springing from the Enlightenment and the emphasis on experience in the Romantic Movement, Friedrick Schleiermacher (1768-1834) created a liberal approach to theology. Schleiermacher is known "the father of liberal Protestant theology," a theology of religious experience.

Schleiermacher recast the content and method of Christianity. He defined religion as "the feeling of absolute dependence." He denied the propositional revelation of the Bible and contended that God could not be described in any objective sense. Theology is the discipline of recording the religious experience in each generation. "...theological statements relate the Christian feeling of absolute dependence to God" (Hoffecker 2001: 1065).

Schleiermacher completely revised the theology of the Christian Church, but his most lasting legacy was his view of the Bible. In his opinion, "No external authority, whether it be Scripture, church, or historic creedal statement, takes precedence over the immediate experience of believers" (Hoffecker 2001: 1065). This contributed to a radical revision of the way Scripture had been viewed.

Embracing rationalism, Schleiermacher and his fellow liberal theologians were embarrassed by reference to miracles in the Bible. Therefore, the inspiration and authority of the Bible were rejected. He wanted to retain the historical Jesus without the miracles and thus he began the search for the historical Jesus.

Albert Schweitzer (1875-1965), a humanitarian activist in Africa, wrote *The Quest for the Historical Jesus* in 1906. However, by the second edition he demonstrated that it was impossible to keep anything of an historical Jesus while separating the supernatural from his life. If you eliminated all of the miraculous in the life of Christ, you had no historical Jesus remaining.

Schleiermacher became the forerunner of liberalism that permeated much of western Christianity and led to the controversies between the liberals and the so-called "Fundamentalists" over the authority of Scripture, the authenticity of biblical prophecy, the deity and resurrection of Christ.

Faith Science

Modern science of the seventeenth century began with men who held to a biblical worldview. Galileo Galilei (1564-1642), inventor of the telescope and father of observational astronomy, and Francis Bacon (1561-1626), formulator of the scientific method which led to the scientific revolution, and Johannes

Kepler (1571-1630), famous for his laws of planetary motion, and John Newton (1642-1726), recognized as one of the most influential scientists of all times, were all born again Christians.

Not all of the early scientists were born again, but they all embraced a Christian worldview with belief in a personal, intelligent Creator of all things. "Christianity is the mother of modern science because it insists that the God who created the universe has revealed himself in the Bible to be the kind of God he is" (Schaeffer 1976: 134). Because the Creator is rational and orderly, we may assume the universe is orderly and rational, operating by consistent laws.

> *The rise of modern science did not conflict with what the Bible teaches; indeed, at a crucial point the Scientific Revolution rested upon what the Bible teaches. Both Alfred North Whitehead (1861-1947) and J. Robert Oppenheimer (1904-1967) [neither were Christians] have stressed that modern science was born out of the Christian worldview...Whitehead said that Christianity is the mother of science because of 'the medieval insistence on the rationality of God.' ...To quote Whitehead once more, the Christian thought form of the early scientists gave them 'the faith in the possibility of science'* (Schaeffer 1976: 132-133).

The 17th century was the age of Isaac Newton (1642-1726), the virtual "saint of science." Newton articulated the law of universal gravitation, the mathematical solutions to the motion of the heavenly bodies. He quantified the density of the earth, explained the motion of the tides and formulated the concept of centripetal force by which an object could orbit the earth and a host of other breath-taking discoveries (Robinson 2004: 130f).

Untold in science books today is the fact that Isaac Newton was a firmly committed Christian who was a lifelong student of the Bible. It has been said that he was more interested in the Bible and the teachings of the Church than he was in science. His view of science was made possible by his belief in a rational, personal Creator.

These first scientists of modern science believed in the uniformity of natural causes in an *open system* in which God could supernaturally intervene with miracles. But "modern science" of the seventeenth century has been transformed into "modern modern science," in the words of Francis Schaeffer. "Modern modern science" believes in a uniformity of natural causes in a *closed system* in which neither God nor any supernatural intervention could interrupt the normal processes of natural laws (Schaeffer 1976: 130-152).

"Modern science" had developed the scientific method based on observation followed by a hypothesis and experiments to prove or disprove the hypothesis followed by an analysis and conclusion. This science is experimental science and was based on observation and experimentation.

"Modern, modern science" excludes God from the equation and includes theories that are not based on observation and testing. This "modern, modern science" is "faith science" because of its faith-based presuppositions. It is naturalistic from beginning to end. Any so-called science that is based on presuppositions that cannot be proven through observation and testing is founded on faith – not faith in God, but faith in nature apart from God. In effect, "modern, modern science" supports the religious dogma of naturalism.

A prime example is that of Charles Darwin (1809-1882) who proposed the origin of biological life through evolution. Ostensibly, his theory rests on evidence that he observed as a Naturalist on the H.M.S. Beagle voyage from 1831 to 1836. Darwin theorized that organisms change over time as they adapt to their environment through natural selection and mutation of genes. Observation of fossils allegedly show a progression of development.

While micro-evolution can be demonstrated scientifically through observation, macro-evolution cannot. No undisputed fossil evidence has been found to show one species transitioning to another species. Though "missing links" have been claimed by researchers, further study has debunked those claims.

Neither can the origins of the universe be proven scientifically. No one has ever demonstrated that something can erupt out of nothing, or that life can spring out of dead matter. Since no one today has witnessed the origins of the universe and life, both evolutionists and creationists must hold to their positions by faith. They cannot prove it through observation and experimentation.

Popular belief for two millennia held that spontaneous generation of life occurred out of decaying matter. They observed fleas suddenly appearing from inanimate matter, maggots arising from dead fish. However, through the experiments of Louis Pasteur in the 19th century, he disproved spontaneous generation. Life does not arise out of non-life.

However, without any proof, evolutionists conjecture that given enough time, billions of years, something can suddenly erupt out of nothing on its own without the all-wise and all-powerful hand of the Creator. Then with the passage of billions of years, a one-celled living organism could be generated out of a primordial soup of chemicals which could eventually evolve into human beings.

The problems with the theory of macro-evolution are massive. Nothing has been proven through observation or experimentation, nor can it be. The more that is learned of the complexity, design and order of the universe, the more difficulty scientists have in explaining the intricate design without a Designer. Natural selection cannot explain the complexity of the molecular systems. It is all based on naturalistic presuppositions that excludes God from the equation.

Natural selection and survival of the fittest have had tragic consequences. What most people do not know is that Darwin sub-titled his book, *Origin of Species: The Preservation of Favoured Races in the Struggle for Life.* Though he was speaking of animal races, the logic of evolution applied to humans. Darwinians spawned the idea of inferiority and superiority of different human races. Spurious comments were made about the Africans such as, "The African was inferior—he represented the missing link between ape and Teuton [whites]."

Evolution contributed immensely to the stigmatic judgement of Africans. In European thinking the simpler the cultures, the more primitive the lifestyles, the more inferior people were. When primates like chimpanzees evolved, they eventually became bipedal and walked upright. Africans were inferior to whites, just as chimpanzees were inferior to Africans. All of life evolved and were graded intellectually with whites on the top and more primitive creatures below.

Heinrich Himmler (1900-1945), leader of the Nazi Gestapo, stated that "the law of nature must take its course in the survival of the fittest." This led to the holocaust and the final solution of annihilating six million Jews. Darwin's evolutionary theory of the survival of the fittest undergirded slavery and racial discrimination by assigning the Negroid race to the bottom of the evolutionary scale of Homo sapiens.

This evolutionary biological theory was taken by later scholars and applied to other areas of human knowledge including religion. When scholars began applying the evolutionary theory to biblical studies the results were catastrophic.

They assumed that the biblical literature evolved naturally with normal human processes unaided by divine revelation.

They taught that Christianity, like all other religions, evolved naturally; it was not divinely revealed. This theory excluded God and the supernatural.

Based on the naturalistic evolutionary progress of culture, theologians have imagined that religion first began with the simple which was the belief in magic. After magic, the human race progressed to belief in spirits residing in trees, rocks and remote ravines. Such beliefs were found among the primitive aborigines living in the heart of Australia and in Africa. These beliefs were called animism, not religion. Finally, religion evolved with belief in many gods (polytheism), progressing to one chief god among many (henotheism), and finally belief in one Supreme Being (monotheism).

According to the proponents of naturalism, the final stage in development of the human race is science when mature, grown up people no longer depend on the "supernatural," but recognize that their lives and their future depend on themselves alone with the use of technology.

Existentialism

Liberalism had placed full confidence in reason apart from any reference to God. Beginning from themselves, rationalistic philosophers tried to find meaning and significance in life, but failed to do so. Philosopher after philosopher came up with his own way of establishing morality and purpose in life, but each proved unsuccessful. Rationalism began with great optimism, confident that rational mankind with science could make progress in the upward ascent to new heights.

Liberal theology represented by Friedrick Schleiermacher had a field day in the 19th century, but gradually lost its appeal as theologians and philosophers became pessimistic. Reason without God took them nowhere. Rationalism became arid and hopeless. This disillusionment with reason led to Romanticism and later to Existentialism.

Existentialism was a philosophical movement with diverse individuals who promoted a few themes, but no doctrines. Many were agnostic or rabid atheists, but not all. Soren Kierkegaard (1813-1855) was a professing Christian who believed in God, although he attacked institutional Christianity as irrelevant.

The themes of Existentialism included: a strong emphasis on the individual; the central role of passions (emotions) as opposed to reason and rationality; and the importance of human freedom. "The existentialists suggest that we live best and are most ourselves in terms of passion." In the area of reason, everything is absurd, they said, but through an act of the will one can become an authentic person. Reason, logic, rationality and verbal propositions were out; passion, feelings, commitment, and a leap of faith were in. Objective truth is gone. For Kierkegaard "passionate commitment" was central to his philosophy (Solomon 2000: 6-7).

> *Humanistic man tried to find himself self-sufficient...His great hope that he could begin from himself and produce a uniformity of knowledge led him, however, to the sad place where his mind told him that he was only a machine, a bundle of molecules [through modern, modern science]. Then he tried desperately to find meaning in the area of non-reason...* (Schaeffer 1976: 169).

We find in history that philosophies are passing fads. Theology which is not grounded in Scripture, but influenced profoundly by the philosophers of the day, wax and wane.

The optimism of confidence in science and reason was the dominant motif of liberalism, but World War One and World War Two shattered that confidence. Replacing liberalism was a pessimistic view of humanity.

Karl Barth (1886-1968): Barth became the agent to revolutionize theology with his *Commentary on Romans* and his thirteen volume *Church Dogmatics.* In many ways Barthian theology was refreshingly conservative. He repudiated liberalism with its attachment to the Enlightenment. Unlike Schleiermacher who rejected the biblical doctrine of total depravity, Karl Barth embraced it. He also stressed grace through Jesus Christ.

But Barth built his theology on a faulty foundation, a Bible full of errors and without propositional truth. He held to the higher critical views of the Bible which undermined its integrity.

Furthermore, he held a distinctively existential view of revelation. God has *not* revealed himself through propositions in Scripture. The Bible is *not* the Word of God, he said, but it <u>becomes</u> the Word of God as God speaks to us through the Bible. Through the Bible God speaks to us experientially and existentially. God's revelation is personal, not verbal. God's Word cannot be studied and exegeted from the Scripture. It can only be experienced.

Like all existentialists, Barth separates reason from experience. Truth is not found in reason but in experience. For Soren Kierkegaard we cannot know truth rationally, so we take a leap in the dark with faith separated from reason.

In the biblical worldview, reason, aided by the Holy Spirit, is an agent in taking steps of faith. Certainty, not a leap in the dark, is based on propositions of truth carefully investigated in Scripture.

Rudolf Bultmann (1884-1976): Bultmann became one of the most influential theologians in the twentieth century. He was heavily indebted to the existential philosopher, Martin Heidegger.

Through Heidegger's influence, many scholars, including Bultmann, have dropped the use of Grammatical-historical hermeneutics which interpreted the meaning of Scripture through a study of vocabulary and grammar within the literary and historical context (De Vries 2001: 545).

According to Heidegger, one is truest to your nature when making decisions. An authentic person is a maker of decisions. Because the essence of a person is making decisions, we should be concerned with the future, not the past, for the future holds options for making decisions, whereas, the past does not.

Bultmann believed that dead traditions and legalistic ethical systems cause a person to avoid making decision and in this way a person becomes inauthentic. Salvation for Bultmann is a radical openness to the future made possible by a saviour, even Jesus Christ, in order to become authentic. But his rejection of virtually all biblical doctrines raises the question of his Christian claims.

> *For Bultmann NT ideas such as the virgin birth, the deity of Jesus, the resurrection of Jesus, the future resurrection of the body, blood atonement for sins, everlasting life, an ethical ideal of human nature, and a salvation history only serve to mislead people about what*

> *salvation really is. These are primitive, 'mythological' ideas that need to be reinterpreted in existentialist terms* (Roberts 2001: 194).

Bultmann became known for his emphasis on demythologizing the Scriptures. His thesis was that "the contemporary humanity, which depends upon a scientific worldview, cannot accept the mythological worldview of the Bible" (Borchert 2001: 333). He therefore believed it was necessary to reinterpret the mythical concepts for twentieth century people. Virtually every major New Testament doctrine he considered mythical and in need of reinterpreting (demythologizing).

While English has only one word for "history," the German languish has two. Using these two German concepts, Bultmann distinguished between *Historie* (meaning the facts of history), and *Geschichte* (signifying the meaning of an event in history). For Bultmann the fact of the bodily resurrection of Christ was "utterly inconceivable." "Easter faith thus becomes faith in the preached word" (Borchert 2001: 334).

Paul Tillich (1886-1995): Tillich ranks with Bultmann and Barth as one of the most influential theologians of the twentieth century. Numerous African theologians cite quotations from these men.

Though influential, comprehending what Tillich said is very difficult. Spiceland says that his philosophy of religious language "is not only difficult to understand – it may indeed be impossible to understand." Spiceland continues:

> *This perhaps derives from the fact that he is attempting to use traditional Christian vocabulary to express essentially alien philosophical concepts, whereas in reality the two are fundamentally incompatible* (Spiceland 2001: 1200).

In fact, this problem is found with many contemporary theologians. They use terminology from historic orthodoxy, like "God," "deity of Christ," or "salvation," but ascribe meaning to those words that is totally different. Their discourse may sound Christian, even orthodox, but in reality they are unorthodox.

A student asked Tillich near the end of his life, "Sir, do you pray?" Tillich replied, "No, but I meditate." Though Tillich used the word, "God," he did not believe in a God as traditionally understood.

Following Tillich's death, "the God-is-dead" theology developed, taking Tillich's theology to its natural conclusion. If there is no God behind the word, "God," why use the term? For all practical purposes, "God is dead" (Schaeffer 1976: 49).

Tillich, like Bultmann, believed that the ultimate meaning of reality can only be understood through the use of myths and symbols which need to be reinterpreted. Tillich, like all liberal theologians, accept the conclusions of higher criticism and reject the factual authority of Scripture.

Higher Criticism

Reference has been made to Higher Criticism so a further word is needed to clarify. Biblical Criticism is divided into Lower Criticism and Higher Criticism. Lower Criticism refers to textual criticism, the study of the manuscript tradition (Hebrew and Greek texts) of the Scriptures. This is a straightforward discipline without distortion taking place as a result of one's presuppositions.

Higher Criticism is the study of the origins of biblical writings including the authorship, date, historical setting and composition of the biblical text. In contrast to Lower Criticism, the results of Higher Criticism depend largely on the presuppositions of the scholars.

If one approaches the biblical text with confidence in the testimony of Christ and his apostles concerning the trustworthiness of the text, one reaches a conclusion consonant with the historic Christian Church. This self-attestation of the Scripture is further verified by archaeological discoveries corroborating the factual statements of the Bible, and by the scientific dating of biblical manuscripts.

If on the other hand one approaches the biblical text as an uninspired, flawed human book which makes unsubstantiated claims and contains historical inaccuracies, one reaches a different conclusion.

For the past 200 years scholars have investigated the authorship and dates of the biblical books with naturalistic, anti-supernatural presuppositions. Sceptical scholars have grounded their study of Higher Criticism in the "historical-critical method" which asserts that "reality is uniform and universal and that one's present experience supplies an objective criterion for determining what could or could not have happened in the past" (Schultz 2001: 555). In other words, since our world today is naturalistically explained, devoid of miracles and the supernatural, we should consign all so-called supernatural accounts to the realm of myth. All reports of prophecies and miraculous events in the Bible must be dismissed as mystical, not historical.

Because we know today that people do not walk on water, raise the dead, or multiply a few loaves and fish to feed 5,000 men, scholars assume that Jesus could not. Therefore, the recorded miracles became evidence that the Gospel writings were not written by eye witnesses, but by the church decades later after Jesus' death which embellished the myths handed down to them.

Prophetic books could no longer be trusted as a testimony of God's ability to foretell the future, but were dismissed as historical documents written after the events, but told as if they were future prophecies. Since prophecy is not possible (all supernatural is rejected), Old Testament prophecies were dated late, after the historical event.

Daniel could not have been written before the rise of Persia, Greece and Rome (Da 2, 7, 8). Jeremiah could not have foretold the 70 year captivity (Jer 25:11-12). Isaiah could not have foretold the rise of Cyrus by name (Isa 44:28, 45:1). All of these "so-called" prophecies were written after the events. Through the study of literary style, vocabulary and content, Isaiah ceased to be the sole author of his prophecy. Biblical scholars competed to discover numerous "Isaiah's." At first it was believed that the Pentateuch could not have been written by Moses because he was illiterate. Later they concluded that the Pentateuch was a compilation of contradictory writings by numerous redactors.

These naturalistic presuppositions are disastrous for a healthy Church. Instead of a Bible inspired by God that can be trusted with a unified theology, we have a Bible without any authority with multiple theologies arising from numerous authors, redactors and editors reflecting their own socio-economic and religious contexts. It is common to hear of numerous theologies such as a Yahwist, a Deuteronomist, Second Isaiah or a Third Isaiah, "Q" in the Gospels, or the Deutero-Pauline letters. We no longer can speak of biblical theology but of contextual theologies arising from different contexts.

Instead of the Gospels being viewed as complimentary presentations for differing audiences, based on eye witness accounts, the Gospels are viewed as conflicting accounts from the early Christian Church which embellished the traditions handed down to them. Instead of viewing historical books of the Old Testament as reliable, accurate reporting of historic events, they are interpreted as inaccurate and fanciful accounts by later editors and redactors who lived hundreds of years after the events.

As more and more biblical scholars adopted these views, seminaries disseminated this unbelief by teaching future pastors and church leaders. And as these pastors began preaching this nonsense in the pulpits, controversies arose, churches split, and gradually Presbyterians, Congregationalists, Methodists, Anglicans and numerous others compromised their theology.

What they preached was a social gospel devoid of any spiritual teaching from the Bible. Emphasis lay in the realm of social, economic, and political change. Churches have become social networks for political and social activists.

Various approaches to Higher Criticism have been developed in the twentieth century including Form Criticism, Historical Criticism, Redaction Criticism and the New Hermeneutics. In recent years social sciences, linguistic and literary studies have been used to interpret the text. Because of the philosophical and ideological presuppositions of these scholars, their conclusions have been destructive of biblical authority.

Despite whatever benefits may potentially accrue from these higher critical methods, Richard Schultz concludes: "...higher criticism has had a profound and largely negative affect on theology over the past century. A diversity of biblical theologies have replaced a unified biblical theology" (Schultz 2001: 556).

Post Modernism

Saint Augustine declared: "You have created us for yourself, O Lord, and our heart is restless until it rests in You" (Augustine).

Biblical Wisdom: Facts of reality are hard facts. According to the Scripture, God created men and women in his own image and for himself. In our sinful state, separated from God, we are restless, seeking, inquiring, and searching for something to fill the emptiness of the soul. Until we find our rest in God through faith in Jesus Christ, we will continue to be restless, searching and unfulfilled. These biblical truths are hard facts and cannot be changed.

Solomon with limitless opportunity searched for something to satisfy his longing heart. Without God in the equation, Solomon saw only vanity. "*Meaningless! Meaningless! ...Utterly meaningless! Everything is meaningless*" (Ecc 1:2 *NIV*). The Message renders this Scripture: "*Smoke, nothing but smoke...There's nothing to anything – its only smoke.*"

Solomon sought fulfilment and meaning in pleasure and laughter, undertaking great projects of planting vineyards, gardens and parks, increasing his herds and flocks, amassing silver and gold, acquiring a harem to delight his heart, becoming wise and pursuing folly. In everything he tried, he experienced emptiness. "*All is meaningless, a chasing after the wind*" (Ecc 2:17).

Concluding his search, at the end of his life, he noted: "*Now all has been heard; here is the conclusion of the matter: Fear God and keep his commandments, for this is the whole duty of man*" (Ecc 12:13).

Human Wisdom: Tracing the philosophies and theologies that are disconnected from God and his Word, we find the same emptiness – smoke, nothing but smoke. Each of the philosophers and liberal theologians make their splash in history, gather fame and followers, only to find that others consider their efforts a failure. This has gone on and on for centuries.

Modernism, arising out of the Enlightenment, emphasized the autonomy of men and women who were free to think as they chose. They repudiated tradition and authority. These rationalists had great confidence in the power of reason which they thought could reason objectively. Disconnecting themselves from God, they were optimistic in their ability to progress. But after making numerous attempts to find meaning and make sense of the world, they sank into pessimism. Man, beginning from himself, apart from God and through reason alone, came up empty.

When Faith Science conceived of human beings as mere biological machines, not made in the image of God, the hopes of a brighter future became muddled. The essence of humanity was reduced to molecules randomly assembled by chance. Instinctively, we know that we are something more than mechanical machines without freedom.

Reacting to modernism the Romanticists disparaged reason and stressed experience and passion devoid of reason, but that failed to yield a satisfying answer. Existentialists turned away from objective truth to discover truth through the struggles of personal existence. Christian existentialists like Karl Barth do not read Scripture to learn objective, propositional revelation but to *experience* a subjective revelation as God speaks to them through the Word. Like all human philosophies, existentialism is fading.

Deconstruction of Truth. According to contemporary philosophers and liberal theologians, truth no longer exists as an objective reality. It is socially constructed and changes with society. Objective truth cannot be known. The Bible contains no truth written in words and propositions. Liberation comes with the deconstruction of "truth" and the reinterpretation of Christianity.

The latest venture into smoke and emptiness is Postmodernism. Moving from modernity and existentialism, they declared bravely that all truth is relative. Friedrich Nietzsche (1844-1900) claimed that all claims of philosophy to offer truth are baseless. We cannot speak of "truth" but only "perspectives" of reality.

This has contributed to the latest craze of Deconstructionism. Initiated in the 1960s by Jacques Derrida, he attempted to deconstruct the text to find ambiguities, inconsistencies and contradictions within the text in order to discover the ideological biases behind the text. The assumption is that history is full of all kinds of domination - racial, gender, economic, political or cultural. Instead of interpreting the text through the study of grammar, context and history in order to discover the original meaning of the author (the grammatical-historical method), the reader tries to learn the cultural and social motives behind the text by deconstructing it and finding its ideological bias.

Various African theologians have used this method for interpreting Scripture. Do they not understand that what they have learned and embraced is western philosophy that has its roots in the western Enlightenment? Therefore, what they present as *African Theology* has been shaped by western presuppositions and preunderstandings? Western naturalistic philosophy underlies much of African Theology today.

They deny any single correct meaning or interpretation of the biblical text. Many meanings are possible, whatever the reader chooses, they say. This becomes a very subjective way of interpreting the Bible as the reader tries to find the hidden meaning by uncovering the motive behind what was written. It has no connection with any objective meaning of the text. Thus the Bible can mean whatever the interpreter thinks it should teach.

> *The deconstructionist does not study the Bible in order to find out the meaning intended by the writer but to attempt to discern the cultural and social motives behind what was written. The deconstructionist is only limited in his interpretation of a passage by his own imagination. To the deconstructionist there is no right or wrong interpretation, and the meaning of the text becomes whatever the reader wants it to be* (Deconstruction 2017: Internet).

This whole approach to language is self-contradictory. Human beings cannot live in a world where the hearer chooses his own interpretation of what is spoken to him. Communication requires defined meanings of words and sentences. Those who promote Deconstructionism are self-contradictory for they insist that people should understand what they intend to say. In the same way, we should understand the text in the way that the authors intended. The future of Deconstruction will be short lived and all those theologies based on this literary theory of interpretation will become passé in the near future.

The great thinkers of this world who fail to acknowledge God and his Word, go round and round, chasing after smoke – nothingness - that finally vanishes. Postmodernism is just the latest experiment in interpreting life without God.

Today we have entered the Post Modern era characterized by certain tenets (Zacharias 2007).

1. **The death of a big-overarching story with coherent meaning (the meta-narrative).** The big story is dead. All that remains are little stories. Without the Scriptures breathed out by the Holy Spirit, we have no biblical theology, only little, disconnected, and contradictory theologies which have no lasting meaning.
2. **The demise of the text.** The reader must decide what the text means for him or her since the author is dead and the original meaning is lost. We no longer use the grammatical-historical hermeneutics to determine the intent of the author. We demythologize and reinterpret and deconstruct the text to find the meaning that suits us in our generation.
3. **The dominion of emotion.** Since reason and thinking are irrelevant, we resort to feelings and emotions. The Word of God breaks through the errant text so that the reader has an existential encounter without any language to describe it. What makes us feel good, what experience gives us meaning, we embrace for a fleeting moment of satisfaction.
4. **The decline of authority.** Since the biblical text has been robbed of authority, the decision of what is right and wrong is individually determined. The multiplication of ideas of what is right and wrong leads either to anarchy or totalitarianism. Ironically, with the loss of authority in the text of Scripture, totalitarianism is on the rise. The politically correct elite today determine what should be believed. All other beliefs are dismissed. Universities no longer tolerate diversity of opinion. They squelch and destroy all conservative and biblical ideas. Tenure is denied those who don't yield to the prevailing postmodern dogmas. With the decline of an authoritative biblical text which has meaning determined by the author, the authoritarian elite determine what is to be accepted and believed.

5. **The loss of logic to govern discourse.** Basic to all logic is the law of contradiction. Logic demands an either/or system of thinking. Either this is true or it is false. Intelligible discourse cannot be carried on when words have no distinct meaning. In Post Modernism the logic of either/or has been replaced by both/and. Truth cannot be discussed as propositions because post modernists demand multiple options between truth and error. They are suspicious of rational and logical forms. They cannot tolerate any discussion of truth in plain propositional terms.

CONCLUSION

The foregoing discussion is most relevant when evaluating African Theologies being produced today.

Much of what is called African Theology is premised on western philosophical and theological presuppositions. No one is able to do theology in a vacuum. Because of the pervasive teaching of Higher Criticism, Existentialism and Post Modernism in western institutions where African scholars have studied, much of African Theology is built unconsciously on western thought and assumptions.

For western elites the Bible has no authority that is binding. This viewpoint has been absorbed by African scholars who have studied under western liberal professors and have read western liberal books. The Bible is only a reference point that can be accepted or rejected or reinterpreted according to the preference of the scholar. Instead of bowing to the authority of Scripture, many African theologians deconstruct the Christian faith and subvert all forms of historic orthodoxy. They seek to reinvent and reinterpret Christianity to suit their fancy.

Though many give lip service to the Bible as a source for doing African Theology, they redefine traditional theological terms according to their personal preference. In effect, these individual African theologians have become their own final authority. Nothing outside of their preference has authority over them.

If African Theology continues on the liberal path chosen by many, we shall see the demise of biblical Christianity in Africa wherever their theologies are embraced. For proof of this statement you only need to examine the western churches that have lost confidence in the authority of Scripture. Believing that the teaching of Scripture is true, we predict that the end result of their theologizing will be "Smoke, nothing but smoke...There's nothing to anything – its only smoke." These African theologies will prove to be unsatisfying, boring and unrelated to the deepest longings of men and women made in God's image.

The following chapter points us to the right direction – away from the perennial problems in Africa to the biblical truths and solutions for humanity's predicament.

5

REFLECTIONS ON TWO FUNDAMENTAL QUESTIONS

The Gospel seed planted in Africa in the late 19th and early 20th centuries has produced a harvest beyond the wildest dreams of those pioneering missionaries. In the same way, what began as a trickle of contributions for African theology in the 1950s and 1960s has mushroomed into a bewildering array of articles and books on the subject.

And just as confusing as the multiplication of Christian denominations in Africa has been, so is the confusion being wrought through the puzzling array of African theologies promulgated year after year.

We would do well to pause for a moment, step back and take a deep breath, to ponder what is becoming of African Christianity? Exactly what is being accomplished by further writings on African theology?

Out of the mouth of Solomon came these words: "*For as he thinks within himself, so he is*" (Pr 23:7 *NASB*). The thoughts of a person determine his character – what he or she says and does. Wrong thinking, based on human opinion, leads to disaster; but right thinking, based on divine revelation, leads to eternal blessings.

The Christian Church grew strong in Europe and America through the faithful preaching of the Word of God. The Bible became their fountain of wisdom. When men and women were transformed by the Truth of God's Word, energized by the Spirit of God, Christians became honest, faithful, diligent, trustworthy, morally upright, hardworking, thrifty, studious, compassionate, and loving. This conduct in turn resulted in a transformed society.

The same phenomenon began in Africa. When young people were taught the Word of God in schools where they learned to read and write, and when they were transformed by the Spirit of God through conversion, they became honest, faithful, diligent and trustworthy. They stood out from their peers and were invited to assume responsible positions of leadership in civil society.

Over time there occurred what is frequently called, "Redemption and Lift." People who are redeemed by the blood of Christ, and nourished in the Word of God, are gradually lifted over generations from poverty to a higher station in life. They don't waste their money on beer and prostitutes; they remain faithful to their spouses and care for their children; they pour their lives into the rearing of their children and provide an education for them. They work hard and spend their money wisely. Over time the positive benefits become evident. And all this begins with right thinking – understanding and embracing the truth of God's Word.

The influential Christian Church in the West began to decline when wrong thinking entered seminaries and universities where pastors and church leaders were trained. Doubts in the integrity of the Scriptures led to unbelief. Like yeast, this unbelief began working its way through the churches, ever so slowly – beginning with the professors, then filtering down to the pastors, and finally into the pews of the lay people. The result in the West is obvious: declining church attendance and membership, and declining influence in society.

When the Bible is dismissed as myth and legend, why continue believing in Christianity? Violence, immorality, and drugs are pandemic in America.

Cathedrals are empty in Europe and churches are turned into museums and mosques. Opinion leaders in the West reject anything and everything taught by Christianity. The very countries which sent missionaries to Africa with the Gospel of Jesus Christ have become mission fields full of sceptics, agnostics, atheists and mostly, people who are indifferent to anything related to the Christian faith. Erroneous thinking of Scriptures has hollowed out Christianity, leading to its decline.

Therefore, we need to pause in this chapter to consider two major issues that must inform every effort to produce African theology in order to ensure a fruitful future for African Christianity: "Who is Jesus?" and "Why was Jesus sent?"

WHO IS JESUS?

The most basic question we must settle before we contemplate doing African Theology is this: "Who is this man called Jesus Christ?"

After years of teaching the Twelve, Jesus asked them, "*Who do people say that I am*?" Their answer reflected the wide range of opinions, stretching from Jeremiah to Elijah or the Prophet. Some even thought that Jesus was John the Baptist raised from the dead!

"*But what about you?" Jesus asked. "Who do you say I am?" Peter exclaimed with believing insight: "You are the Christ [the Messiah], the Son of the living God.*"

"*Jesus replied, 'Blessed are you, Simon son of Jonah, for this was not revealed to you by man, but by my Father in heaven*" (Mt 16:13-18).

There were many opinions of who Jesus was but only one correct answer. Jesus is the Messiah, the Son of God. All other opinions were in error, wide of the mark. The correct response was not concocted by clever intellectuals who devised cunning ways of contextualizing. The identity of Jesus was *revealed* by God and accepted by faith.

Reading through the tomes of African theology we discover various proposals. J. W. Zvomunondita Kurewa, a Methodist minister from Zimbabwe, believes that without a knowledge of African culture and the "composite religious experiences as African people," Africans cannot answer Jesus' question, "Who do you say that I am?" It is not sufficient to know the answer that Peter gave to Jesus by revelation from God, "You are the Messiah." The question demands "a Christological response with African authenticity." Kurewa says, "We cannot imitate Peter" (Kurewa 1980: 182).

Many suggest that Jesus is the African Ancestor or the African King; that Jesus is "the Activist" who came to change the world, or the "Free Spirit" who calls us to enjoy the world. Gabriel Setiloane claims that Jesus is "the most unique unprecedented and so far unrepeated or surpassed human manifestation of Divinity" (Masoga 2017: Internet). What could Setiloane have actually meant by this statement?

What is so tragic is the absence of any serious search of the Scriptures. Who is Jesus? There is only one correct answer and that is found in the Bible. Jesus is the Christ foretold in the Old Testament, the one-and-only Son of the living God. African traditions cannot reveal who Jesus is. Only Jesus Christ himself and his apostles have authority to declare who Jesus is.

Claims of Jesus

Let us first consider the astonishing claims of Christ.

Jesus said, "...*that all may honour the Son just as they honour the Father. He who does not honour the Son does not honour the Father, who sent him*" (Jn 5:23). This is a blasphemous statement, if it were not true, for God jealously guards his worship (Ex 20:3-6). No one should ever dare to rival God.

Jesus declared, "*I am the living bread that came down from heaven. If anyone eats of this bread, he will live forever. The bread is my flesh, which I will give for the life of the world*" (Jn 6:51). Such a conceited statement must surely be challenged. Can this really be true? Those who heard him objected, saying, "*This is a hard teaching. Who can accept it?*" When he doubled down and reaffirmed his teaching, "*many of his disciples turned back and no longer followed him.*"

Jesus acknowledged privately to the Samaritan woman that he was the Christ, the Messiah foretold in the Old Testament (Jn 4:25-26). Jesus also confessed publicly before the Sanhedrin when the Jewish high priest asked: "*'Are you the Christ, the Son of the Blessed One?' 'I am,' said Jesus. 'And you will see the Son of Man sitting at the right hand of the Mighty One and coming on the clouds of heaven'*" (Mk 14:61-62).

Appalled at this, the high priest tore his clothes and said, "*Why do we need any more witnesses? You have heard the blasphemy.*"

Jesus claimed to be the "Son of Man" who would "come in the glory of his Father with angels" (Mt 17:27; Jn 9:35-37). He frequently referred to himself as the "Son of Man" (Mt 16:13, 18:11, 24:27). Within the Hebrew context this title had profound eschatological meaning, rooted in Daniel's prophecy where we read, "*one like a son of man, coming with the clouds of heaven.*" He was given by the Ancient of Days "*authority, glory and sovereign power; all peoples, nations and men of every language worshiped him. His dominion is an everlasting dominion that will not pass away, and his kingdom is one that will never be destroyed*" (Da 7:13-14).

On another occasion the Jews asked Jesus, "Who are you?" Jesus replied, "*Just what I have been claiming all along*" (Jn 8:25). Later on in this discourse with the Jews, Jesus asserted, "*Before Abraham was born, I am*" (Jn 8:58).

This audacious claim is much more than declaring his pre-existence prior to the time of Abraham. "I AM" was the personal Name of the Living God revealed to Moses at the burning bush (Ex 3:1-15). The four Hebrew consonants, known as the Tetragrammaton, are transliterated in our letters as *JHWH or YHWH,* articulated as Jehovah or Yahweh. Jesus here declared in effect, "I am Yahweh!" The Jews fully recognized this and picked up stones to stone him to death for his blasphemy, but Jesus slipped away from them in the crowd.

The claims of Jesus go on and on in the most astonishing manner. Jesus said, "*I am the gate for the sheep. All who ever came before me were thieves and robbers, but the sheep did not listen to them. I am the gate; whoever enters through me will be saved...I have come that they might have life, and have it to the full*" (Jn 10:7-10). The conceit of this statement is appalling if it were not true!

On another occasion Jesus asserted, "*I and my Father are one*" (Jn 10:30). The Jews once again picked up stones to stone him to death, but he asked them why would they stone him? They responded: "*We are stoning you...for blasphemy, because you, a mere man, claim to be God*" (Jn 10:33).

Answering Martha, he replied, "*I am the resurrection and the life. He who believes in me will live, even though he dies; and whoever lives and believes in me will never die*" (Jn 11:25).

Jesus made one audacious claim after another. He declared, "*I am the way and the truth and the life. No one comes to the Father except through me*" (Jn 14:6). This is beyond belief that any human being should be so bold and impudent to claim that no one can approach God the Father except through him. Who is this Jesus?

Philip asked Jesus to show them the Father and they would all be satisfied. Jesus replied, "*Don't you know me, Philip, even after I have been among you such a long time? Anyone who has seen me has seen the Father. How can you say, 'Show us the Father?* (Jn 14:8-9).

As intelligent human beings we must ask ourselves, "Who is this man, Jesus, who makes all these blasphemous and impudent claims?"

We have only three possible answers: either Jesus was a lunatic (a man out of his mind, a crazy man), or he was a fraudster (a charlatan and imposter who knowingly deceived his followers), or he is exactly whom he says he is! There are no other alternatives.

Why should anyone take seriously anything Jesus says if he is a lunatic or a fraudster? There is no point making him some kind of model whom we admire if he is a mad man! We might glean some clever insights from his teaching even if he were a fraud, but we surely would not make him a hero. We would never develop a religion around such a person. But what if Jesus told the truth?

Evidence Supporting Jesus' Claims

So what is the evidence that Jesus is who he claims to be, the Messiah, the one-and-only Son of the Living God?

Miracles of Jesus: The many miracles Jesus performed were intended to be signs, pointing to him as the Messiah foretold in the Hebrew Scriptures. Jesus touched an unclean man with leprosy and cleansed him. He healed the centurion's daughter from a distance. He raised a dead girl and called Lazarus back to life. He healed a woman of a bleeding infirmity which doctors could not cure over a period of twelve years. When Jesus quieted a "furious storm" that threatened the disciples in their boat, the disciples were amazed and asked, "*What kind of man is this? Even the winds and the waves obey him*" (Mt 8:27).

A man born blind received sight through the hands of Jesus. He healed the mute, and the enabled a man paralyzed for 38 years to walk again. Jesus walked on the roiling water of the turbulent Sea of Galilee. He cast out demons from a man whom villagers found unable to control. From a mere five loaves of bread and two small fish Jesus fed 5,000 men besides women and children, and afterwards gathered twelve baskets of food remaining.

The apostle John, who witnessed all the miracles Jesus performed, concluded his Gospel by saying: "*Jesus did many other miraculous signs in the presence of his disciples, which are not recorded in this book. But these are written that you may believe that Jesus is the Christ, the Son of God, and that by believing you may have life in his name*" (Jn 20:30-31).

In reading the Gospels we find a lot of unbelief. The Jewish leaders and many of the people simply could not believe that Jesus was indeed the Messiah whom he claimed to be. Jesus explained their unbelief by saying:

The miracles I do in my Father's name speak for me, but you do not believe because you are not my sheep. My sheep listen to my voice; I know them, and they follow me. I give them eternal life, and they shall never perish; no one can snatch them out of my hand. My Father, who has given them to me, is greater than all; no one can snatch them out of my Father's hand" (Jn 10:25-29).

After all the miracles which Jesus had performed, the Pharisees came to Jesus and said, "*Teacher, we want to see a miraculous sign from you.*"

Blasting their unbelief, Jesus retorted, "*A wicked and adulterous generation asks for a miraculous sign! But none will be given it except the sign of the prophet Jonah. For as Jonah was three days and three nights in the belly of a huge fish, so the Son of Man will be three days and three nights in the heart of the earth."* (Mt 12:38-40).

The most specular sign which confirms the truthfulness of Jesus' testimony about himself is his bodily resurrection from the dead.

The following section on
the death and resurrection of Jesus Christ
is the most important part of this entire book!
Carefully read and reflect!
Your belief or disbelief in Jesus' bodily resurrection
will determine your attitude towards Christ and the Bible.

Death of Jesus: The resurrection is the supreme evidence that Jesus Christ is God come in the flesh as he claimed. However, a major argument against the bodily resurrection is that Jesus never died. Instead, sceptics claim that Jesus simply swooned, losing consciousness, and eventually reviving in the cool of the tomb. We have no evidence for such speculation. If this were so, where could he have gone? How could such a public figure like Jesus disappear into thin air?

On the contrary, medical science has confirmed his death. Dr. Alexander Metherell is a medical doctor (M.D.), board-certified in diagnosis by the American Board of Radiology, who also earned a Ph.D. in engineering (PDF Internet).

Consider the following:

When Jesus prayed in the Garden of Gethsemane, Luke, a physician, reported that Jesus, "*being in anguish, he prayed more earnestly, and his sweat was like drops of blood falling to the ground*" (Lk 22:44). Today this is a known medical condition called "hematidrosis" associated with extreme psychological stress. Anxiety breaks down the capillaries in the sweat glands, resulting in sweating with small amounts of blood. This causes the skin to become very fragile and sensitive, especially with the flogging that followed Jesus' arrest.

When Jesus was later flogged by the Roman soldiers (Jn 19:1), the torture was extreme. The Roman soldier used a leather, braided whip with metal balls and sharp bones woven into the braided leather. These balls caused deep bruises and the sharp bones cut the skin. The back became so deeply lacerated that the spine was exposed. Eusebius, a third century historian, described Roman flogging of his day. "The sufferer's veins were laid bare, and the very muscles, sinews, and bowels of the victim were open to exposure" (PDF Internet).

This caused excruciating pain which led to hypovolemic shock, meaning, a loss of large amounts of blood. This led to a craving for fluids and fainting or collapsing. Evidence of this hypovolemic shock is that Jesus collapsed on the Via Dolorosa under the burden of the cross which he was forced to carry.

The Roman soldiers stretched out Jesus' arms on the cross bar of the cross and drove metal nails, five to seven inches long, into the wrist of the arm (considered part of the palm in the language of the day). This fulfilled Old Testament prophecy, "*They pierced his hands and feet*" (Zec 12:10).

By driving the nail into the wrist, this provided a solid position to hold the body to the cross. But the pain was excruciating. By driving the nail into the wrist it crushed the largest nerve, causing extraordinary pain that was unbearable. In fact, the pain was literally beyond words to describe, so the Romans invented a new word to describe it. "Excruciating" means literally, "out of the cross." Jesus suffered excruciating pain when the nails were driven through the median nerve. Nails were also driven through the feet to hold the body on the cross. This fulfilled the Old Testament prophecy (Ps 22:16; Zec 12:10; c.f. Jn 19:31-37).

When the cross was erected and dropped into the hole in the ground, his lacerated back from the flogging triggered enormous pain. Worse still, the arms were wrenched six inches, dislocating both shoulders, causing horrendous pain. This fulfilled Old Testament prophecy, "*all my bones are out of joint*" (Ps 22:14).

Death on the cross was caused by asphyxiation (lack of oxygen). Because the outspread arms stretched the diaphragm, the lungs were pressed inward, forcing all air out of the lungs in the inhaled position. In order to breathe, the crucified person had to push up with his legs. Exhaustion would eventually set in and the person died for lack of oxygen when he could no longer stretch his legs.

Because the following day was the Sabbath, the Jews did not want bodies hanging on the cross on their holy day, so they asked Pilate to break their legs (Jn 19:31). This would lead to immediate asphyxiation since the victims could no longer push up with their legs which had enabled them to breathe.

But when the soldiers came to Jesus, they noticed that he was already dead and so they did not break his legs, fulfilling Old Testament prophecy, "*Not one bone was broken*" (Ps 34:20).

One of the soldiers, desiring to make sure that Jesus was dead, "*pierced Jesus' side with a spear, bringing a sudden flow of blood and water*" (Jn 19:31-37). According to Dr. Metherell, this is clear evidence that Jesus had died while still on the cross.

The hypovolemic shock causes a sustained rapid heart rate which leads to heart failure, which in turn leads to a collection of fluid in the membrane around the heart. This is called "pericardial effusion." Fluid also collects around the lungs, called "pleural effusion." When the spear was thrust into the side of Jesus, possibly the right side, it penetrated the lung and pierced the heart. Removing the spear triggered an outpouring of blood and the gushing flow of fluid from the pericardial effusion and pleural effusion.

Dr. Metherell concluded, "There is absolutely no doubt that Jesus was dead."

Dr. William D. Edwards concurs. In 1986 he published an article in the Journal of the American Medical Association which concluded: "Clearly, the weight of the historical and medical evidence indicates that Jesus was dead before the wound in his side was inflicted...Accordingly, interpretations based on the assumption that Jesus did not die on the cross appear to be at odds with modern medical knowledge" (PDF Internet).

Instead of unsupported speculation and theories, we need to accept the testimony of Scripture, confirmed by medical science, that Jesus Christ did indeed die on the cross. He bore such excruciating suffering in his body because of his love for us. Moreover, he experienced the throbbing agony of being separated from his eternal Father because he had become a sacrifice for sins, bearing our sins in his own body. This is truly amazing grace.

Resurrection of Jesus: When Jesus voluntarily "*gave up his spirit*" and died on the cross between two convicted thieves, Joseph of Arimathea received permission from Pilate to bury Jesus' body in his own newly hewed tomb in which no one else had been buried.

The Jewish leaders feared that Jesus' disciples would steal the body at night and claim that Jesus had been raised from the dead, so they received permission to seal the tomb. "*Take a guard*," Pilate told them, and "*Go make the tomb as secure as you know how.*" They put a seal on the stone and posted a guard (Mt 27:57-66).

An examination of the evidence for this miraculous sign should convince everyone, but it never has. From the beginning there were doubters. The Jewish leaders, who heard first-hand reports from eye witnesses about his resurrection, bribed the soldiers to lie and spread falsehood throughout Jerusalem.

Note the compelling evidence for the resurrection of Christ:

(1) The tomb was empty. Peter and John ran to the tomb to check out the report of the women who first discovered the empty tomb. What they found was astonishing. Not only was the tomb empty, but they found the "*strips of linen lying there, as well as the burial cloth that had been around Jesus' head. The cloth was folded up by itself, separate from the linen*" (Jn 20:6-9). The body was not snatched hastily in a frantic effort to steal the body, for the cloth that had been around Jesus' head was "folded up" and lying separately.

(2) Evidence for the empty tomb is abundant. The disciples returned to Jerusalem and preached a risen Saviour (Ac 2:24; 4:2). This preaching would have been soundly denounced and totally rejected if the tomb were not empty. The Sanhedrin was greatly disturbed by the preaching of Jesus' resurrection and arrested the apostles on two occasions. Gamaliel, a prominent Pharisee, stood up and urged them not to put the disciples to death, saying, "*Leave these men alone! Let them go! For if their purpose or activity is of human origin, it will fail. But if it is from God, you will not be able to stop these men; you will only find yourselves fighting against God*" (Ac 5:38-39). How could Gamaliel have suggested to the unbelieving Sanhedrin Council that the apostles' preaching might be from God if Jesus' body was still in the tomb? They knew the truth!

Not only do the Gospels testify to an empty tomb, Jewish and Roman sources do as well. Josephus and other Jewish writings admit to an empty tomb. "Dr. Paul Maier calls this 'positive evidence from a hostile source, which is the strongest kind of historical evidence. In essence, this means that if a source admits a fact decidedly not in its favour, then that fact is genuine'" McDowell 2017: Internet).

The fact is that no shred of historical evidence has been found to repudiate the report of an empty tomb.

(3) The seal on the tomb was broken. The Roman seal, which was placed on the tomb stone, represented the full authority of the Roman government. Historically, anyone found to have broken a Roman seal would have received the severest punishment of crucifixion upside down. The fact that no one was accosted and held accountable was due to the fact that the chief priests paid a "large sum" to the soldiers in order for them to say that the disciples came at night and stole the body while they were sleeping. Bribes are paid for people to lie, not to tell the truth (Mt 28:11-15).

(4) Women first reported Jesus' resurrection. The men in Hebrew culture did not trust or believe the witness of women. When Mary Magdalene, Joanna, Mary the mother of James and the others ran to tell the Eleven, we read, "*But they did not believe the women, because their words seemed to them like nonsense*" (Lk 24:11). If the Gospels had been fabricated and written by those who had not witnessed the resurrection, they would never claim that women were the first witnesses of the empty tomb.

(5) The disciples had numerous personal encounters with the resurrected Jesus.

(i) Mary Magdalene spoke with and touched Jesus outside the garden tomb (Jn 20:10-18).

(ii) Jesus broke bread in the home of the two individuals whom he met on the road to Emmaus (Lk 24:13-35).

(iii) Jesus suddenly appeared to the disciples in a room with locked doors for fear of the Jews. He showed them his pierced hands and side to prove that he was really the risen Christ (Jn 20:19-20).

(iv) On another occasion he appeared to them. "*They were startled and frightened, thinking they saw a ghost. He said to them, 'Why are you troubled, and why do doubts rise in your mind? Look at my hands and my feet. It is I myself! Touch me and see; a ghost does not have flesh and bones, as you see I have'*" (Lk 24:37-39). Evidence abounds in the resurrection accounts that the disciples were not gullible and readily disposed to the idea that Jesus had risen from the dead. They still did not understand that the resurrection of the Christ was foretold in the Hebrew Scriptures. These are not fabricated accounts, but testimonies of eye witnesses that these events had actually taken place.

(v) On another occasion Jesus appeared to his disciples who had decided to go fishing. He cooked fish for them and said, "*Come and have breakfast*," then Jesus ate with them (Jn. 21:12).

(6) The doubting disciple believed. The apostle Thomas had not been with the other disciples when Jesus first appeared to them in a closed room. Despite the reports from the other disciples, Thomas would not believe that Jesus had been raised from the dead. He said, "*Unless I see the nail marks in his hands and put my finger where the nails were, and put my hand into his side, I will not believe it*" (Jn 20:25). When Jesus reappeared to the Eleven in a locked room with Thomas present, Jesus invited him to put his finger in his hands and side. When Thomas did, he exclaimed, "*My Lord and my God*" (Jn 20:28). Convincing physical evidence persuaded a doubting apostle.

(7) Jesus appeared to hundreds of followers on one occasion. Paul reports that Jesus "*appeared to more than five hundred of the brothers at the same time, most of whom are still living, though some have fallen asleep*" (1 Co 15:6). Individuals may be deceived but it would be unprecedented for 500 to be deluded all at once!

(8) The disciples were willing to die for their testimony that Jesus rose from the dead. All of the apostles were witnesses to the life, death, resurrection and ascension of Jesus Christ. Most became missionaries, taking the Gospel to other nations where they met their death.

Persuasive evidence for the resurrection of Jesus Christ is the willingness of each of these apostles to die for what they believed and knew to be true. Would any one person, let alone nearly a dozen men, be willing to die individually and separately for preaching a lie which they knew was not true in foreign lands far from their friends? (Wellman 2017: Internet).

Some accounts of their deaths are historically established, though others cannot be verified and read more like hagiography. Here we mention just a few.

Peter was crucified upside down in Rome. Thomas was a missionary to India where he reportedly was stabbed by a sword and died from the wound. Paul died at the hands of the Romans in Rome. Andrew was reportedly crucified on an X shaped cross in Greece. James was beheaded with a sword. Matthew was impaled to the earth by spears and then beheaded in Ethiopia. Bartholomew (Nathaniel) is said to have been martyred in Armenia.

(9) The remarkable growth and spread of the apostolic Church. Unlike Islam which spread through the sword, the Christian Church expanded under severe persecution through the witness and preaching of the Gospel. At times the Roman Emperors made determined efforts to annihilate Christians and destroy the Christian Church. The more Rome persecuted, the more the Church grew. We can say with Tertullian in the second century that "the blood of the martyrs is the seed of the Church." Persecution only increased the number of believers. This remarkable fact points to the supernatural nature of the Christian Church. Jesus Christ is indeed the Lord, the risen Christ who is the Saviour of the world.

(10) The day of worship changed to Sunday. Jews had always worshipped on the Sabbath, the seventh day of the week. This day was sacred and they would never annul that practice, for the Sabbath day worship was enshrined in the Ten Commandments.

And yet we learn that the early church, comprised of Jewish believers, changed their day of worship from the seventh day of the week to the first day. This practice began as Christians gathered on the first day of the week to break bread together (Ac 20:7), and to bring their offerings to the Lord (1 Co 16:1). John the Apostle speaks of "the Lord's day," a day belonging to the Lord, referring to the first day of the week (Rev 1:9). Only because of this factually confirmed historical event of Jesus' bodily resurrection would Jewish Christians consent to making such a change.

(11) The Authenticity of the Gospels. The evidence in the four Gospels compel us to believe that these were eye witness accounts. Matthew and John were apostles. Mark was a close companion of Peter. Luke, the other Gospel writer, was not a disciple but a companion of the apostle Paul. As a medical doctor, Luke was an educated man who researched the life of Christ thoroughly. He "carefully investigated everything from the beginning" and read the various written accounts that had already been made by "eye witnesses" (Lk 1:1-4).

What appears to be clear from the Gospels, that these were eye witness accounts, has been cast into doubt by unbelieving scholars. Most biblical scholarship today, apart from conservative evangelicals, reject the traditional dates, authorship and authenticity of the Gospels. Instead, they ascribe late dates for the Gospels which they think were written by early church fathers who embellished the myths handed down to them. Their opinions, however, are based on their naturalistic assumptions with no historical evidence.

The fact is that no historical documents have been more exhaustively studied than the New Testament, including the Gospels. Names of people and places have been proven repeatedly to be historically accurate through archaeological discoveries and comparison with ancient documents.

Luke's account in the book of Acts has been examined exhaustively by classical scholars and historians. The scores and scores of names for people and places have been researched in detail and shown to be accurate, the obvious result of eye-witness accounts. If Luke was accurate in the writing of the Acts of the Apostles, we have every reason to be sure that his companion work, *The Gospel of Luke,* is likewise accurate.

Dr. Josh McDowell answered a university student who doubted Christianity by saying:

> *After more than 700 hours of studying this subject, I have come to the conclusion that the resurrection of Jesus Christ is either one of the most wicked, vicious, heartless hoaxes ever foisted on the minds of human beings — or it is the most remarkable fact of history* (McDowell 2017: Internet).

William F. Albright, who in his day was the world's foremost biblical archaeologist, said:

> *We can already say emphatically that there is no longer any solid basis for dating any book of the New Testament after about A.D. 80, two full generations before the date between 130 and 150 given by the more radical New Testament critics of today*" (McDowell 2017: Internet).

Brooke Foss Westcott, an English scholar, said:

> *Taking all the evidence together, it is not too much to say that there is no historic incident better or more variously supported than the resurrection of Christ. Nothing but the antecedent assumption that it must be false could have suggested the idea of deficiency in the proof of it* (McDowell 2017: Internet).

Serious minded Christians have every right to be confident in the authenticity and authority of the Gospels, being written by eye witnesses. We have every reason to believe in the bodily resurrection of Jesus Christ from the dead.

Lee Strobel, with a bachelor's degree in journalism and a master's degree in law, was an award-winning legal editor of *The Chicago Tribune* where he served for fourteen years. He won the State of Illinois' highest honour for public service journalism and together with a team of journalists won the top award for investigative reporting in Illinois.

An avoid atheist, he became angry when his wife yielded her life to Jesus Christ. Their marriage was jeopardized because of his rage against Christianity. Only science mattered to him, facts must be based on observable evidence. He plunged into extensive research to prove that Jesus did not rise from the dead.

It was a long struggle, but after examining all the evidence he was compelled to bow his proud heart and accept the evidence that Jesus did indeed rise from the dead. The consequences were huge. He surrendered his life to the Lord and became a pastor. He has traveled throughout the United States and the world, sharing his testimony to encourage believers and challenging sceptics. From the evidence supporting the bodily resurrection of Jesus Christ, Lee Strobel was converted from an atheist to a full-hearted believer in Jesus Christ as Lord and Saviour (Lee Strobel Internet).

Prophecies Fulfilled in Jesus: Not only are the miracles, especially the resurrection of Jesus, compelling testimony to the authenticity of Jesus' claims, the Old Testament prophecies also bear witness.

This historical figure, Jesus Christ, did not pop up in history out of nowhere. A serious reading of the Hebrew Scriptures demonstrates that the whole Old Testament points to the advent of Jesus who is the Christ. As Augustine wrote, "The New Testament is concealed in the Old Testament; the Old Testament is revealed in the New Testament."

Immediately after the creation accounts and the description of Adam and Eve's sin, God foretells the coming of a Saviour. The seed (offspring) of the woman would be bitten in the heel by the serpent (a painful, although non-lethal wound), but in turn the offspring would crush the serpent's head (a mortal wound) (Ge 3:15). God then provided a covering for their shame and guilt by slaying an animal and clothing them with the animal skin, the first biblical reference to the shedding of blood (Ge 3:21).

From the very beginning of the Bible we find God's plan of redemption through the shedding of blood by an animal sacrifice who typified Jesus Christ. He became "*the Lamb of God who takes away the sin of the world!*" (Jn 1:29). Satan, "that ancient serpent called the devil, or Satan" (Rev 12:9), did inflict a painful death on Jesus. But in turn we read that Jesus "*shared in [our] humanity so that by his death he might destroy him who holds the power of death – that is, the devil...*" (Heb 2:14).

The New Testament is replete with references to the fulfilment of Old Testament prophecies. Here we mention a few.

Jesus is:

- A prophet like Moses (Ac 3:22, 23; cf. Dt 18:15),
- A priest after the order of Melchizedek (Heb 5:6, 10; cf. Ps 110:4).
- A king, the greater Son of David (Ro 15:12; cf. 2 Sa 7:11-16).

We read that Jesus

- was born of a virgin (Mt 1:23; cf. Isa 7:14)
- was born in Bethlehem (Mt 2:6; cf. Mic 5:2)
- sojourned in Egypt (Mt 2:15; Hos 11:1)
- grew up in Nazareth of Galilee (Mt 2:23)
- was anointed by the Spirit (Lk 4:18-19;cf. Isa 61:1f)
- performed miracles (Mt 11:5-6; cf. Isa 35:5-6)
- spoke in parables (Mt 13:35; cf. Ps 78:2)

The passion of Christ is the pivotal moment in the life of Jesus with one-third of the Gospels devoted to the final week leading up to his death. We read of many prophecies fulfilled during that time frame:

- His triumphal entry into Jerusalem (Jn 12:12-16; cf. Ps 118:25-26; Mt 21:5; cf. Zec 9:9)
- His betrayal by Judas (Jn 13:18; cf. Ps 41:9)
- His price of 30 pieces of silver and the purchase of the potter's field (Mt 27:6-10; cf. Zec 11:12-13)
- His disciples forsake him (Mt 26:31; cf. Zec 13:7)

- Jewish rejection of Jesus (Jn 12:38-40; cf. Isa 53:1)
- Jesus "opened not his mouth" (Mt 27:12-14; cf. Isa 53)
- They pierced his hands and feet (Jn 19:31-37; cf. Ps 22:16; Zec 12:10)
- The soldiers divided his garments and cast lots for the tunic (Jn 19:23-24; cf. Ps 22:18)
- He cried out, "*Why have you forsaken me*?" (Mt 27:46; cf. Ps 22:1
- He lamented, "*I thirst*" (Jn 19:28; cf. Ps 69:21)
- Not one bone was broken (Jn 19:31-37; cf. Ps 34:20; Ex 12:46)
- Resurrection from the dead (Jn 20:8, 9; cf. Ps 16:10).

After Jesus' resurrection, he rebuked his followers for not understanding and believing what the Old Testament had prophesied about him, saying:

> "*How foolish you are, and how slow of heart to believe all that the prophets have spoken! Did not the Christ have to suffer these things and then enter his glory?" And beginning with Moses and all the Prophets, he explained to them what was said in all the Scriptures concerning himself* (Lk 24:25-27).

Conclusion

Since Christ fulfilled the Old Testament prophecies, since Christ did rise bodily from the dead, we are confronted with the life-altering question that Pilate asked the Jews. "*What shall I do, then, with Jesus who is called Christ*?" (Mt 27:22). A decision is demanded. Do we reject him as our Lord and Saviour, or do we bow in worship with faith and obedience?

To accept Jesus as Lord and Saviour is to trust in Christ for our salvation from sin and to embrace his teachings. We cannot be true disciples of Christ if we are not committed to Jesus' commands. We are not free to pick and choose what we want to believe.

Most main-line Protestant denominations in Africa belong to the World Council of Churches and hence subscribe to the doctrinal confession of the W.C.C. The official pronouncement of the W.C.C. is quite impressive! "The World Council of Churches is a fellowship of churches which confess the Lord Jesus Christ as God and Saviour according to the scriptures..." Who could object to that?

The problem is that the members do not ascribe to the historic meaning of the words. If "the Lord Jesus Christ" is God and Savior "according to the Scriptures," then we know who Jesus is.

Jesus cannot be Lord at all if he is not Lord of all. That includes our beliefs and worldview. This is the most basic question that must be answered before we attempt to do any study of Scripture and seek to build a biblical theology.

WHY WAS JESUS CHRIST SENT?

According to the Scriptures, Jesus did not come to the earth on his own. "*For God so loved the world that he* ***gave his only Son***..." (Jn 3:16a). More than that, God "***sent his Son***..." (Gal 4:4a). Jesus came from God with a mission to accomplish.

Jesus became the first missionary with Good News from God. No missionaries were sent from Israel to other nations under the Old Covenant except Jonah, and he was sent to proclaim "bad news" of God's coming judgement (Jnh 1:1).

Jesus is called the "apostle" in Hebrews (3:1). The English word, "apostle," is the transliteration of the Greek noun meaning "messenger" or "envoy," and is derived from the verb meaning "to send away." The English word, "missionary" is derived from the Latin noun meaning "sent one." Thus the English words, "apostle" and "missionary" mean literally the same thing, the latter derived from Latin and the former from Greek. Therefore, Jesus became "the apostle," or missionary ("sent one"), sent by God the Father.

The purpose for which Jesus was sent was threefold: (1) to save lost sinners from their sins; (2) to vanquish Satan and his demons; (3) and to inaugurate the Kingdom of God.

To Save Lost Sinners from their Sins

The purpose was salvific, to bring salvation to lost sinners who were in bondage to sin. Jesus was sent for a specific purpose: "*to redeem those under law, that we might receive the full rights of sons*" (Gal 4:4b). "*...that whoever believes in him shall not perish but have eternal life*" (Jn 3:16b).

This is indicated by the three-fold announcement of Jesus' birth to Mary, Joseph and the shepherds.

Announced at Christ's birth: When Gabriel appeared before Mary to announce the virgin birth of God's Son, he said, "*You will be with child and give birth to a son, and you are to give him the name Jesus*" (Lk 1:31). The name, "Jesus," was a common name among the Jews and is the Greek form of the Hebrew name, Joshua. It means "the Lord is salvation" or "the salvation of the Lord."

When Joseph, to whom Mary was engaged, learned of Mary's pregnancy, an angel from the Lord appeared to him at night and said, "*...what is conceived in [Mary] is from the Holy Spirit. She will give birth to a son, and you are to give him the name Jesus, because he will save his people from their sin*" (Mt 1:20-21).

The Jews were waiting for a political Saviour who would liberate them militarily from their enemies. This is clear from Zechariah's song of praise when he said: "*He has raised up a horn of salvation for us...salvation from our enemies from the hand of all who hate us...*" (Lk 1:69, 71).

During the first century the Jews were under the oppressive rule of the Roman Empire. Jews were not free, but were kept under the thumb of the imperialists. The Jews yearned for liberation.

Although the Jews thought that their promised Messiah would rescue them from their imperial masters, God made clear in the annunciations that Jesus in his first advent would "*save his people from their sin*." Jesus, the Saviour, would not save Israel from their Roman bondage, but would redeem them from their spiritual bondage to sin.

When God announced the birth of his Son to the shepherds, the angel said, "*I bring you good news of great joy that will be for all the people. Today in the town of David a saviour has been born to you; he is Christ the Lord*" (Lk 2:10-11).

These shepherds were not common, ordinary shepherds. They were watching over sheep on the plains east of Bethlehem where the watch-tower Migdal Eder was located. According to the Mishna, the flocks pastured there were destined for temple sacrifices. The daily sacrifices of lambs for sin required a constant, unending supply. A popular belief held that the Messiah would be revealed from this "tower of the flock" (Shepard 1963: 32). These shepherds were humble and pious, well versed in the Mosaic Law, temple worship and prophetic teaching.

That great Messianic prophecy of the Suffering Servant in Isaiah 53 is profound. No doubt the shepherds were familiar with it. The Suffering Servant would become a sacrificial lamb on whom the sins of the lost sheep would be placed.

> *But he was pierced for our transgressions, he was crushed for our iniquities; the punishment that brought us peace was upon him, and by his wounds we are healed. We all, like sheep, have gone astray, each of us has turned to his own way; and the LORD has laid on him the inequity of us all...he was led like a lamb to the slaughter, and as a sheep before her shearers is silent, so he did not open his mouth*" (Isa 53:5-7).

The sacrificial system of the Old Testament was extensive and explicit. Sacrifices were continually offered, morning and evening, and on many special occasions. These sacrifices were intended to propitiate God who was aggrieved by the sins of his people. Without propitiation through his blood, all sinners would be under God's judgement. By laying hands on the head of the sacrifice, the sins of the people were symbolically transferred onto the lamb who died in the place of the sinner.

It was not without significance that John the Baptist pointed to Jesus twice and announced, "*Look, the Lamb of God, who takes away the sin of the world*" (Jn 1:29, 35). John saw in Jesus the fulfilment of Isaiah 53.

Proclaimed by Jesus: Throughout his ministry, Jesus Christ proclaimed that the sin issue was his focal point. Jesus made it clear that he had authority to forgive sins (Mk 9:5, 10). During his ministry Jesus frequently ate with "sinners" and associated with those deemed reprehensible by the Pharisees. This aroused numerous criticisms. But Jesus declared, "*I have not come to call the righteous, but sinners to repentance*" (Lk 5:32).

After one such criticism for his association with "sinners," Jesus told the parable of the Lost Sheep. When the shepherd found the lost sheep, he joyfully put it on his shoulder and returned to the 99 sheep still in the sheep pen "who did not need to repent" (Lk 15:1-7). This was a clear rebuke of the Pharisees and a forthright claim that Jesus' mission was to save sinners. Elsewhere Jesus said, "*I am the good shepherd. The good shepherd lays down his life for the sheep*" (Jn 10:1ff).

The salvation Jesus came to bring was neither political, social nor economic emancipation. Salvation from sin was far more basic and essential. It was salvation from God's wrath on sinners who disobey God. "*Someone asked him, 'Lord, are only a few people going to be saved?'*" (Lk 13:23). Jesus responded by saying the door is narrow and many will not enter. At the last judgement

Jesus will say to many, "*I don't know you or where you come from. Away from me, all you evildoers! There will be weeping there, and gnashing of teeth...*" (Lk 13:27-28). In fact, Jesus frequently accompanied his teachings with warning of hell fire (Mk 9:43-48; Lk 12:4-5).

But Jesus did not come on his first advent to sit on the seat of judgement to judge all sinners. The apostle John declared, "*For God did not send his Son into the world to condemn the world, but to save the world through him. Whoever believes in him is not condemned, but whoever does not believe stands condemned already because he has not believed in the name of God's one and only Son*" (Jn 3:17).

Accomplished by Christ's Death: As the Good Shepherd, Jesus came to lay down his life for the sheep. This was his ultimate purpose of his first advent.

During the first half of his ministry, he publicly taught and performed miraculous signs to verify his identity. But mid-way through his ministry, on the foothills of Mt. Hermon in Caesarea Philippi, Peter made his confession of faith in Jesus, "*You are the Christ, the Son of the living God*" (Mt 16:16).

At that point Jesus changed the nature of his ministry from public to private. He began preparing his disciples for his pending death. We read: "*From that time on Jesus began to explain to his disciples that he must go to Jerusalem and suffer many things at the hands of the elders, chief priests and teachers of the law, and that he must be killed and on the third day be raised to life*" (Mt 16:21; c.f. 17:22). Jesus kept heading toward Jerusalem and reminding the Twelve that he would be betrayed, condemned to death and crucified, but raised to life on the third day (Mt 20:17-19).

Salvation from our sins was accomplished by Christ's death and the shedding of his blood. This is prominent throughout the New Testament (Ro 3:24-25; Heb 9:26-10:14; 1 Pe 1:18-19).

Conclusion: The Gospels clearly state that Jesus came for the purpose of redeeming lost sinners.

Jesus did not come as a political activist. Never once do we read that he encouraged insurrection or resistance to the Romans. Jesus' teaching undermined all hatred, violence and insurrection. Jesus advocated mercy, meekness, peace-making, and forgiveness. He instructed his disciples to turn the other cheek when struck by someone, and to forgive their enemies (Mt 5).

When the Jews tried to trap him, they asked Jesus whether they should pay taxes to Caesar. Knowing their duplicity, he asked, whose portrait was found on the denarius. When they replied, "Caesar," Jesus responded, "*Then give to Caesar what is Caesar's, and to God what is God's*" (Lk 20:22-25). When Peter used his sword to strike the servant of the high priest who arrested Jesus, he ordered Peter to put his sword back in its place, "*for all who draw the sword will die by the sword*" (Mt 26:52).

Neither was Jesus a social activist. He warned against greed, saying: "*Watch out! Be on your guard against all kinds of greed; a man's life does not consist in the abundance of his possessions*" (Lk 12:13-21). This was followed by a parable, warning against fools who strive to become rich, but forget their impending death when they will lose all earthly wealth.

Instead, he urged his disciples to "store up" treasures in heaven where their treasure cannot be lost. "*For where your treasure is, there your heart will be also*" (Mt 6:21-24). No one can serve two masters. You either serve God with all your heart, or you serve Mammon, the god of wealth.

In fact, Jesus had many negative comments about material riches. When a young rich man asked him what he needed to do to inherit the kingdom of God, Jesus' reply was: "*...go, sell your possessions and give to the poor, and you will have treasure in heaven. Then come, follow me*" (Mt 19:21). Instead of focusing on material gain, or material security, Jesus taught contentment and trust in God.

The primary purpose of Jesus' first advent was to offer his life as a sacrifice for the sins of his people.

To Vanquish Satan and his Demons

Men and women are not only sinners, they are enslaved to Satan in his dominion of darkness. The second purpose of Christ's first advent was to vanquish Satan and his demons.

Origin of Evil Spirits: According to the Scriptures, God is surrounded by myriads of angelic beings who worship and serve him continually (Isa 6; Rev 4-5). Apparently, at some point, a portion of these holy angels rebelled against God, including the chief adversary of God, though not much is said in the Bible about this. Compare Isaiah 14:12-15 and Ezekiel 28:11-19.

The chief adversary of God is Satan, also called the devil. The Bible implies that Satan is a demon (Lk 10:17-20). Jude refers to "*angels who did not keep their positions of authority but abandoned their home*" (Jude 6). Clearly, at some point in time these beautiful angelic beings whom God created good, rebelled against him and became evil spirits.

In the Bible these fallen angels are referred to as "demons," "unclean spirits" and "evil spirits" (Dt 32:17; Mk 1:24ff; Ac 19:12ff). These rebellious angels who became "demons" and "evil spirits" are allied with fallen men and women who are part of the kingdom of darkness, ruled over by the prince of the power of the air (Eph 2:2).

According to the Scripture, idolatry is not empty superstition. A spiritual dynamic emanating from Satan and his legions inspires and activates pagan worship. In Psalm 106 God castigates Israel for mingling among the nations and adopting their customs. He then stated:

They worshiped their idols, which became a snare to them.
They sacrificed their sons and their daughters to demons.
They shed innocent blood the blood of their sons and daughters,
whom they sacrificed to the idols of Canaan... (Ps 106:34-38).

Sacrifices offered to the idols in Canaan were actually sacrifices offered to demons. The same teaching is found in the New Testament. Paul stated:

Do I mean then that a sacrifice offered to an idol is anything,
or that an idol is anything?
No, but the sacrifices of pagans are offered to demons, not to God, and I do not want you to be participants with demons
(1 Co 10:19-20).

Satan was Rendered Powerless by the Cross: God not only sent his only Son to save lost sinners, he sent Jesus to deal a lethal blow to Satan, the arch enemy of God. Christ's death on the cross not only accomplished our salvation from sin, it also vanquished the devil. He crushed the head of the serpent (Ge 3:15).

Since the children have flesh and blood,
he too shared in their humanity
so that by his death he might destroy him
who holds the power of death – that is, the devil... (Heb 2:14).

According to Hebrews one purpose for Christ sharing our humanity by being born of a virgin, was "*so that [in order that] by his death he might destroy*" the devil.

The word, "destroy," can be misleading because Satan will never be annihilated. He will spend eternity in the Lake of Fire prepared for the devil and his angels (Rev 20:10). Rather, the purpose was to render the devil powerless and make him ineffective in his hold of death over those in Christ.

The Message reads: "*By embracing death...he destroyed the Devil's hold on death.*" The grip is gone. It has been destroyed. The devil has been rendered powerless over us. Through Christ Christians may overcome all temptations. Through faith in Christ, Satan no longer has any grounds to accuse the believer. The penalty of sin has been paid.

Although Satan still roams about "*as a roaring lion, seeking whom he may devour*" (1 Pe 5:8), he is powerless over believers who entrust themselves to the Lord

One may ask, "How did Christ's death make the devil powerless? How did the devil lose his grip on death?" The power of Satan over sinners is based on sin and its consequences. Through Satan, sin entered the world. Because the just penalty of sin is death, Satan wielded this power over sinners, continually accusing them before the throne of God.

Furthermore, sinners are under the dominion and control of Satan. They are in the kingdom of darkness. God could not justify sinners apart from Christ's death. But when the guilt of sin on a repentant believer is removed through the blood of Christ, the Christian is plucked from the dominion of Satan and brought into the Kingdom of God's Son (Col 1:13).

Christ's death destroyed Satan's power over believers.

The Evil Spirits were Disarmed by the Cross: The Scriptures teach:

And having disarmed the powers and authorities,
he made a public spectacle of them,
triumphing over them by the cross (Col 2:15).

The "rulers and authorities" are the spiritual powers of darkness, as we read in Ephesians 6:12: "*For we do not wrestle against flesh and blood, but against the rulers, against the authorities, against the cosmic powers over this present darkness, against the spiritual forces of evil in the heavenly places*" (Eph 6:12 *ESV*).

On the cross Jesus Christ *disarmed* the evil spirits. This rare word in the Greek for "disarm" makes the emphatic assertion that the evil spirits have been stripped of their power and authority. Their future damnation has been rendered certain and their present ability to exercise dominion over believers has been stripped away. They are disarmed.

The imagery of a triumphal procession portrayed here is graphic and arresting. Roman armies marched against their enemies throughout the Mediterranean world. Time after time the Roman armies prevailed over their enemies. The triumphant general returned to Rome with his victorious soldiers and their captive enemies. In a great triumphal procession and to the applause of Rome's residents, the generals led the victorious army through the city followed by their humiliated captives.

The Bible speaks of making "a public display" of the captives, literally, "exposing" them to humiliation, having triumphed over them through Christ. The *Message* paraphrases this graphically: "*He stripped all the spiritual tyrants in the universe of their sham authority at the Cross and marched them naked through the streets*" (Col 2:15b). This is an accomplished fact. These evil spirits have been "stripped naked," and publicly humiliated under Christ's rule. It is our responsibility to deal with the powers of darkness in this light.

We know that evil spirits continue to exercise power, but it is limited and circumscribed. The devil does play havoc with those who are not active in faith, with those who have not protected themselves with the armour provided by God (Eph 6:10-18).

But the evil spirits are <u>*unable*</u> to molest believers who trust in Christ. Paul indicates that we do *wrestle* against these evil powers, but not in our own strength. Christians can stand and resist with the armour of God. Victory is never in doubt. Believers can "stand firm" and not be defeated for the evil spirits have been disarmed by the cross, and Satan has been rendered powerless over believers.

To Inaugurate the Kingdom of God

The purpose of Christ's ministry was to vanquish his foes, rescue sinners from their enslavement to sin, and inaugurate his rule over all creation.

Preaching of the Kingdom of God was prominent in Jesus' earthly ministry. (The Gospel of Matthew, written to the Jews, substitutes "heaven" for "God" – "the Kingdom of Heaven.") After John the Baptist was put into prison, "*Jesus went into Galilee, proclaiming the good news of God. 'The time has come,' he said. <u>'The kingdom of God is near</u>. Repent and believe the good news!*" (Mk 1:14-15). The kingdom of God was central in Jesus' preaching.

The Rule of God: The "Kingdom of God" is not so much the "realm" of God's kingdom as his "rule" over the lives of people. "The Kingdom of God" is the sovereign rule of God. Unregenerate men and women are living under the rule of Satan (Jn 12:3). Men and women in their fallen, sinful nature are enslaved to sin as they seek to be autonomous and independent of God's law. They follow the ways of the world, the ways of "*the ruler of the kingdom of the air, the spirit who is now at work in those who are disobedient*" (Eph 2:2). Jesus preached the sovereign rule of God over the forces of evil and demonstrated his power over the evil one. To enter the kingdom of God one must be born again by the Spirit of God (Jn 3:3, 5).

A prominent part of Jesus' ministry was exorcism, casting evil spirits out of those who were demon possessed. Jesus declared, "*If I drive out demons by the Spirit of God, then the kingdom of God has come upon you*" (Mt 12:28). Casting out demons was a visible demonstration of Christ establishing his rule over all creation.

The Present Reign of Christ: Unknown to the Jews, the Kingdom of God would come in two phases. The parables on the "mysteries [secrets] of the kingdom of God" (Mt 13) disclose that the first phase of the kingdom will not come with brute force. This spiritual kingdom comes through the preaching of the Word of God with the enemy sowing tares among the wheat. God's kingdom will grow slowly from the smallest mustard seed to become a large tree.

In this sense the Kingdom of God is already present spiritually as men and women submit to the rule of God through faith in Christ.

The Messiah (the "anointed one") is the greater son of David who takes the throne of David and rules as king (2 Ki 7; Ps 89:33-37). The Jews who witnessed Jesus' ministry associated the Davidic kingship with Jesus. They had hoped for a political rule but were disappointed. The spiritual nature of this kingdom was reaffirmed during Jesus' trial. Pilate asked him:

> *'Are you the king of the Jews?'*
>
> *'Is that your own idea,' Jesus asked, 'or did others talk to you about me?'*
>
> *'Am I a Jew?' Pilate replied. 'It was your people and your chief priests who handed you over to me. What is it you have done?'*
>
> *Jesus said, '<u>My kingdom is not of this world. If it were, my servants would fight to prevent my arrest by the Jews. But now my kingdom is from another place</u>.'*
>
> *'You are a king, then!' said Pilate.*
>
> *<u>Jesus answered, 'You are right in saying I am a king</u>. In fact, for this reason I was born, and for this I came into the world, to testify to the truth. Everyone on the side of truth listens to me'*" (Jn 18:33-37).

Jesus is the Messiah, the Spirit anointed King (Lk 3:21-22), the greater son of David (Mt 1:1ff). He launched the Kingdom of God in his own Person by declaring its coming and demonstrating his authority over the evil spirits. Through his death on the cross he disarmed the powers and authorities and triumphed over them (Col 2:15). This first phase of the Kingdom of God, explained in the parables on the "secrets" or "mysteries" of the Kingdom (Mt 13), is spiritual and non-political.

The Kingdom of God, however, arrives in two phases. It is a case of the Kingdom of God being "already" present but "not yet" fully present. The spiritual, non-political aspect of the Kingdom of God is "already." It has come and can be found wherever men and women hear the Gospel, repent of their sin, and accept Jesus Christ as their Lord and Saviour.

The Future Reign of Christ: The visible reign of Christ, the "not yet" aspect of the Kingdom, will occur at the Second Advent when Christ, the Son of Man, will come in the clouds to assume authority over all peoples with an everlasting dominion that cannot be destroyed (Da 7:13-14). Jesus alluded to this at the Last Supper (Lk 22:16).

What is important for us to understand is that in no way is Christ's present kingship or his inauguration of the Kingdom of God a political event. In this phase of the Kingdom, it is spiritual with Christ reigning in the hearts of believers.

The Role of the Church and Christians in Society: Something more needs to be said, however, concerning the role of the Church and individual Christians in society.

The role of the Church in this world, according to New Testament teaching and modelling, is to glorify God by:

- Leading God's people in worship.
- Teaching God's people the whole counsel of the Word of God to equip them for works of service (Eph 4:7-13).

- Evangelizing the lost by heralding the Gospel of saving grace in Christ Jesus.
- Discipling all nations by sending missionaries into all the world to evangelize the lost and teach converts everything Christ commanded (Mt 28:16-20).

The ministry of the Church is spiritual. The church's responsibility to the believers is to teach them *the whole counsel of the Word of God*. This surely includes the teaching of the Old Testament. The Hebrew prophets repeatedly chastised Jewish leadership for social injustices as well as idolatry and personal sins.

Micah, for example, rebuked his fellow Jews for defrauding a man of his home, taking bribes, being dishonest in business, and dealing unjustly with the poor and defenceless. What God required was "*to act justly, love mercy and to walk humbly with God*" (Mic 6:8). Other prophets likewise condemned the trampling of the poor to the dust and denying the oppressed their due justice (Am 2:7). Does this prophetic ministry apply to the Church?

We need to remember that these prophets were addressing God's covenant people living under a theocracy. God had made a covenant with the descendants of Abraham to be their God and they would be his people. The Law was given to which they were obligated.

This was a totally different situation from today when most national and local civic leaders are not born again. They are not disciples of Jesus Christ. What they need primarily is not coercion to act justly but a spiritual conversion so that they will become new creatures in Christ Jesus. The primary mission of the Church is spiritual, fulfilling the four mandates given above.

This view is not popular in many circles, but it is a biblical truth. The principle problem of injustice in society is not due to unbelievers, but due to the failure of Christians to follow in the footsteps of Jesus. If all Christians, both within the church and in society, would live honest, unselfish lives, corruption and injustice would greatly decrease.

The teaching of Jesus and his apostles includes both personal morality and social justice – of exercising leadership with justice, showing compassion for the poor, paying a just wage on time, and "loving your neighbour as yourself." Pastors should include the teachings of Christ and his apostles, as well as the Old Testament prophets, in their biblical preaching of social ethics.

The role of the believer is quite different from that of the church. Each Christian is gifted by God to serve with a particular mission in life (Eph 2:10). Believers need to be equipped for their vocation, whatever that may be, to shine brightly in society as a witness for Jesus Christ and serve as salt and light among the peoples. God calls Christians to public service in government. They should be both wise and courageous in their advocacy for justice and honesty.

Should Christians take part in civil uprising against injustice? Paul lived under the oppressive rule of the Roman imperialists. Yet he admonished the Christians in Rome:

> *Everyone must submit himself to the governing authorities, for there is no authority except that which God has established...Consequently, he who rebels against authority is rebelling against what God has instituted...* (Ro 13:1-2)

Although Christians should live obediently under the rule of law of government, Christians live under a higher law, the Law of God. Hence, whenever a government mandate contravenes the law of God, the Christian must obey God rather than man (Ac 4:19-20).

What of laws that are unfair and unjust? Within Jesus' ethical teaching, public pleas for justice and passive resistance against unjust overseers can be blessed by God when done peacefully and with love. A Christian who prayerfully considers what he or she should do, may engage in civil disobedience if it is non-violent, prayerfully inspired and following the ethic of Christian love for his neighbour rather than for love of self. That Christian should also be willing to accept the penalty for non-compliance.

When sinners become saints they should be compelled by the Spirit and from the heart to act justly, love mercy and treat others as they wish to be treated. Christians should seek to alleviate poverty and injustice. In this way they can become salt in society.

However, poverty and injustice are mere symptoms of a deeper problem. Because of sin against God, men and women act selfishly with all the acts of the sinful nature (Gal 5:19-21). Therefore, Jesus' primary mission was to save sinners, not only from the wrath of God, but also from their sinful natures. Like yeast working its way through the dough, the Holy Spirit gradually permeates society and penetrates to the deepest levels when God's people are obedient.

Take slavery for an example. This inhumane and grievous practice was widespread in the Roman Empire. Though the apostles, as leaders of the apostolic church, never resisted slavery overtly, they undermined it with the Christian ethic of love. See how this is done in Paul's letter to Philemon, a slave owner. Masters of slaves were taught that God shows no favouritism. Both slave and free are equal in God's sight. Masters should therefore not threaten their slaves, but treat them with magnanimity, knowing that God rewards according to what good they do in this world (Eph 6:9). In this way God undermined the very idea of slavery. Eventually, slavery was made illegal in the Western world through the conscience of Christians who exerted influence in government.

As the Church and the individual Christian live under the rule of God in this age, they must seek God's wisdom to maintain priorities in life.

CONCLUSION

The Christian Faith is not of human origin. Shrewd men have not written, edited and redacted the Bible to create a cleverly written religious document called the Bible. Therefore, we need to learn from Scripture what our emphases should be in doing African Theology.

Jesus Christ is the heart of the Christian Faith. Christianity is nothing without Jesus, the one and only Jesus spoken of in the Gospels and in the writings of his apostles. Remove the supernatural from Christianity and you have nothing but an empty, meaningless and futile way of life. Shred away the miraculous from the historical narrative of Jesus Christ, and you have nothing more than a human sage whose words are offensive and incomprehensible.

Though Jesus demonstrated and proved his divine nature and origins, educated, clever scholars cannot know him apart from God's saving grace. As Jesus joyfully prayed through the Spirit:

I praise you, Father, Lord of heaven and earth, because you have hidden these things from the wise and learned, and revealed them to little children. Yes, Father, for this was your good pleasure.

He went on to say:

All things have been committed to me by my Father. No one knows who the Son is except the Father, and no one knows who the Father is except the Son and those to whom the Son chooses to reveal him (Lk 10:21-22).

Christian theology does nothing for anyone apart from genuine faith in Jesus Christ. This comes not through shrewd, intellectual efforts but through humble repentance of sins and faith in the only One who offers eternal, abundant, and liberating life in this world, and unending life in the world to come.

The historic Christian faith, grounded in revealed Scriptures which cannot err, testifies who Jesus is and why he came to this earth. African Theology is relevant and has staying power whenever it is grounded on Jesus Christ and his teaching.

6
ISSUES ARISING FROM AFRICAN THEOLOGY

As in every scientific discipline, issues arise that require further thought and research. For those who do African Biblical Theology, this chapter explores several of the issues that need further clarification in the African context.

CHRIST AND CULTURE

Crucial in the discussion of African Theology is one's view of African culture. Since many African Theologians believe African culture, including African Traditional Religion, are sources of doing African Theology, we need to evaluate the nature of culture.

In 1951 Richard Niebuhr published *Christ and Culture* which has been cited frequently for well over half a century. It was a monumental contribution to the topic of Christian attitudes toward culture (Niebuhr 1951).

He suggested three basic ways in which Christians have viewed culture throughout history: Christ against culture, Christ of culture, and Christ above culture. Within the third view (Christ above culture) Niebuhr suggested three further variations.

African Theology raises the profound question of how Christians should understand their culture. Many African theologians propose that culture should be one of the sources for doing African Theology. So the question is asked: Is culture good or is it evil? Or is culture a little bit of both, or is culture a neutral vehicle for humans to use at will? How can we determine what our attitude should be toward culture?

Without attempting any major treatise on the subject, and without interacting with Niebuhr's proposals, several ideas are laid out which need further thought.

Definition of Culture

Anthropologists have noted that culture is a product of human imagination and creativity. Louis Luzbetak examined various definitions for culture and noticed five components.

Culture is "a way of life," a "total plan for living" that is "functionally organized into a system," is "acquired through learning," and is "a way of life of a social group" (Luzbetak 1970: 59-60).

Language as part of culture, reflects culture. Learn a language and you have learned the essence of that culture. A uniquely designed way of life, organized by each social group, includes everything that humans learn in life from infancy.

The elements of culture include: social organization, economic systems, forms of government, customs and traditions, arts and literature, and religion. Though listed last, religion forms the heart of every culture for religious beliefs permeate all of culture. Values and norms spring from religious beliefs.

Culture includes material objects produced by the people. These material products are relatively easy to change. African material culture has been transformed beyond recognition, particularly in the cities. Material culture includes everything from housing and clothing, dishes and utensils, communication with cell telephones, radio and TV, education with classrooms, chalkboards, desks and chairs, transportation with cars, buses, and taxies, governments with parliament buildings, mace, wigs and robes. African material culture has been turned upside down and few Africans oppose this. But material culture is not the deep-seated beliefs of the traditional worldview which resist change.

The belief system includes beliefs in the Creator God, divinities, nature spirits, ancestral spirits, mystical powers of magic, witchcraft and sorcery; it includes the causes of sickness and death, health and prosperity, and the need for divination to determine the causes of misfortune. Beliefs provide an explanation for everything that happens (Gehman 2005: 20).

A basic question must be asked: How do we determine whether any or every aspect of a particular culture is appropriate for Christians to use? Is culture good, bad or neutral?

Biblical Perspective

If culture is the creation of human beings, then we can inquire from Scripture whether human beings are good, bad or neutral?

We find in Scripture that human beings are both good and bad, created in the image of God and totally ruined by sin.

When God created Adam and Eve, he created them in God's own image (Ge 1:26). This means that: (1) human beings are personal, like God who is personal, a self-conscious being with ability to think, make decisions and feel emotions; (2) human beings are godlike in their ability to exercise dominion on the earth as vice-regents of God, serving under his sovereign direction; (3) human beings initially reflected the moral character of God (Gehman 2005: 34-37).

Because Adam and Eve disobeyed God, they and their descendants suffered the consequences of their sin, namely, physical, spiritual and eternal death (Ro 5:12; Eph 2:1). Spiritual death meant that their thinking was futile (Eph 4:16-17), they were enslaved to sinful desires (Ro 1:24), and their emotions became unstable, ranging from simmering anger to lustful temptations, from greed to jealousy (Eph 4:22).

Paul concludes that "*Jews and Gentiles are all under sin. There is no one righteous not even one...no one seeks God. All have turned away...there is no one who does good, not even one...There is no fear of God before their eyes*" (Ro 3:9-18).

The image of God in human beings has been smudged, twisted and distorted, but something of God's image is still evident. Men and women are totally depraved in the sense that every aspect of human nature has been sullied by sin, but they are not absolutely depraved. They still have a conscience, convicting of wrongdoing and affirming their good conduct, although it is not a reliable judge. They may still show kindness and love, honesty and faithfulness, concern for right and wrong.

The Bible teaches not only that individuals are sinful by nature, it also speaks of a "world" that is hostile against God and animated by the powers of darkness. "The world represents an organized force, a power or order that is the counterpoise to the kingdom of God" (Erickson 1998: 661).

This "world order" is mentioned by Paul not in a neutral way. Paul wrote that before believing in Christ the Ephesian Christians had been dead in transgressions and sins, "*in which you used to live when <u>you followed the ways of this world and the ruler of the kingdom of the air</u>, the spirit who is now at work in those who are disobedient. <u>All of us also lived among them at one time,</u>*

gratifying the cravings of our sinful nature and following its desires and thoughts" (Eph 2:2-3).

Culture is the creation of the human race. It stands to reason that if unbelievers spend their lives 'gratifying the cravings of [their] sinful nature," whatever they touch will be tainted by their sinful nature. Therefore, permeating all of human culture is a structure of evil opposed to the law of God, a world order that is hostile to the Kingdom of God.

"The world" as expounded in Scripture is not to be equated with culture as such, for "the world" is uniformly described as evil and hostile to God. But "the world" is manifested in culture and is expressed throughout culture. Paul warns the Colossians not to become captive to the "*deceptive philosophy, which depends on human tradition and the basic principles of the world rather than on Christ*" (Col 2:8) (Gehman 2005: 44).

Not only is culture tainted by sin because sinners have created it, the Bible also teaches that "the world" is under the dominion of the devil (Eph 2:2). John teaches: "*The world is under the control of the evil one*" (1 Jn 5:19). There is a spiritual dynamic which moves the world system in ways that are antagonistic to the law of God (Gehman 2005: 44).

Conclusion

Scripture addresses the question of "culture" indirectly. It would appear beyond any doubt that culture is tainted with sinful elements that must be expunged. The big question is: How do we determine what is acceptable for Christians and what is not? Is Scripture our final authority or is personal opinion final? Do we pick and choose from culture and Scripture what we believe is relevant for us? Or does Christ exercise his authority over our thinking?

Within these parameters we need to probe further the nature of culture. Since contextualized theology includes culture in the equation, we need a more biblical understanding of how we should evaluate African cultures.

UNITY AND DIVERSITY

African Theology has arisen in part as a reaction to colonial and missionary denigration of Africans and their culture. From the human point of view, the response of Black Theology is quite understandable. Africans have suffered grievously under Apartheid.

The question arises, however, do we perpetuate segregation and accent our differences? Do we develop African Theology separate from historic Christianity simply because Christianity began in the Middle East and prospered in Europe where the historic creeds of the Church were formulated, such as the Nicene Creed? Or do we emphasize our unity in Christ?

Unity in Humanity and Grace

Instead of separating and dividing ourselves from others, we find a great emphasis in Scripture on our unity both in our humanity and in Christ.

Unity of Humanity: Paul's visit to Athens is instructive. The city of Athens was the leading city of the ancient Greek empire under Alexander the Great (356-323 BC). Athens became the birthplace of democracy. Its great cultural achievements in the fifth century before Christ laid the foundations for western civilization. The New Testament was written in Greek.

Paul was not impressed, however, by the splendour of Athenian architecture and its historic significance, but was appalled by their idolatry. The men of

Athens "*spent their time doing nothing but talking about and listening to the latest ideas*" (Ac 17:21). These men invited Paul to share his ideas on Mars Hill, also called the Areopagus which meant "hill of Ares," the Greek god of thunder and war, the equivalent of the Roman god, Mars.

Paul usually preached in the synagogues to Jews and Jewish proselytes. In contrast to his typical approach to the Jews by presenting Christ as fulfilment of God's past revelation to the Hebrews, Paul's point of contact for the Athenians was the inscription to an idol, "*To an Unknown God.*" In one sense this idol demonstrated the depths of Athenian idolatry. Paul had been "*distressed to see the city was full of idols.*" For fear of neglecting some unknown god, they erected this additional idol among the many others.

"*Now what you worship as something unknown,*" Paul said, "*I am going to proclaim to you.*" He began with creation. Then he declared, "*From one man he made every nation of men, that they should inhabit the whole earth...*" (Ac 17:26).

The Athenians prided themselves in being the only Greeks on the mainland who never migrated to that place. They alone were the original settlers of the area. But in fact their pride was misplaced. Professor F.F. Bruce comments:

> *All mankind was one in origin – all created by God and all descended from one common ancestor. This removed all imagined justification for the belief that Greeks were innately superior to barbarians, as it removes all imagined justification for parallel beliefs today. Neither in nature nor in grace – neither in the old creation nor in the new – is there any room for idea of racial superiority* (Bruce 1960: 358).

Instead of the words, "*from one man*" in the more recent Bible translations of the Bible, the Authorized Version (King James) translates Acts 17:26, "*from one blood.*" The truth is that the unity of the human race is proven by the blood types. We have types A and B, types O and Rh-positive, and Rh-negative in every race and ethnic group throughout the world. The assumption that Africans have one blood type, Caucasians have another type and Asians a third type is untrue. If I need a blood transfusion, my biological son may not have my own blood type, but an African will.

> *For almost every gene we know, either everybody in the world has the same form of the gene, in which case all human beings are the same or if there's variation, the frequencies of the different variants are the same relatively speaking, close to the same, in Africans, Asians, North Americans, Austro-Asians, and so on...So there's little differentiation* (Lewontin 2017: Internet).

The fact is that we all belong to one race, the human race. Our blood and genes prove it and Scripture teaches it.

Unity in Christ: What is true in nature is also true in grace: Christians are *one* in Christ. Unity in the Body of Christ is pivotal.

When the Holy Spirit was poured out at Pentecost, all the first believers in Jesus Christ were Jews. The Church continued to grow in Jerusalem and the surrounding areas of the Jewish homeland.

But when the Gospel was received by the Gentiles, this created a measure of inner conflict, for the Jews had always separated themselves from the Gentiles, and considered the Gentiles inferior to them. We read in Acts 10-11 of Peter's reluctance to meet with Cornelius, a Roman centurion. But God demonstrated the equality of these Gentile believers with the Jewish believers. Peter reported to the Church in Jerusalem that "*the Holy Spirit came on them as he had come on us at the beginning*" (Ac 11:15). God had made no difference between the Jews and the Gentiles. Peter concluded by saying, "*So if God gave them the same gift as he gave us, who believed in the Lord Jesus Christ, who was I to think that I could oppose God?*" (Ac 11:17).

Throughout the New Testament we read of unity between all believers, regardless of their ethnicity. Paul wrote:

> *But now in Christ Jesus you who once were far away have been brought near through the blood of Christ. For he himself is our peace, <u>who has made the two one and has destroyed the barrier, the dividing wall of hostility...His purpose was to create in himself one new man out of the two</u>, thus making peace and in this one body to reconcile both of them to God through the cross, by which he put to death their hostility...For through him we both have access to the Father by one Spirit* (Eph 2:13-18).

Not only were the Jewish and Gentile believers united in one body by God himself, the Christians were exhorted to make every effort to maintain that unity because of what united them. Paul exhorted the Ephesians,

> *<u>Make every effort to keep the unity of the Spirit</u> through the bond of peace. There is <u>one body</u> and <u>one Spirit</u> – just as you were called to <u>one hope</u> when you were called – <u>one Lord</u>, <u>one faith</u>, <u>one baptism</u>; one God and Father of all, who is over all and through all in in all* (Eph 4:3-6).

The unity of all believers is not only because they are baptized into one body, the Church of Jesus Christ. They are also united with "one hope," "one Lord, one faith, one baptism."

All believers have "one hope." The great hope of all believers is the eager expectation of their future inheritance at the return of Christ. Peter urges Christians, "*Set your hope fully on the grace to be given you when Jesus Christ is revealed*" (1 Pe 1:13). Paul speaks of "*the hope that is stored up for you in heaven*" (Col 1:5). This "one hope" is future and it unites all believers. We all groan with afflictions of one kind or another, and eagerly wait for the redemption of our bodies (Ro 8:24), when "*there will be no more death or mourning or crying or pain*" (Rev 21:4). Liberals mock our eschatological hope for the return of Christ as "pie in the sky," but that is the biblical truth which all Christians should embrace with "one hope."

All believers have "one Lord." A lord is both owner and sovereign. Believers are the possession of Christ who is also their Lord. This refers to the possession and authority of Christ. They belong to the Lord who is their Master. Christians are not their own for they have been bought with the price of Christ's death on their behalf (1 Co 6:20). All Christians are subject to his teachings. Their hearts and lives are under his control

All believers have "one faith." Usually, "faith" is taken in the subjective sense, "to have faith in someone." But there are instances where faith is also an object, a statement of what Christians believe, a creedal statement of faith. Paul wrote elsewhere that he preached "the faith" (Gal 1:23). Clearly, this refers to the object of faith. It seems best to understand the "one faith" in Ephesians 2 as an object of faith, namely, the fundamental doctrines of the Christian faith.

It is also possible to understand "the faith" in Ephesians 2 both in the objective and subjective sense. Christians not only embrace the "*one faith delivered to the saints,*" but they subjectively believe and accept that teaching. Thus Christians are united by the "one faith" they profess outwardly, and with one accord they believe it inwardly.

However, it is difficult to eliminate the natural, grammatical and lexical meaning of the text which affirms that "the faith" is the objective set of beliefs that unite all believers.

Jude, the brother of Jesus Christ, wrote a few decades after Jesus death, "*I felt I had to write and urge you to* _*contend for the faith*_ *that was once for all entrusted to the saints*" (Jude 3). Looking beyond the apostolic church and the departure of the apostles, Jude urges that "the faith" that had been entrusted to the saints by the apostles, should not only be kept, but actively and aggressively protected by contending for it. Believers should "fight" to preserve "the faith."

The apostles predicted a time when "the faith" would be distorted and repudiated. Peter foresaw in the last days "scoffers" would come who would deny that Jesus would return again (2 Pe 3:3-4). John forewarned that the antichrist would come who would deny that Jesus is the Christ (1 Jn 2:22; 4:3).

In view of this inevitability, Jude exhorts Christians to "*contend for the faith.*" They need to "fight" for the faith boldly but always graciously, speaking the truth in love (Eph 4:15).

Paul admonished the Thessalonians, "_*hold*_ *to the teachings [or traditions] we passed on to you, whether by word of mouth or by letter*" (2 Th 2:15). The Greek verb for "hold" refers to a masterful grip, holding fast to the "traditions" and hence closely united to them. It is a continuing imperative with an ongoing and unceasing command to keep on holding to the teachings so that they will not go away.

In Paul's first letter to his son in the faith, he admonished Timothy, "_*Guard*_ *what has been entrusted to you*" (1 Ti 6:20). The Greek word for "guard" comes from a banking term used in the Greek world, of placing something of value as a deposit in a bank for safe keeping. The Gospel, which was taught by Paul, was more precious than gold and must be preserved safely, like keeping money in a bank.

Underlining the importance of Paul's concern, he repeated his admonition in his second letter to Timothy, "_*Guard the good deposit*_ *that was entrusted to you – guard it with the help of the Holy Spirit* (2 Ti 1:14). Paul repeats the analogy of banking. The 'good deposit" is the Gospel and Timothy is charged to protect the Gospel so that it will not be lost or damaged.

Even in Paul's day heresies arose. Paul pronounced a curse on those who taught a "different gospel" which in fact is "no gospel at all." For emphasis Paul repeated himself twice, "*let them be eternally condemned*!" (Gal 1:6-9).

Of course, believers do not all agree on many aspects of theology. Christians differ widely on "peripheral" doctrines, but they are united on the essentials, the fundamentals of the Faith. This "Faith" unites all believers. For example, all Christians, both Roman Catholic and Protestant have historically embraced the Nicene Creed without altering the intended meaning of the authors.

All believers have "one baptism." Through baptism all believers are baptized "into Christ" who died on the cross and rose again from the dead. Therefore, all believers are in one body.

> *You are all sons of God through faith in Christ Jesus, for all of you who were baptized into Christ have clothed yourselves with Christ. There is neither Jew nor Greek, slave nor free, male nor female, for you are all one in Christ Jesus* (Gal 3:26-28).

Diversity in Culture and Ethnicity

From our study of Scripture, unity should be in the forefront of all our theologizing. We are one in Christ and one in our Faith. But this does not eliminate our differences.

The very text given above, which underlines equality and unity of all Christians, implicitly acknowledges continued differences. Equality of the sexes does not eliminate their differences in gender or in their maternal or paternal roles. Equality of Jews and Greeks does not change their ethnic and cultural identities. The Jerusalem Council laid down the rule that Jewish believers could not compel Gentile believers to live like Jews (Ac 15:19-21).

God has demonstrated his love for diversity in all of creation. Consider the fascinating range of flowers and trees, fish and mammals. The world is full of dazzling, bewildering diversity.

Even so among human beings. Are diverse cultures evidence of God's curse or blessing? Each culture potentially brings a different perspective on life and emphasizes different strengths.

Christian faith does not eliminate diversity. In the last book of the Bible we read of believers from every "*tribe and language and people and nation*" worshipping before the Lord (Rev 5:9). Moreover, "*The glory and honour of the nations will be brought into it [the new Jerusalem]*" (Rev 21:26). Far from demanding uniformity, God delights in diversity. Diversity will be preserved in heaven.

Individuals in the Body of Christ have differing gifts, each one needed in the building up of the Church of Jesus Christ (Ro 12:3-8). The local church is blessed when a wide range of gifts is present.

But instead of complimenting each other, individuals with their sinful nature strive to be the big man. The problem with diversity in this fallen, sinful world is that pride, envy, jealousy and enmity creep in. Emphasizing diversity is dangerous. Think of the conflict between families, clans, tribes, nations and races. This world is being torn apart by hatred and violence.

The church in Corinth had an internal conflict with differing factions, each claiming primacy – those who followed Paul or Apollos, Peter or Christ. As Paul tried to resolve this conflict, he asked the question: "*For who makes you different from anyone else? What do you have that you did not receive? And if you did receive it, why do you boast as though you did not*?" (1 Co 4:7).

Conclusion

Should we be proud of our tribal identity, or of our nationality or race? On one occasion when I was teaching an adult Sunday School class in retirement, the subject drifted to pride in being an American. The discussion became quite animated when I expressed reticence in saying, "I am proud to be an American," something that Americans frequently say and sometimes sing. The refrain of one song reads: "I'm proud to be an American where at least I know I'm free...And I'd gladly stand up next to you and defend her still today. Cause there ain't no doubt I love this land! God bless the U.S.A."

I told the Sunday School class, "I would feel very uncomfortable when talking with my African friends to say, "I am proud to be an American." What would that say about our relationship? Instead of unifying us, I would be differentiating myself from them and bragging about my nationality. Such talk only creates barriers and misunderstanding.

Paul's comment to the Corinthians is apropos. "*What do you have that you did not receive? And if you did receive it, why do you boast as though you did not*?" I can honestly say, "I'm thankful to be an American." There have been many benefits that have come to me as a result. But pride? I did nothing to become an American. My mother, an American citizen, gave birth to me. On what basis can I be "proud" to be an American?

Should I say, "I'm proud to be a white person?" What in all the world could that mean? Should Africans say, "I'm proud to be a black African?" That is a question that needs to be explored by African Christians.

In my view, based on my understanding of Scripture, any tendency to brag about my racial, cultural or national identity falls short of being gracious, loving and humble. Eulogizing racial or cultural identity can only divide, not unite.

As grateful as I am that I was born in America to my parents, I am most thankful that they led me to Christ and that I am now a child of the King of kings, and a joint heir with Jesus Christ. That is the heritage which I cherish most.

Yes, I come from the Pennsylvania Dutch who migrated from German Switzerland to the United States in the 1800s. This means that I like Sauerkraut (finely cut cabbage that has been fermented), Schnitz un knepp (ham with dried apples and dumplings), chow chow (pickled relish made from tomatoes, onions, carrots, beans and peas) and a host of other delicious foods prepared best in Lancaster County, Pennsylvania, and found in such buffets as "Shady Maple" or "Good and Plenty."

We are all defined by our ethnic backgrounds with varying cultural preferences. But what is our defining identity? What does the Scriptures say about Christians, those who have been born by the Spirit and belong to Christ? Who are we?

According to the Scriptures: "*You are a chosen race, a royal priesthood, a holy nation, a people for his own possession*" (1 Pe 2:9).

Our primary identity is in neither our biological race nor our nationality. Christians belong to a "chosen race" (Jn 10:26-29). God calls out his people who have been chosen before the foundation of the world.

- *[God] has rescued us from the dominion of darkness and brought us into the kingdom of the Son he loves, in whom we have redemption, the forgiveness of sins* (Col 1:13).
- *You received the Spirit of sonship...we are God's children. Now if we are children, then we are heirs – heirs of God and co-heirs with Christ...* (Ro 8:15-17).
- *You were dead in your transgressions and sins, in which you used to live when you followed the ways of this world and of the ruler of the kingdom of the air, the spirit who is now at work in those who are disobedient...But because of his great love for us, God, who is rich in mercy, made us alive with Christ...And Christ raised us up with Christ and seated us with him in the heavenly realms in Christ Jesus, in order*

that in the coming ages he might show the incomparable riches of his grace, expressed in his kindness to us in Christ Jesus (Eph 2:2-7).

- *...in Christ we who are many form one body, and each member belongs to all the others* (Ro 12:5)
- *For you know that it was not with perishable things such as silver or gold that you were redeemed from the empty way of life handed down to you from your forefathers, but with the precious blood of Christ...* (1 Pe 1:18).

The primary identify of all believers in Jesus Christ is our Christian identity. We have been rescued from the dominion of darkness and brought into the Kingdom of God; we have been raised from spiritual death and given new life in Christ; we have been made heirs of God and joint-heirs with Christ; we are members of the Body of Christ.

Because our citizenship is in heaven, we are "aliens and strangers in this world" (1 Pe 2:11). We are called upon to "live as strangers" in this world (1 Pe 1:17).

We are all members of one human family, diverse as we may be, and if we are believers in Jesus Christ, we have been baptized into one Body, the Body of Christ, holding to "one faith" and "one hope."

SYMPTOMS AND ROOT CAUSES

Symptoms

All nations have symptoms of social malaise and malignancy. When governments seek to resolve those problems, they can only deal with the symptoms, and not the root causes.

In every society, to one degree or another, we find poverty, unemployment, homelessness, drug addiction, illiteracy, violence, inequality, injustice, and oppression.

How do governments undertake to address these festering problems? For the hungry they deliver financial aid and food, for the homeless they offer shelter, for drug addiction they provide drug rehabilitation, for violence they incarcerate, for inequality they redistribute the wealth through taxation, for injustice they enact new regulations. These actions may alleviate the problem for some people for a period of time, but they do not address the root causes.

Let's take the problem of poverty as an example. Why are people poor? The deep seated causes of poverty are complex and diverse. Families are poor for a great variety of interrelated reasons – alcohol or drugs, squandering of wealth, divorce, inability to obtain a living wage, bearing children outside of marriage, discrimination based on race or tribalism, unjust government leaders or employers, inability to gain a good education, oppression by capitalists – and on and on the list goes. The poor are voiceless without any place to turn for assistance.

Helping people in their needs is noble and desirable. For the Christian, this is biblical. We can be thankful for governments that do seek to alleviate the problems that fester in society.

Christians above others are responsible to help where they can, individually and corporately. Christians need to be in the vanguard of calling for justice and helping the weak and vulnerable. By banning together in parachurch organizations, Christians can do much to alleviate suffering. In fact, the Lord rebukes those who fail to lend a compassionate hand. Teaching people how to fish is far better than giving them fish. Better to be self-reliant than dependent.

The Psalmist enquires of the judges: "*How long will you defend the unjust and show partiality to the wicked? Defend the cause of the weak and fatherless; maintain the rights of the poor and oppressed. Rescue the weak and needy, deliver them from the hand of the wicked*" (Ps 82:2-4).

The Proverbs offer wisdom: "*He who oppresses the poor shows contempt for their Maker, but whoever is kind to the needy honours God*" (Pr 14:31). "*He who is kind to the poor lends to the LORD, and he will reward him for what he has done*" (Pr 19:17). The prophets of the Old Testament castigate those who hoard plunder, but oppress the poor and crush the needy (Am 4:1).

A tiny Old Testament commandment, lost among the scores of other commandments, was plucked from obscurity by Jesus and made the second most important commandment in the Bible. "*Love your neighbour as yourself*" (Dt 19:18; Mt 22:39). Repeatedly, this command is enunciated in the New Testament, first of all by Jesus (Mt 19:16), then by Paul (Ro 13:9). James declares this to be "the royal law found in the Scripture" (Jas 2:8).

Jesus set the golden standard for benevolence when he enunciated the Golden Rule: "*So in everything, do to others what you would have them do to you, for this sums up the Law and the Prophets*" (Mt 7:12). Others like Confucius gave the negative version, "*What you do not like if done to yourself, do not to others*" (Henry 1973: 266). But Jesus goes beyond restraint. He enunciated a positive axiom of universal benevolence towards those in need. Charity towards others summarizes the last six of the Ten Commandments (Gal 5:13-15).

Jesus applied this principle of benevolence to all classes, races and nationalities. In the Parable of the Good Samaritan Jesus stated explicitly that benevolence should be shown beyond the confines of one's own ethnic, racial or economic status. Loving your neighbour is loving anyone you meet who is in want. Showing compassion to all those in need, even your enemy, is the mark of a child of God (Lk 10:25-32).

Therefore, Christians are commanded by our Lord to show love and kindness in practical ways to those in need, even though their needs are merely symptoms of deeper issues.

Root Cause

As important as it may be for Christians and the Church to lend a helping hand to those in need, the Church has an even higher calling: to preach the Good News of saving grace to those who know not the Lord, and to teach the whole counsel of the Word of God to believers so that they may live godly lives and fulfil God's purpose for them.

For African Theology to focus mostly or exclusively on the visible, tangible problems plaguing society, it lacks faithfulness to the Word of God. Forsaking the God-given calling for the sake of agitating for justice is a failure with eternal consequences.

Let's review the symptoms of social malaise and malignancy mentioned above: poverty, homelessness, drug addiction, illiteracy, violence, inequality, injustice, and oppression. What is the root cause of all those sores in human societies? It is sin!

Sin has many manifestations, both individually and socially. Because of idolatry, greed, pride, envy, jealousy, covetousness, hatred, dishonesty, unfaithfulness, adultery, immorality, drunkenness and a host of other sins, our societies are festering with incurable sores. These sins are deep-seated and ingrained within the heart, for *"The heart is deceitful above all things and beyond cure"* (Jer 19:9). Social and political activists cannot cure the sinful heart.

The Jews were greatly concerned with external and ceremonial cleanliness, but Jesus reminded them that bad conduct cannot be fixed by outward cleansing. He taught: *"But the things that come out of the mouth come from the heart, and these make a man unclean. For out of the heart come evil thoughts, murder, adultery, sexual immorality, theft, false testimony, slander"* (Mt 15:18-19).

On another occasion Jesus taught the same truth but added, *"Make a tree good and its fruit will be good"* (Mt 12:33-35). A bad tree cannot bear good fruit.

In this fallen, sinful world, governments, civil societies and Christians are called upon to conduct themselves honestly, justly and benevolently. But the most that unbelievers can do is to treat the symptoms and minimize the pain and suffering that springs from our sinful natures.

Only the Church of Jesus Christ knows the remedy for the root problem in society. Secular and Christian organizations can devote themselves to political confrontation, but the Church should retain her focus on spiritual things. For the Christian Church to become a mere social and political activist is to desert her high and holy calling.

EARLY CREEDS AND GREEK PHILOSOPHY

African theologians claim their right to use African traditional religion and culture to re-imagine and reshape Christian theology because, they say, "westerners" have shaped their European brand of Christian theology through Greek philosophy and culture. Since theology is cultural, they believe, there are many theologies, and Africans need their own contextual theology.

We have no intention of delving into the question of the early church fathers engaging with Greek philosophy. Many volumes have been written concerning that. Our focus is on the fourth and fifth century creeds, namely, the Nicene Creed of 325 that was reaffirmed and enlarged in 381 at the Council of Constantinople. This alone is our focus.

Alleged Hellenistic Influence

African theologians claim, in sync with western liberal theologians, that during the fourth century Trinitarian controversies, Christian theologians "drew heavily on the dominant forms of abstract and speculative Greek philosophy, namely, Neo-Platonism." Orobator continues, "Our ways of talking about the Triune God today bear the burden of this Greek legacy" (Orobator 2008: 37).

According to Ezigbo, when Jesus asked Peter, "Who do you say that I am? Peter with his Jewish background, said, "You are the Messiah." But when the question was asked in the Greek context, by using Greek intellectual materials they replied, "...begotten of his Father before all worlds...being of one substance with the Father" (Ezigbo 2010: ix-x). The problems with the fourth and fifth century creeds, we are told, are two-fold: they are limited in value due to their western cultural perspective, and secondly, they are very technical, hard to understand, and cannot be adapted to the African context and circumstances of today's Christians.

Theology is "culture-bound," according to Pobee, first encrypted in Jewish tradition and then influenced by "views and concepts out of Hellenistic syncretism, especially the mystery religions" (Pobee 1992: 154f).

According to Boulaga, "Christianity is heir to Greek reason and continuation and crown of the Judiac revelation" (Boulaga 2002: 30). Since this Hellenistic, abstract thinking is not meaningful to Africans and an impediment to faith, the All Africa Council of Churches in 1973 declared:

> *Speaking for Africa, what we cannot buy is Western Civilization, culture or whatever you want to call it. Its Roman-Greek thought-forms and modes of expression are the swaddling-clothes that we need to tear open in order to get to the Christ...we attempt to break the seal of Western thought forms and culture so that we can come face to face with Christ and in Him see ourselves...and others* (Setiloane 1986: 35).

We need to explore this question: "Is the Christian doctrine of the Trinity, as expressed in the Nicene Creed, really shaped by Greek philosophy?"

The Nicene Creed

We shall not delve into the broader question of how Christian theologians interacted with Greek philosophy and utilized it to develop Christian theology. But we shall examine the Nicene Creed, first formulated in AD 325, and finalized at the Council of Constantinople in AD 381. Is the Nicene Creed truly biblical? Has it been influenced by Greek philosophy? Can Christians today disavow it and remain orthodox, biblical Christians?

Following is the Nicene Creed of AD 381, each phrase numbered for biblical references given below and for further comments.

1. **We believe in one God**,
2. the Father Almighty,
3. maker of heaven and earth,
4. of all things visible and invisible.

5. **And in one Lord Jesus Christ**,
6. The only-begotten Son of God,
begotten from the Father before all worlds.
7. Light of Light,
very God of very God,
begotten, not made;
8. being of one substance with the Father (*homoousion tõ patri*);
9. by whom all things were made;
10. who for us men, and for our salvation, came down from heaven;
11. and was incarnate by the Holy Spirit of the virgin Mary,
and was made man;
12. he was crucified for us under Pontius Pilate;
13. he suffered and was buried,
And the third day he rose again, according to the Scriptures,
14. and ascended to heaven and is seated
on the right hand of the Father;
15. from thence he shall come again with glory,
to judge the living and the dead; His kingdom shall have no end.

16. **And we believe in the Holy Spirit, the Lord, the Giver of life,**
17. who proceeds from the Father,
who with the Father and the Son together is worshipped and glorified, who spoke by the prophets.

18. We believe in one holy catholic and apostolic Church.
19. We acknowledge one baptism for the forgiveness of sins.
20. We look for the resurrection of the dead,
and life of the world to come. Amen.

1. Ex 20:2, 3; Mk 12:29-31
2. Eph 4:6; Mal 2:10
3. Ge 1:1; Isa 44:24
4. Col 1:16; Ro 1:20
5. 2 Co 1:3; 1 Th 1:10
6. Jn 3:16; Rev 1:8; Heb 1:5, 6; Mt 3:17; 14:33; Ps 2:7
7. Jn 1:1, 5; 8:12; 1 Jn 1:5; Jn 8:58; 20:28; 1 Jn 5:20; Ps 2:7; Heb 1:5; Jn 14:9; Col 1:15
8. Jn 10:30; Isa 44:6; Rev 1:8; Php 2:6; Jn 10:38; Col 2:9; Jn 17:21
9. Jn 1:1-3, 10; 1 Co 8:6; Col 1:15-17
10. 1 Th 5:9; Ac 4:12; Jn 6:51, 38; Jn 14:6; Ac 10:43
11. Mt 1:18; Lk 1:27, 35; Php 2:6-7; Ro 1:3
12. Ac 2:36; Mt 27:2, 24-26; Mk 15:15
13. Mt 16:21; Mk 15:46; Lk 24:5-7; 1 Co 15:3-4
14. Jn 20:17; 1 Ti 3:16; 1 Pe 3:21, 22; Ac 1:9; Mk 16:19
15. Ac 1:10-11; Rev 1:7; Jn 5:22; Ac 10:42; Lk 1:33; Da 7:13-14; Rev 11:15; Heb 12:28
16. Jn 14:16-17; 16:7-11; 2 Co 3:17; Ac 5:3,4; Jn 3:5; Tit 3:5
17. Jn 14:26; 15:26; Lk 11:13; Mt 28:19; 2 Pe 1:21
18. Jn 17:20-23; Eph 4:1-6; Col 1:18; Heb 12:23; Php 4:3; 1 Ti 3:15; Eph 2:19-20; Ac 2:42
19. Mt 28:18, 19; Eph 4:5; Lk 24:47; Ac 2:38; 1 Pe 3:21; Ro 6:3, 4
20. 1 Co 15:12-22; Jn 3:16; 5:9

Analysis of the Nicene Creed

Nicene Creed is Biblical: First, we note that every affirmation in the Nicene Creed is taught by the Scriptures. The biblical references are given above so that everyone can confirm for themselves that the Nicene Creed is biblical. The fourth century church fathers did not create this creed by appropriating Greek concepts from Neo-Platonism or Mystery Religions. They did not accommodate their theology to Hellenistic thought, but instead, they tried to be faithful to the revealed Word of God. This creed cannot be dismantled and dismissed unless we also choose to dismiss the authority of Scripture.

Nicene Creed is Ecumenical: This creed is ecumenical (worldwide). During the Council of Nicaea, approximately 250 to 318 bishops came from every corner of the Christian Church, including Egypt. During the second ecumenical council held in Constantinople in AD 381, the bishops reaffirmed the Nicene Creed. Because the Council of Nicaea had not clarified the deity of the Holy Spirit in AD 325, the Nicene Creed was enlarged to include affirmations about the Holy Spirit. During the third ecumenical council in Chalcedon in AD 451, the Nicene Creed was again reaffirmed.

Those who dismiss the Nicene Creed as western and enmeshed in Greek philosophy must reckon with the fact that both the Eastern and Western branches of the churches, including North Africa, participated in this consensus. In fact, several of the chief contributors to the Nicene Creed, directly or indirectly, were theologians from North Africa including Tertullian (c. 155 – c. 230) of

Carthage, Origen (c. 184 – c. 253) of Alexandria, and Athanasius (296-373) of Alexandria.

Those theologians today who claim that the Nicene Creed is unintelligible should remember that the hordes of Germanic tribes who invaded Rome were called Barbarians because they knew not Latin or Greek and were strangers to the Graeco-Roman culture. Yet they eventually embraced the Nicene Creed when they became Catholics. Martin Luther, the German Protestant Reformer, endorsed it. So did all Christians worldwide in many different cultures until the Enlightenment in Western Europe sowed seeds of doubt and unbelief.

Their problem was not the abstract, philosophical language, but the concept of the Trinity. They rejected the supernatural, the spirit world, divine revelation, miracles and prophecy. They rejected the God who is revealed in the Bible. For this reason they cannot comprehend the Nicene Creed. It needs to be demythologized, Bultmann said. Many African theologians have sat at their feet, learning and believing these western theologies of post-modernism which in turn have formed their presuppositions and preunderstanding as they write African theologies.

The Nicene Creed and Greek Philosophy: The doctrinal issues debated at Nicaea were absolutely critical for Christianity for they centred on Jesus Christ, his Person and purpose in coming; it sought to state carefully the relationship of Jesus Christ and the Holy Spirit to the one eternal God.

These Christian leaders were absolutely committed to belief in one and only one true God, the Creator of heaven and earth as revealed to Israel and written in the Holy Scriptures by the Hebrew prophets. And yet Jesus had revealed himself, both in his teaching and through his resurrection, that he was truly God (see Chapter 5).

These men, living in the Graeco-Roman world and using both Latin and Greek, were conversant with the philosophies of the day which contributed to the Greek language vocabulary. During the fourth and fifth centuries heated discussions and debates enveloped these Christian leaders.

Contrary to common belief, the danger which threatened the Church was not persecution from enemies outside the Church, but from "the Greek menace" that made them vulnerable to syncretism from within the Church. Kenneth Scott Latourette, the historian of international repute, made this keen observation:

> *As it moved out into the non-Jewish world it was in danger of so far conforming to that environment that it would sacrifice the essential features of the Gospel. The threat was especially acute from Hellenism and the atmosphere of the Hellenistic world...The danger was not conformity to polytheism, for against that Christians were quite adamant. It was more subtle and therefore more to be feared. It was the incorporation of some of the attitudes of the Hellenistic mind. One of these was the confidence in philosophy as the way to truth, or, in a less thorough-going conformity, the attempt to think through and present the Gospel in the categories of Greek philosophy. In the process the Gospel might be distorted or obscured* (Latourette 1975: 122).

This intrinsic danger of syncretism was serious because the Greek and Roman converts were steeped in the philosophies of Platonism and Neoplatonism. These pagan views persisted deep in their minds and thinking.

The Church held tenaciously to a core of divinely revealed truths:

(1) "The unity of God was basic."

(2) "The deity of each of the three persons, Father, Son and Holy Spirit."

(3) "The Threeness and the oneness of God are not in the same respect." Though the Trinity seems to defy logic (God is both one and yet three), the contradiction is only apparent, not real. For the doctrine of the Trinity teaches that God is one in one sense, but three in another sense.

(4) "The Trinity is eternal."

(5) "In the final analysis, the Trinity is incomprehensible. We cannot fully understand the mystery of the Trinity" (Erickson 1998: 363f).

As these church leaders debated these theological issues, controversies arose when Christian leaders proposed doctrines that were contrary to the prevailing beliefs. Arius (c. 250-236), a presbyter from Alexandria, Egypt, in his desire to protect monotheism, denied the deity of Christ. He taught that Christ was not eternal, but had a beginning by the creative act of God prior to time.

Jean Sabellius (c. 215), a third century priest from Rome, made another attempt to avoid polytheism. He proposed that God was three in manifestation of forms, not in essence. This became known as modalism, or Sabellianism. The one God appeared in the Old Testament as Yahweh, in the Gospels as Jesus, and in the Church as the Holy Spirit.

In order to protect orthodoxy, the Nicene Creed was written in AD 325 and further expanded and ratified in AD 381. The creed is not, for the most part, an abstract or static statement. The Nicene Creed is full of activity and very concrete with reference to actions taken in time and space.

The one part of the Creed which we might call abstract is found in numbers 6-9 above and should be understood in the light of the Christological controversies threatening the orthodoxy of the Church in the fourth and fifth centuries from Arius and Sabellius. It was Athanasius of North Africa who effectively countered Arianism through persuasive arguments based on biblical exposition.

The key affirmations are these (Noll 2000: 57-59):

(1) Christ is *"very God of very God."* Repudiating Arius who claimed that Jesus Christ was a created god, the Nicene Creed affirms that Jesus is God in the same sense that the Father is God. The Father and Son may be different in the tasks they perform or in their inter-personal relationships, but in their essence or nature, they are one.

(2) Christ is *"of one substance with the Father."* The word, *homoousios* (*ὁμοουσιος*), means "same substance." This affirmation led to great controversy because the Greek word, *homoousios,* is not found in the Bible, but was a technical term used in philosophy. A large part of the Church preferred the word, *homoiousios,* meaning "similar substance." The addition of the little Greek letter, iota (ι), created heated debate. Finally, "of one substance with the Father" was approved because it restated what had already been affirmed, "very God of very God," and because Jesus himself had said, "*I and the Father are one*" (Jn 10:30).

(3) Christ was *"the only begotten Son of God," was "begotten, not made."* "Begotten, not made," diverges from the teachings of Arius. The catholic Christians affirmed the eternality of Christ – Jesus had no beginning.

The King James translation of the Greek word, *monogenes* (*μονογενης*), ("only begotten") in John 3:16 and in similar passages is somewhat misleading. Jesus was neither created by God to become a god, nor was he "begotten" as we speak of children being "begotten" of their parents. Jesus had no beginning. He is eternal. The word, *μονογενης,* simply means "only." Jesus is the "unique" Son of God, the "one-of-a-kind" Son of God (Bauer 1957).

The more contemporary translations of John 3:16 read, "the only Son" (ESV) or "the one and only Son" (*NIV*). The Jehovah's Witnesses are in gross error when they follow Arius by falsely translating John 1:1, "the Word was **a** god" and consider Jesus a created being.

The word, *μονογενης,* does mean literally, "only begotten," as found in the Nicene Creed and the Authorized Version. Some argue that in light of John 1:13, it should be translated as "the only begotten Son" as in John 3:16.

However, the Bauer Greek Lexicon argues that in that case, *μονογενης,* ("only begotten") should be understood as *protatakas* (*πρωτοτοκος*), (meaning "firstborn"), and taken in a figurative sense of Christ as "the first-born of a new humanity which is to be glorified, as its exalted Lord is glorified (Ro 8:29; Heb 1:6; Rev 2:8).

Though the Nicene Creed was approved by the bishops in the first Ecumenical Council in A.D. 325, large numbers of Christians found difficulty with it. Human logic argues against the Trinity. It seems more logical to say that Jesus was "like" God in his nature or substance, rather than saying that he was of the "same" nature or substance. Besides, the term, *homoousios,* had a lengthy history in Hellenistic philosophy and is not found in the Bible.

However, through the compelling efforts of Athanasius, and the persuasive evidence of Scripture, the Nicene Creed was finally accepted by the whole Catholic Church, East and West, North and South. If we accept the teachings of Scripture, the divinity of Christ ***is*** a doctrinal verity. Jesus is not a created god with a beginning – another god – but he is one with the true eternal God.

One of the clearest passages in the epistles is in Romans 9:5: "*To them [the Israelites] belong the patriarchs, and from their race, according to the flesh, is the Christ who is God over all, blessed forever, Amen*."

The question arises, did the early Church Fathers accommodate the Greek culture and absorb Greek philosophy in their creedal statements? The clear evidence in the Nicene Creed is that they did not. The Trinity as described in the Nicene Creed surely is not rooted in Greek philosophy. The church fathers used Greek vocabulary which had been used in Greek philosophy, but they used the words only to communicate divinely revealed truth in Scripture. Just as the apostle John used the Greek word, *logos,* but proceeded to fill it with meaning far different from that which was taught in Greek philosophy.

Mark Noll comments,

> *The Nicene Creed has remained for nearly seventeen centuries a secure foundation for the church's theology, worship, and prayer. Not only does it succinctly summarize the facts of biblical revelation, but it also stands as a bulwark against the persistent human tendency to prefer logical deductions concerning what God must be like and how he must act to the lived realities of God's self-disclosure. And it*

> *powerfully restates the realities of Christ's divine nature, his incarnation as a human being, and the work of salvation he accomplishes for his people. The turning point in Christian history represented by the Nicene Creed was the church's critical choice for the wisdom of God in preference to human wisdom* (Noll 2000: 59).

Status of Creedal Statements

The Nicene Creed, like all other creeds, is man-made. Creeds are not divinely inspired and breathed-out by God. They remain subject to the authority of the written Word of God. A Christian Creed, like all doctrine, is a human effort to state a human understanding of what the Scripture teaches. Some creeds are in error and need to be discarded. But the Nicene Creed has stood for seventeen hundred years because the universal Church believes it is biblically based.

Creeds are also culturally impacted. The Nicene Creed was composed in the fourth century within the Graeco-Roman world in order to combat a particular kind of error. Eleven hundred years later, Melanchthon, on behalf of the Lutherans, composed the Augsburg Confession to combat perceived errors in the Roman Catholic Church. These and all creeds are time bound, but that does not mean that they are time barred and useless for later generations.

May Christians in Africa compose their own creed? Why not, unless they cease to base their affirmations on Scripture? An African creed written by Evangelicals might indeed be useful in order to combat the errors threatening the African Christian Church. But this can be done without repudiating the Nicene Creed which has been the bedrock of universal Christian orthodoxy. We should not study Scripture in a vacuum as if we were the first Christians to think through the biblical teachings of the Triune God. Christians have a rich heritage and we should learn from those who have gone before.

The biblical teaching that the one Creator God is Three-in-One is truly a mystery, but truly biblical. Suggestions for using African traditions and metaphors to illustrate and explain the biblical teaching could prove to be challenging if one desires to be faithful to Scripture without re-inventing Christianity.

James Kombo, an evangelical African scholar, is committed to the biblical doctrine of the Trinity and defends the Nicene Creed. He has researched extensively and thought deeply on the subject, and has published a noteworthy proposal for an African Biblical Theology of the Trinity seen through African eyes. He sought to be true to Scripture, saying. "If we wish to articulate any aspect of Christian doctrine, we must be prepared to be students of the Holy Scriptures" (Kombo 2007: 254).

But he also believes that "African theology needs to entrench the doctrine of the Trinity in its own cultural milieu" (Kombo 2007: 9). Early church creeds should be reinterpreted or translated for the African context (Kombo 2007: 77). Using "the African intellectual tools or symbols" will help translate the doctrine of the Trinity (Kombo 2007: 7f).

Kombo is clearly committed to the early church creedal statements on the Trinity. They are relevant, he says. Africans do not need to formulate the doctrine of the Trinity afresh, as if the church in whose tradition it stands never did anything to that effect. Africans cannot ignore the creeds (Kombo 2007: 77).

His ideas are worthy of consideration within the context of his commitment to biblical revelation and the value of the Nicene Creed.

In no way is our apologetic defence of the Nicene Creed intended to deny the influence of Greek-Roman philosophy and culture on the discussions of the early church fathers. Western theologians did interact with philosophy and utilized its vocabulary in their theologizing.

But they Christianized Greek vocabulary, such as *ουσια* (being) and the Latin word, *persona* (person), to convey biblically revealed truth. In much the same way that the translations of the Scriptures into African languages used the vocabulary available with all of their cultural and religious nuances to translate biblical revelation, and in the process, changed their meanings. What must be strongly stated is that Christian theology was not syncretized in the fourth and fifth centuries with Greek philosophy.

Tertullian in the third century, for example, is the first known person to have used the word Trinity. As a trained lawyer he employed terms familiar with the law courts. He was the one who suggested the Latin word, *substantia* (or substance), derived from Roman legal terminology, to refer to the essence or nature of God. He further suggested the Latin word, *persona* (or person), to refer to the three members of the Godhead (Latourette 1975: 145).

None of these Greek or Latin words are adequate to describe the mystery of the Trinity. A "person" in our thinking is an individual separate and autonomous from other "persons." In Tertullian's thinking, "person" was a word in Roman law where it meant "a party in a legal action." This is not the relationship of the Father, Son and Holy Spirit as revealed in the Scriptures. The three Persons of the Trinity are not three separate entities. The word, *persona* (person), is very deficient for it does not say precisely what God has revealed of himself.

Human language is inadequate to communicate fully the wonders of the Creator God, but it is sufficient for God to reveal something of himself. The belief that God is one in essence and three in persons has withstood the test of time because, like persons, the Father, Son and Spirit commune with each other and interact with each other. Each one has a different function in the procuring of our salvation. Yet they are not three separate entities, but the Three-in-One eternal God.

Efforts have been made to illustrate or explain the Trinity, but inevitably they fall short or convey erroneous ideas. In some respects the best illustration of the Trinity, in my opinion, is a triangle with each point representing a different Member of the Trinity. Each point shares the same triangular "essence" of the triangle. Though the Father, Son and Holy Spirit communicate with each other and have different tasks to perform, each Person shares the same essence or nature. Wherever the Father is (omnipresent), the Son and the Holy Spirit are. Whatever attributes the Father has, the Son and the Spirit share the same. Whatever worship the Father receives, the Son and Spirit receive the same.

Is this a mystery? Yes, but a glorious mystery. And the Church Fathers at the Council of Nicaea were enabled by God to express the biblical teaching in an admirable way that still affirms the orthodoxy of the Christian Church today although all human effort to express the mysteries of the Godhead fall short.

AFRICAN ANCESTORS IN AFRICAN THEOLOGY

Among many African communities the ancestor cult is the most dynamic and dominant feature of their worldview. This has led many African theologians to seek ways of incorporating the ancestors into African Theology, but no consensus has arisen how this might be done.

Perspective of African Theologians

Many African theologians believe that provision should be made in Christian theology for remembering and honouring African ancestors. Setiloane (b. 1922) declared: "...to take the ancestors from an African is robbing him of his personality" (Setiloane 1978: 406). C.G. Baeta (1908-1994) wrote, "The Africans live with their dead" (Bediako 1995: 216).

Jean-Marc Ela, born in Cameroon in 1922, became a diocesan priest, a professor and author of theology, philosophy, social sciences, and an advocate for Liberation Theology. He asked the question, "Can we be at peace with our conscience, if conversion requires that we live separated from the dead of our family, without any possibility of contact with them in the periods of crisis?" (Ela 1988: 31). He further inquired, "Is there any place in our life in Jesus Christ for maintaining a relationship between the living and the dead? Or must Africans break their relationships with their ancestors if they are to be converted to the gospel?" (Ela 1988: 18).

Edward Fashole-Luke, born in 1934 in Sierra Leone, an Anglican priest and former teacher in Fourah Bay College, was one of the first Africans to suggest that African ancestors should be included in the Communion of Saints found in the Roman Catholic and Anglican churches. He feared that all would be lost "unless the Churches develop a theology of the Communion of Saints that will satisfy the passionate desire of Africans, Christian and non-Christian alike, to be linked with their dead ancestors" (Glasswell 1974).

Agbonkhianmeghe Orobator, a Jesuit priest, finds "deep resonance in [his] traditional beliefs and understanding of the meaning of life" whenever he professes "faith in the communion of saints and the resurrection of the dead." He finds support for this in the apocryphal writings (Sirach 44-49) and in Hebrews 11:4-39 (Orobator 2008: 105-106).

He claims that not any African becomes an ancestor, only those who fulfil certain conditions before they die. One must leave a positive legacy, model an exemplary character with life-enhancing skills and behaviour (Orobator 2008: 107f). This, he asserts, is much the same as the process known as canonization in the Roman Catholic tradition (Orobator 2008: 107).

The heading that commences his discussion on ancestors is telling: "Our Fathers and Mothers who art in Heaven." As a Roman Catholic Christian, he is taught to assist with prayers the dead who are suffering judgement in purgatory.

In like manner Orobator believes Africans should pray for their ancestors who have lived their lives consistent with the Beatitudes in Matthew 5. If you treat others with respect and compassion, if you mourn over injustice, if you work tirelessly for justice, equality and human dignity etc., "such a person," Orobator claims, "is indeed covered by the blood of Jesus, and his or her life is totally dedicated to God." He recommends that prayers should be offered for all noble Africans in this manner:

> *Kwame Nkruma, champion of the unity of all African nations.*
> *Response: Present!*

> *Patrice Lumumba, champion of the democratic freedom of the African peoples. Response: Present!*
>
> *Julius Nyerere, Promoter of Ujamaa and African family solidarity. Response: Present!"* (Orobator 2008: 112).

Others believe the African ancestors should be the prism through which Christian Christology and Ecclesiology should be viewed. Ka Mana, Professor at Institut Protestant de Theologie de Porto-Nova in Benin, proposes that salvation in Christ should be interpreted through the perspective of the African ancestors. He declares:

> We view it [salvation in Jesus Christ] from the primordial place where our ancestors of old handed down to us great wisdom, tools of knowledge, customs and lifestyle, through which we may welcome Jesus Christ as one of us, deep within the 'grove of initiation,' in this ancestral hearth, vital energy which determines our identity as a people, civilization, and culture (Mana 2004: 3).

Ka Mana of Congo also views "salvation in Jesus Christ" "against the background of all our religious ideals and spiritual powers where Christianity occupies an equally important place alongside Islam and African traditional religions" (Mana 2004: 3).

Contrary to the many African theologians just mentioned above, however, numerous African Initiated Churches have repudiated the ancestral cult. This African Christian movement of African Initiated/Independent Churches is hailed by many African theologians as the most authentic African expression of Christianity. It is, therefore, quite ironical that many African Independent Churches which broke away from the mission founded churches continue to repudiate the ancestral cult. However, the movement is not unified. Ancestors "still play an important role and are to be respected and obeyed" among some AICs in South Africa

But "the most frequent response" of African Initiated Churches toward the ancestors is "*confrontation* as many AICs reject the ancestor observances" (italics original). They reject the ancestors' appearances to Christians. "New Pentecostal and Charismatic churches usually give an unqualified rejection of ancestors and as we've seen, they're the most confrontational of all AICs with regard to traditional beliefs" (Anderson 2001: 203). "...a Spirit-inspired confrontation with the ancestor observances has usually replaced traditional beliefs with Christian alternatives...Many AICs have effectively reduced dependence on ancestors in the lives of their members, although some believe that ancestors reveal themselves to African prophets and must be respected" (Anderson 2001: 204).

Other African theologians have raised the question whether a focus on past African traditions is relevant in a dynamically changing Africa of the twenty-first century. Ezigbo observes, "The issue of reuniting with their ancestors was undoubtedly a primary concern of the majority of African peoples in the early era of the Western missionary expeditions. It is, however, doubtful if it is still a major concern of many of the present-day Africans who are seriously losing their grasp of the sense of community that characterized the traditional society" (Ezigbo 2010: 32).

Examination of Kwame Bediako's Views

We need to examine more closely Bediako's view of the African ancestors and their place in Christianity.

Biographical Sketch of Bediako: Kwame Bediako, born in 1945 in Accra, Ghana, and a self-described evangelical with distinguished academic credentials and reputation, demands careful consideration of his views on ancestors. His parents were nominal Presbyterians, though his father frequented the local ancestral shrine. Kwame himself was disinterested in Christianity during his youth. While studying in Bordeaux, France, "he was collared, like Saul on his way to Damascus." When struck that "Christ is the Truth, integrating principle of life as well as the key to true intellectual coherence," he felt an "irresistible force" compelling him to read the Bible through many times. Through this reading of Scripture he was "soundly converted to Christ" (Bediako 2004: xii).

Following his conversion he felt led to study theology which began at London Bible College and concluded at the University of Aberdeen, earning his Ph.D. under the internationally renowned Professor Andrew Walls. His thesis, completed in 1983, is entitled, *Theology and Identity: The Impact of Culture upon Christian Thought in the Second Century and Modern Africa.* It was published in 1992.

In the words of Keith Ferdinando, this book is "indeed a *tour de force*, one of the most substantial scholarly contributions to an issue that is central for African Christianity, and which deserves the courtesy of serious reflection and careful probing and response" (Ferdinando 2007: 124).

Returning home, Bediako was ordained in the Presbyterian Church, Ghana, and began teaching. He founded and directed the Akrofi-Christaller Memorial Centre for Mission Research and Applied Theology, a creative and innovative achievement. The Centre specializes in African theology, language and cultural studies in order to Africanize the Gospel.

His studies for his PhD were formative and shaped his development of African Theology. He chose to study four church fathers: Tatian and Tertullian who stressed discontinuity between Christianity and Greek culture, and Justin and Clement of Alexander who emphasized continuity. For modern African theologians he chose: Bolaji Idowu, a Nigerian Methodist who promoted a "radical continuity;" Vincent Mulago, a Congolese Roman Catholic who set forth a "less radical" continuity; John Mbiti, a Kenyan Anglican, a main stream liberal stressing continuity; and Byang Kato, a Nigerian evangelical who stressed "a radical discontinuity" (Bediako 2004: 54f).

Bediako chose to emulate Justin and Clement of Alexandria, champions of continuity, even though, in his own observation, the theological emphasis of discontinuity has a long and reputable history. He believed that it was essential to gain a new understanding of African primal religions which had been ignored or denigrated by the missionaries. Bediako sought to recover a positive view of ATR in order to develop "a creative African evangelical Christian apologetics..." (Bediako 2004: 37).

Bediako's Proposals: Since the ancestors were "the most powerful aspect of religious life" among many Africans, Bediako concluded, "It becomes essential, therefore, that there should be a Christian theology of ancestors" (Bediako 1995: 216). This is a common theme among African theologians, though unique among professing evangelicals.

Bediako's theology of ancestors must be understood in light of his emphasis on continuity between Christianity and African Traditional Religion, and his view of the universality of Christ. This was buttressed by the examples of Justin and Clement of Alexandria. These early church fathers rejected the pagan, polytheistic religions of the Greeks and Romans, but looked favourably on the Socratic tradition, one narrow strand of Greek philosophy not followed by the masses. Justin and Clement believed this continuity was due to partial illumination through the universal presence of the Logos, based on John 1:9. The pre-incarnate Word was operating within the non-Christian world, they believed.

On this basis Bediako declared that the Gospel was known partially by the Africans and were saved thereby. "...the cross-cultural transmission did not bring Christ into the local African situation...Christ, already present in the situation, called in His messengers so that by proclamation and incarnation, He might be manifest" (Bediako 1995: 226). "Local ancestors who prepared the way for the coming of the Gospel emerge as fellow witnesses in the 'multitude that no one could count...'" (Rev 7:9-10). A doctrine of the Communion of Saints, in this sense of the cloud of witnesses, therefore becomes the outcome of a theology of ancestors" (Bediako 1995: 226).

Evangelical Affirmations of Bediako: Seeking to develop a Christian theology of ancestors is surely a challenge. Unlike other African theologians, Bediako tries to maintain his evangelical convictions. He is Trinitarian and holds to the authority of Scripture. He believes in the deity and humanity of Christ and his centrality in Christianity with his atoning death and the necessity of faith. Though ancestors are "worthy of honour" for the benefits they have brought, "Christ has done infinitely more." "Jesus Christ surpasses our natural ancestors also by virtue of who he is in himself." Ancestors are human but Christ is "the Son of the Father (Heb 1:1ff)" (Bediako 1990: 40f). Furthermore, "once Jesus Christ comes, the ancestors are cut off as a means of blessing and we lay our power-lines differently...God's saving activity towards us is focused on Christ, mediated through the Holy Spirit" (Bediako 1995: 217). Bediako devotes himself to "the evangelical affirmation of the uniqueness of Jesus Christ in the religiously plural environment in which most of us live..." (Bediako 2004: 37).

Mythologizing African Traditional Religion: However, troubling questions arise from his positive assessment of African Traditional Religion and his embrace of African ancestors in Christian theology. Westerners, who are troubled by the supernatural aspects of the Bible, choose to reinterpret the Bible by demythologizing it – reinterpreting biblical accounts of miracles, prophecies and the supernatural to mean what they did not mean originally.

Many Africans do the reverse with African Traditional Religion. They idealize the past, and in effect, they mythologize African traditions to make them appear what they never were. Bediako claims that it is "the myth-making imagination of the community itself which sacralises them [ancestors], conferring upon them sacred authority...the potency of the cult of ancestors is *not* the potency of ancestors themselves; the potency of the cult is the potency of myth" (Bediako 1990: 40). Instead of theologizing about the ancestors as they were traditionally venerated, he mythologizes them, omitting their darker side while eulogizing their imaginary positive role.

Belief in ancestors varies greatly among the 1,000 African communities. What is true in one community is not true in another. Africans who have grown up in ATR must make the final call. This surely is not in my area of experience or expertise. But in my limited research I have discovered that ancestors in Kenya are not benevolent. They may bring benefits, but they also frighten the living with many afflictions. Nor do the living welcome ancestors for fellowship. They are feared because they make incessant demands of sacrifices to the point of impoverishment. Furthermore, the cult of the ancestors retarded progress for they demanded that the living hold on to African traditions. Christians with whom I have spoken do not treasure their memories of the ancestor cult, but found joyful relief in their deliverance from spiritual captivity.

Continuity between Christianity and African Traditional Religion: Bediako's theology of ancestors relies heavily on the theology of continuity expounded by Justin and Clement of Alexandria, second and third century theologians, and the puzzling text in John 1:9. He is unconvincing! Keith Ferdinando observes:

> *...in the light of two millennia of Christian reflection, it is a long step from this single enigmatic text to a positive evaluation of non-Christian religion, including African traditional religion. To the extent that one might look for a substantial biblical foundation for Bediako's arguments, as opposed to one based on the arguments of second century theologians, this must be judged one of the more vulnerable points in his case* (Ferdinando 2007: 126).

The relationship of Christianity with African Traditional Religion is contentious. Although Bediako classifies Byang Kato with "radical discontinuity," evidence demonstrates that he did believe in a measure of continuity with African culture. And although Bediako identifies with "continuity," he in fact does not embrace everything in ATR. Few theologians hold to absolute continuity or discontinuity between ATR and Christianity. Elsewhere I have argued that the biblical position is one of "continuity/discontinuity" (Gehman 1989: 396-402). You can find evidence for continuity between ATR and Christianity as well as discontinuity.

Basis for Determining Truth and Error: The problem is, however, on what basis does one determine what is right and what is wrong? What elements of ATR might be considered continuous with the Christian faith and what are discontinuous? Assuming that we must reject certain teachings and practices of a non-Christian religion, what criteria should be used to make that judgement? We have seen that in most cases the decision is based on personal preference of the theologian.

For evangelicals the normative standard by which we judge something is the written Word of God. If we accept the finality of Scripture, one is severely challenged to defend a positive theology of ancestors, even in the prescribed way of Bediako.

A compelling argument can be made that the spirits manifested in the ancestral cults worldwide are not the spirits of the departed, but evil spirits (Gehman 1999: 177-187). Because this is such a difficult and contentious issue, let us lay that argument aside and assume that Africans are in actual contact with their departed ancestors, the living-dead.

Communication with the Dead is Divinely Forbidden: Communication with the dead in Africa is intimately connected with mediums, and the Bible clearly condemns any consultation with mediums. Israel was commanded not to imitate the religious practices of the Canaanites when they entered the

Promised Land. God declared, "*Let no one be found among you...who practices divination or sorcery, interprets omens, engages in witchcraft, or casts spells, or who is a medium or spiritist...*" (Dt 18:10-11). God further commanded, "*Do not turn to mediums or seek out spirits, for you will be defiled by them. I am the LORD your God*" (Lev 19:31).

Furthermore, any attempt to contact the dead was utterly forbidden. No one was permitted to "consult the dead" (Dt 18:11). Late in Israel's history, during the monarchy, many Jews were drawn to the dead, seeking their guidance and help. But Isaiah declared, "*When men tell you to consult mediums and spirits, who whisper and mutter, should not a people inquire of their God? Why consult the dead on behalf of the living? To the law and to the testimony!*" (Isa 8:19-20).

The Medieval Catholic Church accommodated pagan practices by teaching people to pray to and for the dead. Roman Catholic Africans today promote the idea that angels can replace divinities and the ancestral cult prepares the ground for the Communion of Saints. They argue, "The strong attachment to ancestors makes it easy to promote both devotion to the saints and prayers for the departed" (Bediako 1995: 216). For Protestant Evangelicals, however, the notion of praying for or to the dead is appalling. It is contrary to God's revelation. Scripture offers no support.

In view of these forceful prohibitions against the cult of ancestors, it would seem abhorrent to identify them with the "Communion of Saints." Furthermore, Bediako feels that "by virtue of [Christ's] Incarnation, death, resurrection and ascension into the realm of spirit-power, [Jesus] can rightly be designated, in African terms, Ancestor, indeed Supreme Ancestor" (Bediako 1995: 217). Bediako, hereby, seeks to make ancestors an integral part of Christology and Ecclesiology – the theology of Christ and the Church.

Dubious Basis for Incorporating Ancestors in Theology: Naming Christ as "Supreme Ancestor" in African tradition is a stretch of the imagination. Ancestors are by their very nature antecedent and progenitors of the living. As Bediako says, they are "natural" ancestors and he affirms that Christ does not correspond with ancestors in this way. He argues that "natural ancestors" remain human and "cannot ultimately be rivals of Christ in Christian consciousness" (Bediako 1995: 217f). Therefore, I assume, he does not feel it is harmful to incorporate them in Christian theology.

Bediako uses tortuous logical arguments with specious presuppositions to argue his case. He claims:

> *...a theology of ancestors is about the interpretation of the past in a way which shows that the present experience and knowledge of the grace of God in the Gospel of Jesus Christ have been truly anticipated and prefigured in the quests and the responses to the Transcendent in former times, as these have been reflected in the lives of African people.*
>
> Furthermore, he writes, "*a theology of ancestors becomes, therefore, the corollary and unavoidable by-product of the continuity of God in African experience...If the God of African pre-Christian tradition has turned out to be the God of the Christians, then it is to be expected that He has not left Himself without testimony in the past* (Bediako 1995: 224f).

While agreeing with Bediako that God has not left himself without a witness among any people (Ac 14:17), it is a groundless assumption that ancestors were Christ's witnesses. Why not magicians or sorcerers? Why not divinities or diviners? When Paul declared to the Lycaonians that God "has not left himself without testimony," he points to the rains and bountiful food as God's witness. He did not refer to their religion beliefs which he described as "worthless things."

Bediako makes an unjustified assumption that ancestors were saved, members of the Communion of Saints, and preparers for the coming of Christ who now supersedes them. If the decision is not left up to the personal judgement of a theologian, then Scripture should have the final say.

To include African ancestors in the Communion of Saints raises many basic theological questions. Are African ancestors included in Paul's sweeping judgement of human beings in Romans 3:9-18? Since "all have sinned" and "the wages of sin is death," on what basis can we say that these ancestors were redeemed by Christ? What evidence do we have that African ancestors before the preaching of the Gospel were saved by faith? Faith in whom? Orobator believes that by obeying the beatitudes, they are covered by the blood of Jesus and are saints who were "totally dedicated to God" (Orobator 2008: 110). This is salvation by works, contrary to biblical teaching (Eph 2:8-9).

Bediako does not go that far explicitly, but he does believe that Africans have "lived exemplary lives." How then are they saved from their sins? By their "exemplary lives"? Bediako does not say, but what he does state is dubious:

> *Local ancestors who prepared the way for the coming of the Gospel emerge as fellow witnesses in the 'multitude that no one could count...' (Rev. 7:9-10). A doctrine of the Communion of Saints, in this sense of the cloud of witnesses, therefore becomes the outcome of a theology of ancestors* (Bediako 1995: 226).

Bediako's commitment to continuity, based on little more than the view of two second and third century theologians, allows him to create an African theology of ancestors that cannot be founded on the Scriptures. Instead of focusing on ancestors as evidence of God's prevenient grace, why doesn't Bediako speak of their pre-Christian knowledge about God? That would have firm footing in the Bible. But Scripture also indicates that this knowledge about God was suppressed by the Africans (Ro 1:18ff), and there is an abundance of evidence for this in ATR. This leaves Africans where all humanity are left: utterly dependent on the grace of God.

Many believe that Paul's preaching in Athens supports continuity with non-Christian religions. In contrast to African ancestors with all of their negative baggage, Paul took the least offensive item from the Athenian paganism to preach Christ. Paul declared, "*Now what you worship as something unknown I am going to proclaim to you*" (Ac 17:23).

When Paul first entered Athens he was "*greatly distressed* to see that the city was full of idols" (Ac 17:16 *NIV*); in other words, he was "provoked" (*NASB*), a strong word in the Greek meaning that Paul was "*irritated*." *The MESSAGE* paraphrases this by saying: "*The longer Paul waited in Athens for Silas and Timothy, the angrier he got – all those idols! The city was a junkyard of idols.*"

Paul did not see idolatry as a preparation for the Gospel. He took the least offensive idol, one devoted to "an unknown god," the one with the least pejorative ideas attached to it – they knew *nothing* about this god – and used it as a bridge, a point of contact, to declare the Good News of the living God.

And at the close of his sermon he called on these Greeks to "*repent*" because one day God would judge the world with justice (Ac 17:30-31). As theologians we can see God's prevenient grace preparing the way for the preaching of the Gospel, but their required response before God was to *repent* before standing at the judgement of the great white throne (Rev 20:11).

Conclusion

I remember vividly attending a theological conference in 1974 at the Brackenhurst Conference Center near Nairobi, Kenya. African theologians read their papers on the topic of ancestors. Prominent among them was Professor Edward Fashole-Luke, an Anglican from Sierra Leone, who read a paper on "Ancestor Veneration and the Communion of Saints." He questioned why Africans should not pray to and for their ancestors if westerners are encouraged to pray to the saints?

I heartily agreed with him, but lamented the direction he was taking in promoting the incorporation of dead Africans, who knew not Jesus Christ, to be part of the Communion of Saints, and then encouraging Christians to pray to them. As we turned to questions and discussion, I heard some evangelical Anglicans sitting nearby commenting in hushed tones, "We are in big trouble!"

Yes, indeed! The Church is in "big trouble" when they turn away from the clear teaching of Scripture. How sad that evangelical Christians should bypass the Protestant Reformation and turn back to the errors of medieval Roman Catholicism which accommodated pagan practices! Where can you find any biblical support for prayers to Mary and the saints? Where can you find evidence that we should bypass Jesus Christ as the one Mediator between God and man, and instead plead for help from the dead?

How sad when African Christians, in reaction to wrongs done in the past, should seek dignity and self-esteem by reimagining their past religious practices and clothe them in Christian garb! Rephrasing Isaiah 8:19-20, "*Why pray to the dead on behalf of the living? Instead, we should seek divine guidance and help from the living God through Jesus Christ and from his holy Word.*"

Why presume to take God's place and declare that the dead are among the saints? God is merciful and no doubt has revealed himself especially to those whom God chooses to save. But it is not our prerogative, apart from the declared Word of God, to theologize unilaterally according to our personal preference.

When Abraham pleaded with God for his nephew, Lot, who lived in Sodom, he prayed, "*Far be it from you to do such a thing – to kill the righteous with the wicked, treating the righteous and the wicked alike. Far be it from you! Will not the Judge of all the earth do right*?" (Ge 18:25). When troubling questions arise about our ancestors who never heard the Gospel, our faith should be in God who will do what is right, trusting in his mercy, grace and justice, rather than theologizing on baseless theories and erroneous traditions. Our hope is in God and in his Word, not in theologians and their home-spun theologies.

7

A NEW WAY OF DOING AFRICAN THEOLOGY

The first six chapters of this book have prepared us for this final chapter. African theologians have every need and right to study Scripture for themselves to seek an understanding of God's will for their own lives in Africa. Context is important when addressing particular issues and perspectives.

As the living Body of Christ we are interdependent with one another throughout history and the world. We learn from one another. But African Theology, if it is to be built on a solid foundation, must be based entirely on the Scriptures, "the word of God [that] stands forever" (Isa 40:8). We approach Scripture with confidence in its integrity and historical trustworthiness. Our confidence in God's Word is based on Jesus Christ who rose again from the dead. And we interpret the Bible to learn the author's intention and meaning, and then apply it meaningfully to our own lives through the illumination of the Holy Spirit.

Scores of evangelical African theologians have been providing a lasting legacy for the African Church to build them up in the Faith. For those who have adopted a sceptical understanding of Scriptures from the modern western worldview, it would seem prudent for them to reconsider their approach to the Bible in view of the overwhelming evidence of Christ's bodily resurrection from the dead. A major paradigm shift is needed before they can ever hope to provide the African Church with edifying helps in biblical studies.

African Christian Theology Revisited assumes that God's Word has the final authority over whatever we may proclaim. This chapter, however, moves on to a proposed new methodology for doing theology.

It has become a virtual shibboleth to say that African culture focuses on the community. Kinship is a dominant feature of African life. Individuals do not exist, only persons in relationship. "I am because we are; and since we are, therefore I am," in the words of John Mbiti (1969: 104).

If this is true, then it would seem that doing African theology should be done in community and in relationships. This would be in contrast to western ways of doing theology, an individual cloistered inside a building lined with thousands of books. The western traditional way of composing a book is library and archival research by individuals. For a PhD dissertation field research may be included as the budding scholar prepares questionnaires and engages in interviews.

The new way of doing African Theology recommended in this book is the communal, inter-personal approach. The wealth of knowledge in Africa is not found primarily on the printed page in libraries, but in the hearts and minds of the Africans themselves. To do African Theology one should dialogue with individuals while studying Scripture together.

Following are several fruitful models which follow this approach.

THE THEOLOGICAL ADVISORY GROUP

My experience which took me down this fruitful trail was my involvement with the Theological Advisory Group, a research and renewal group in the Africa Inland Church, Kenya (A.I.C.).

The need was straightforward. Pastoral leadership recognized numerous issues that plagued the church. In the western church, rich in resources, one could attend seminars, or read books and journals on the subject. These possibilities rarely exist in Africa. God's Word has the answer, but how do we ascertain God's word for any particular issue? How do we apply biblical teaching to the African context?

The answer was a research *team* of trained pastors who would meet together periodically, search the Scriptures, do field research, and collectively discuss and share ideas for resolving the problem. Providentially in God's timing and direction, the A.I.C. National Bible Schools Committee (NBSC) embraced the concept of the Theological Advisory Group (TAG) and appointed me as the Coordinator and Manuscript Drafter for TAG.

The NBSC was composed of the Principals representing nearly twenty Bible training institutions within the Africa Inland Church, Kenya, as well as Theological Education by Extension and Christian Education. The role of the NBSC was to appoint the members of the Theological Advisory Group and approve whatever was produced by the research teams. The role of TAG was to choose the topics for research, appoint the members of the research team and approve whatever they produced. Thus, whatever was written for publication was approved by the research team of pastors, approved again by the members of TAG, and finally approved by the NBSC.

The First Two Research Teams

After brief deliberation the members of TAG decided that the first research project should be on prayer. This may seem a bit odd, but there were three underlying reasons: first, an increased prayer life in the A.I.C. was a definite need, a definitely *felt* need; secondly, the Bishop of the A.I.C. was himself a man of prayer and often spoke of the need for more prayer in the A.I.C.; and third, TAG was mindful of the need to tread softly on the issue of innovative ideas in theology, not wanting the older leadership of the Church to feel unnerved by younger men suggesting new ideas. TAG needed first to prove themselves supportive of the church and to be non-threatening.

After a couple of years the second topic for research chosen was worship, how to improve worship in the Africa Inland Church. TAG chose this topic because they concluded that Christians did not really understand worship. This was complimentary to the first topic. If both the prayer life and worship of Christians could be renewed, the A.I.C. would truly become a revitalized body of believers.

Each research team met once every three months for a period of three nights and two full days over 30 months. We met in a facility owned by the A.I.C. where food and lodging was provided. Through the experience of the first research team on prayer we learned that the appointment of 10-14 members for the research team was the optimum number because several members would inevitably find it difficult to meet every time. The presence of approximately eight participants proved ideal. Research team members consisted mostly of pastors, trained at different academic levels. For the worship team two local Bible College teachers also participated.

In both projects the members desired to accomplish two goals: first, to study the issue from the Scriptures and apply what we learned to the context, and secondly, to seek ways of communicating these truths to the Church. The end goal was not publication, but edification of the Church.

The coordinator of TAG served both as the chair, secretary, and manuscript drafter. The discussion by the pastors was mutually inspiring. *Every* person made significant contributions. No one was insignificant. We needed each other. One contribution inspired a further insight. As the Scriptures teach, "*As iron sharpens iron, so one man sharpens another*" (Pr 27:17). These pastors knew their people and their churches well, and they knew the Scriptures.

During the three-month interval between our meetings, the pastors were assigned to do field research among their people on particular topics. A questionnaire was prepared to inquire from church members their views on different aspects of prayer and worship within the church. Bible School students were enlisted throughout Kenya to conduct this survey with approximately 1,300 questionnaires returned.

Our purpose for meeting was to research for TAG, but I discovered that these pastors anticipated these meetings for the blessings they received. Busy in their ministry, they found these quarterly gatherings a respite. Their empty fuel tanks were filled through Christian fellowship with colleagues in ministry, daily times devoted to prayer and exhortations from Scripture, and learning from one another through dialogue.

The conclusion of the research team on prayer included a Bible study workbook on prayer with a leader's guide. Thousands of books were sold and hundreds of Bible study groups formed to study the biblical teaching on prayer. Seminars were conducted with church leaders in each linguistic community of the A.I.C. to examine the present state of prayer in the church and to encourage a return to the prayer emphasis found in the apostolic church. Two retreats were arranged for the Bishop and his administrative staff to explain and promote the emphasis on prayer. In God's providence and unknown to us, a man, burdened with prayer renewal and with prayer renewal experience in the United States, applied to the Africa Inland Mission at that very time and joined us in promoting prayer renewal. This effort has continued for over 25 years.

The research team on worship included two publications: one was a Bible study workbook on worship, comparable to the one on prayer, together with a leader's guide. Questions were asked and space provided for students to write their answers in the workbook, while teachers were given help in conducting the inductive study of Scripture. A second book was called, *A Worship Guide: How to Improve Worship in the Africa Inland Church.* This was a practical manual, a how-to-do-it book with many suggestions for improving each part of the worship liturgy.

In order to make this an ongoing effort to improve worship in the churches, a large seminar was conducted for all A.I.C. Bible School and Bible College teachers. The intention was to incorporate worship renewal in the Bible Schools and Colleges. They would become the instruments for improving worship in the churches by training future pastors.

In both cases, prayer and worship, effort was made to make this research practical. The end result was not merely publication, but edification of the church. Theology is not meant for the classroom, but for lay men and women so that they might grow into maturity in Christ.

Extensive notes of all discussions were made by the secretary during the meetings of the Research Team. Every contribution was recorded. It was truly exciting to see how one thought led to another, and then to another and to another. Discussion, if skilfully led, can produce insights that a lone individual does not have. But the discussion must be led artfully in order to avoid meandering and mere talk for talking sake. Discussion can become fruitless and tiresome if not guided toward the projected goals.

The coordinator then became the manuscript drafter who creatively fashioned the many thoughts to form a book. When the research team approved the draft, the manuscript was then given to the members of TAG (Bible School and College teachers) who critiqued it and gave final approval. This process was concluded by giving the revised manuscript to members of the National Bible Schools Committee (Principals of the Bible Schools and Colleges) who gave their final approval.

Authoring a book is a gift which requires graduate training. Not all graduate students are gifted as authors, but all authors of publications need graduate training in research and writing skills. This was a hard lesson learned through experience. All trained pastors can make valuable contributions. They all have insights and understanding, both of their people and of Scripture. But they may not have the gift of writing, nor the training necessary.

The TAG Research Team on Marriage

The third TAG project for research was marriage and family in Africa. Multiple books can be bought from the West on the topic marriage and family, but they are oriented to a totally different culture. Marriage and family in Africa is uniquely different and surely must take on an African flavour. This topic proved to be ideal for collective research.

Early on the research team decided that if we are considering "African Christian marriage and family," we need to understand African traditional marriage. As a result massive effort was made, both in field research with interviews, and through library research. The findings were presented at the quarterly research seminars and dutifully recorded.

If we are being practical, they concluded, we need to understand the marriage laws in Kenya, so we invited a Christian attorney to come and explain the African Christian Marriage Act in Kenya.

The biblical teaching on marriage was basic. For this we were able to use biblical studies produced elsewhere. In order to distinguish between biblical teaching and cultural practices, we listed ten essentials for a genuinely Christian marriage.

A whole range of issues were then researched to determine an African Christian view of them including: family planning, renewal of weddings, polygamy, marriage of widows and widowers, single parents, separation, divorce and marriage, the single state. We studied the problems arising from childlessness, separation from one another because of employment, unfaithfulness of one spouse, wife beating, disagreements over finance, problems with parents and parents-in-law, and disagreement over child rearing.

They considered the issue of choosing a spouse ("courting and dating"). They researched the main features of a Christian marriage in Africa which included: engagement with parental involvement and consent, exchange of gifts (payment of dowry), the wedding ceremony and feast.

They considered the Christian family with the responsibilities of each member according to the Scripture. Ten Commandments for a healthy Christian marriage were presented.

In brief, this research team covered the whole gamut of Christian marriage and family in Africa. This eventually became a first-class textbook with 223 pages. It has been used as a textbook in multiple institutions throughout Kenya, inside and outside of the Africa Inland Church.

Each topic of research determines the range of involvement of participants. Marriage and Family in Africa is the best possible example of this collegial approach. It was truly an exciting and fulfilling experience for all participants. Not only did it produce a noteworthy textbook, it energized and educated seasoned and experienced pastors. One pastor had married hundreds of couples, but he testified that he had learned so much. This research team ended up having the fewest members attending, sometimes only four or five. But since they were all widely experienced, each research seminar produced a wealth of insight.

The Fourth TAG Research Team

The fourth topic for TAG research was very different from either worship or marriage. *The Holy Spirit and the Church in Africa Today* by its very nature is primarily a study of Scripture. The study naturally grew out of the explosion of Pentecostal and Charismatic churches in Africa. So the research team made an historical study of the Pentecostal and charismatic movement: its root, origin and evaluation of these churches in Kenya.

The study of Scripture, however, was the primary focus. Even so it was framed by the debates swirling around the Kenyan churches. One chapter with 50 pages dealt with Pentecost and the baptism in the Spirit and the initial sign of tongues. Another chapter with 55 pages explored "Those Controversial Gifts: Healing, Prophecy and Tongues." This became a 441 page textbook which has even been used in Kenyan government universities.

Conclusion

When Scott Theological College was preparing to become a chartered private university to grant her own degrees, the Commission for Higher Education required Scott to have a Department of Research. Dr. Titus Kivunzi, the Principal, requested that TAG should become that Research Department. I will thrilled because this would ensure that the TAG ministry would continue with many Kenyan faculty, fully qualified, who could serve as a manuscript drafters. Up to this point the members of the research teams did not have either the level of education or the gift to serve as manuscript drafter.

Alas, this move to Scott became a huge disappointment. One teacher agreed to take on the challenge of leading a research team, the Principal and Governing Council arranged to grant him a sabbatical for the TAG research, but at the last moment he relented and said he would prefer a vacation to a sabbatical for field research.

Without any further manuscript drafters, Scott Theological College (now Scott Christian University) has no functioning Department of Research and, apart from the sale of the TAG books already published, TAG is effectively defunct.

But the lessons learned from the fruitful endeavour of TAG offer an effective method of doing African theology. The core idea of TAG can be adjusted to various situations.

A church leader, such as a bishop, priest, or chairman of a church region or diocese, who is gifted and educated, would find this approach in doing African theology a mutually profitable endeavour. By appointing 10-14 pastors to participate in a research team, the church leader could disciple these men, invigorate their spirits through fellowship, prayer and Bible study, stimulate their minds with new ideas, and explore how a particular problem in the church can be resolved through biblical teaching. An adequately trained and gifted pastor would have a marvellous opportunity to mentor his elders through this group research.

Teachers in Bible Schools and Colleges desperately need sabbaticals so that their minds and spirits can be refreshed and renewed. In most Bible institutions they are encumbered with a heavy teaching load, and may even pastor churches on the weekends. They cannot continue this way without mental fatigue and burn out. The mind needs refreshment with new insights and understandings.

The key to making this happen is commitment to doing a TAG-like research project. "Where there is a will, there is a way" is a slogan with much truth. If an institution or a church leader is determined to do field research with the collaboration of colleagues in ministry, a way can be found to make it happen.

OTHER MODELS OF COMMUNAL RESEARCH

Several other research projects utilized in Africa offer helpful insights.

The Christian Learning Materials Centre

CLMC is a "semi-autonomous cooperative venture established by the AEAM" (Breman 1996: 308f). It was founded in 1981 in Nairobi, Kenya, to "create Bible teaching materials for African churches **written by qualified nationals** explaining, illustrating and applying within their cultural context – NOT OUTSIDERS. This facility was based in Africa for ongoing publications in several languages" [emphases original] (Coon 2016: email).

The method of team work to develop Sunday School materials was creatively designed by Roger Coon, the Managing Director. Through consultation with Roger, this team work methodology was adapted for use by the Theological Advisory Group.

Four assets were needed to write Sunday School materials for all ages: biblical knowledge, educational knowledge, educational development knowledge, and African cultural knowledge. This new method of CLMC was designed to enable Africans do the writing of African materials at a time when Africans lacked some of those assets.

For example, no African had educational development knowledge. An overall curriculum plan for all ages needed to be developed for Sunday Schools. The teaching of biblical knowledge had to be related to the educational needs of the different ages.

By the early 1980s Africans had been trained in education. Teacher Training Colleges had functioned for many years. All of the writing staff had master's degrees in education. By using the team work methodology the product was not just one person's outlook, but the work representing various viewpoints, cultural backgrounds, and family backgrounds (Coon 2016b: P.I.).

One person did the curriculum planning in consultation with the team of African parents and African teachers. At this point the Curriculum Planner was an expatriate, Joyce Coon, who had professional training in both biblical knowledge and educational development of children. She did the curriculum development year by year, and within each year, the things to be covered each period.

The procedure for writing the CLMC Sunday School materials followed these steps (Coon 2016: Email):

- The biblical curriculum planning was prepared, related to the educational development of each age group.
- The writing of lessons as defined in the curriculum plan were assigned to one African staff writer for each age level.
- The resultant drafts were typed and copies circulated to all writing staff and then returned to the writer with comments.
- The draft was then revised by the writer and recirculated again for comments, but not returned to the writer. Instead, they all met together as the editorial team which went over the comments. The Managing Director chaired the meetings, but the Africans as a group made the final decisions. After discussion, agreement was made on the changes and given to the writer to incorporate those recommendations.
- The manuscript was then prepared for final layout and published.

Initially, CLMC had ten staff, half national and half expats. The five nationals were the writers. During the first ten years of CLMC this team produced graded Sunday School materials for all ages from the youngest to adult.

The ten year goal, to staff CLMC solely by nationals, was achieved. By 1991 Dr. Buconyori, with qualifications in theology, Christian education and curriculum development, was appointed the Managing Director and Roger Coon retired.

However, the pattern of team writing has continued. With 1,000 ethnic communities in Africa, a team effort is valuable to gain differing perspectives. In order to prepare "truly African life-related Bible teaching materials," it is prudent to use this team approach.

Team research and writing is less efficient than individual efforts. It is time consuming and for this reason it is not used much in the United States. It also diffuses the glory of writing a publication and distributes the recognition to numerous individuals. But the benefits are enormous. Team research and composition is not only African but a recognition that multiple perspectives on the application of Scripture is inherently more enriching.

Africa Study Bible

The production of the *Africa Study Bible* was a humongous team effort continent-wide. While the Bible translation itself was the *New Living Translation*, published by Tyndale House Publishers in the United States, the notes were all prepared by Africans. The writers chosen were scholars, pastors and elders, reflecting the diversity in the African continent with 1.2 billion people. The theological perspective was evangelical while allowing for differences on non-essential issues.

The 316 authors came from 50 countries, including Anglophone and Francophone countries, Portuguese and Arabic speaking countries. While the writers were located in their respective residences, they communicated with the editorial team by email based in Nairobi, Kenya.

Before anything was officially approved for inclusion in the *Africa Study Bible*, 14-20 individuals reviewed, edited and proof-read each note and article.

The supervising editor, Dr. John Jusu, Dean of the School of Professional Studies in the Africa International University, reviewed and commented on every item submitted, often sending it back to the writer for revision.

A team of editors worked to standardize the articles so that the comments in the *Africa Study Bible* would speak with a unified voice.

These edited articles were then submitted to a group of ten African theological scholars to review and make further suggestions for improvement.

Then an "experienced Bible editorial team" made further revisions "according to the African scholars' suggestions, and edited the articles and notes for clarity."

This was followed by further review and revision by two senior Ph.D.-level theological editors, book by book.

The final step was to edit the copy for reading level and accessibility by the target audience.

"This rigorous and exhaustive process" was necessary to assure that the *Africa Study Bible* "speaks with the highest quality as a trusted resource for the church" (Africa Study Bible 2016: A23).

Whenever excellence is sought in doing African Theology, one must be diligent to assure high quality. Could one or two individuals have written and collated all the African proverbs and stories, African Touch Points, Application Notes and Learn Notes? No doubt they could have done so in much less time and with much less expense! But quality is costly and time consuming. The multiple perspectives and viewpoints enrich the *Africa Study Bible* and ensure its long-term value for the African Church. The extensive and collaborative effort made this a truly enduring *African* Study Bible.

Bible Translation

Bible translations can surely be made by one individual. J.B. Phillips translated *The New Testament in Modern English*; Kenneth Taylor translated *The Living Bible Paraphrased*; Richard Francis Weymouth translated *The New Testament in Modern Speech.*

However, most translations are collaborative efforts overseen by Bible Societies or editorial committees. One example is "the common language translation of the Bible into Kikamba. It was a "meaning-based" translation, not a literal word-for-word translation. The purpose was to have it flow naturally in grammar and easy to understand.

Rev. Charles Kimwele, one of the translators, outlined the procedure which they followed (Kimwele 2017: email).

- Each of three translators on the team was assigned a passage to translate into Kikamba from the Revised Standard Version. Other English translations were consulted at times.
- Team revision was made when the three translators met together and worked their way through the translation, approving the final translation with a unanimous recommendation.
- This approved translation was then submitted to a translation consultant of the United Bible Society who visited the translators to establish the quality of the translation.
- The translation was then submitted to a team of reviewers drawn from different churches, giving a wide representation in terms of age and sex. They went through the translation to get a feel of the accuracy, naturalness and ease of reading and understanding. Corrections were made and inserted in the text.

- The text was then polished and prepared for publication.

Admittedly, Bible translation is not the usual way of doing African theology as we generally think of it. Nevertheless, the selection of the vernacular vocabulary and phraseology involves translation of biblical truth into the mother tongue. Bible translation is incarnational work for it takes biblical revelation expressed in Hebrew and Greek and makes it intelligible in a particular culture.

Ideally, this requires many minds and a joint effort to do a trustworthy job. Handling God's Word is a sacred responsibility. Warnings abound in Scripture about twisting, misrepresenting, adding or purging what God has revealed. *Every word of God proves true...Do not add to his words, lest he rebuke you and you be found a liar* (Pr 30:5, 6). John the Apostle warns his readers against adding or taking away from God's revelation given to him (Re 22:18-19).

Lecturers Writing Textbooks

Throughout the vast continent of Africa there are no doubt thousands of teachers in Bible Institutes, Bible Schools, Bible Colleges, Seminaries and Christian Universities. Among them can be found scores of lecturers who are potential contributors to the important project of developing a literary African Biblical Theology.

Dr. Samuel Weje Kunhiyop (Ph.D.) from Nigeria is one of those whose life experiences give us insight into the making of a Christian theologian (Kunhiyop 2017). Dr. Kunhiyop is an accomplished and prolific writer and international speaker. In addition to lectures and papers presented on scores of occasions at meetings and conferences on three continents, including a United Nations workshop, he has written stellar textbooks in great demand in Christian colleges and universities. He is married to Yelwa Tugga and has children ands grandchildren.

Dr. Kunhiyop was born on September 24, 1954, in a "typical African home with its customs and ideas." His grandfather was a "native and traditional doctor" who "combined the spiritual and physical elements in his practice." This experience has helped Dr. Kunhiyop teach and write from personal knowledge of traditional African beliefs and practices.

He came to faith in Christ at an early age when his teacher read from John 3:16. He was later baptized as a Christian in 1972 in the River Kaduna. Following this he was discipled and taught the Bible by Rev. Yakubu Boye. His education included Kagoro Bible College (1975-1979) for a Certificate; Jos ECWA Theological Seminary (1980-1984) where he earned his BA in Theology; Western Seminary in the United States (1986-88) for his MA in Exegetical Study; and Trinity International University in Deerfield, U.S.A. (1988-1993) for a Ph.D. in Systematic Theology. Ten years later he did further post-doctoral studies in the Global Research Institute, Pasadena, California.

Returning to Nigeria in 1993, he began teaching as Professor of Theology/Ethics in ECWA Theological Seminary, Jos, Nigeria.

Theologically, he was grounded in his biblical faith through his extensive training in evangelical institutions. He writes, "The Bible is very fundamental to me in all my writing. So I would say that my biblical and evangelical foundations are my watch words" (Kunhiyop 2017b: Email).

But his training overseas had extracted him from his African roots. After seven years abroad in the United States, he says, "I was no longer very conversant with Nigeria." Even his English accent was transformed into an American accent which made it difficult for his students to understand him. In his first year of teaching he "basically dumped the course load" of his philosopher/theologian professor in Trinity Divinity School on his students. Fortunately, he was sensitive enough to engage with the students.

At the conclusion of a course on Biblical Theology he gave an evaluation form to all the students. He asked them, "What lesson did you learn from this course?" One of the students wrote, "I learnt absolutely nothing."

This comment he took seriously. From that time on he began to listen more to the students instead of insisting on his own way. "I started asking myself serious questions on what would make my lectures more understandable and relevant," he said. That became the foundation of the books that he has written.

From that day onward he began seriously to develop his lectures to make them more relevant. At that time he had no thought of writing a textbook. His only thought was to work hard in teaching theology in a relevant and meaningful way. He dialogued with students and engaged with them in personal discussions. This helped to restore his African perspective. He revised his notes year after year until his notes had the mark of mature thought that was connecting with his students.

God has gifted him both with ability and a motivation to write. He has honed his skills by writing articles for publication for secular and religious audiences, and presented papers on various topics. No doubt the disciplines he learned in writing his numerous theses for his B.A., M.A. and Ph.D. helped prepare him for this ministry. There is also found within him an inner drive and desire to write.

Part of his education included observing and interrogating his grandfather who was a traditional doctor. Samuel questioned some of his beliefs and practices. For example, Samuel challenged his grandfather when he communicated with the spirits through a stone. "I basically told him," Samuel said, "that he was just fabricating some things he claimed the stone told him." His grandfather said nothing but just looked at him and smiled.

Dr. Kunhiyop's main concern is to teach his students the truth of Scripture, properly interpreted, and this is from an evangelical perspective. He desires to "take every thought captive for Christ." "Whether it is African or Western thought," he writes, "I subject it to Scripture to make sure that it is true, but I also seek to make it relevant to the African Christian in his situation. As I say, African Christian theology is about scratching where people are itching" (Kunhiyop 2017b: email).

His major source of motivation is his students. They ask all kinds of questions and tell many stories. They challenge him by alleging that he is not African enough because he questions African beliefs. For example, he questions many stories about witchcraft. "*To me*," he writes,

> *just because I am an African doesn't mean I cannot question issues. From my late father and grandfather, there are many unanswered questions on witchcraft belief to the extent that they would prohibit the children getting involved in witchcraft. They believed strongly that witchcraft is divisive and destructive and that we should stay away from it. With this background, I have challenged many beliefs such as witchcraft, polygamy, demonic spirits etc.* (Kunhiyop 2017b: email).

If God has called you to be a teacher of God's Word, you are blessed to have this wonderful privilege. Love the Lord your God with all your heart, soul, strength and mind. Be diligent in studying the Scripture so that you can teach your students God's will for their lives. "*Be diligent to present yourself approved to God as a workman who does not need to be ashamed, accurately handling the word of truth*" (2 Ti 2:15 *NASB*)

His advice is: "Dialogue with your students, and intermingle with lay Christians. Interact with them so that you can learn how to expound Scripture relevantly to meet their every need."

CONCLUSION

For most teachers God's calling is for them to be the best teachers. But for some teachers, God may have gifted you to write articles and books that can help a wider range of people.

Spiritual gifts come in varying degrees and the Bible says that the Spirit "*gives them to each one, just as he determines*" (1 Co 12:11). If God has gifted and called you to write, this requires discipline and commitment. Writing is not easy and quick. Ask any successful writer! Faithfulness in preparing daily teaching lessons – refining, researching, and improving your notes – is a first step in developing mature and relevant thought. After years of teaching, Dr. Kunhiyop took one full year to write a textbook.

Theology is not for debate by the elite. Theology – a knowledge of God and his will for mankind – is meant for practical application, to lead men and women into a believing and obedient relationship with Jesus Christ. The growing number of godly, faithful *task theologians* in Africa today are models to follow.

CONCLUSION

This book is deeply concerned with the development of theologians in Africa who are faithful to Scripture. But what kind of theologians are most needed?[2]

The classic definition of theology given by B.B. Warfield states: "Theology is the science of God and his relationship to man and the world." Systematic Theology is devoted to a "unified formulation of truth" derived from divine revelation which is then applied to human life.

This kind of theology, represented by so many systematic theologies from the West, sometimes called "Dogmatic Theology," is often abstract and seemingly unrelated to life. Pick up most systematic theologies from the West, and you find highly refined, abstract logic designed to provide "a scientific" and "unified formulation" of biblical truth. Theology is neatly arranged in logical categories but with little application to life. Theological debates rage over dichotomy or trichotomy, the number and organization of the angels, supralapsarianism or infralapsarianism. How does all this impact the common man anywhere in the world?

While there will always be a need for systematic theologians who faithfully seek to systematize the teachings of Scripture, we need to develop another kind of theologian. Instead of mere professional scholars surrounded by books and isolated from the common Christian in the local church and village, we need *task theologians*. The need for task theologians around the world, and especially in Africa, is very great.

A *task theologian* is out in the battle field, working in the trenches and engaged in spiritual warfare as he or she is building the Church of Jesus Christ. He is fully engaged in evangelism and discipling, bringing believers to maturity in Christ. He teaches them the biblical truth as it applies to them in their context. A *task theologian* is one who knows biblical teaching and can relate it and apply it contextually to the believers in order to ground them in their faith.

The apostle Paul is a model of the *task theologian* which is needed. Paul was immersed with biblical understanding of the Old Testament which he learned at the feet of Gamaliel. Furthermore, he knew Jesus Christ in a living and personal way and was taught by the Holy Spirit. In his missionary endeavours to plant churches where Christ had not been preached, he grounded the converts in biblical truth. Read any of his letters to these churches. They are filled with theology. But that theology is practically related to the particular needs and problems which they faced.

The Christological passages of Paul, for example, are embedded in practical concerns. Paul's teaching of the incarnation of Christ in Philippians 2:4-11 provided a model of humility for the Philippians who were deeply divided. The supremacy of Christ as found in Colossians 3:15-20 was written to correct the incipient Gnosticism present in Colosse.

Everywhere you turn in the New Testament epistles you find profound theology designed to affect the practical lives of Christians. In fact, theology forms the basis for all practical exhortations for Christian conduct. The profoundly rich theology of Romans 1-11 is followed by practical exhortations, beginning with

---

[2] This conclusion has been adapted from my editorial in the *African Journal of Evangelical Theology*, Volume 16.1, 1997, pages 1-2.

the appeal in Romans 12:1, "***Therefore,*** *I urge you, brothers, in view of God's mercy, to offer your bodies as living sacrifices..."*

Biblical, practical and relevant systematic theologies are greatly needed for Africa. *African Christian Theology*, authored by Dr. Samuel Kunhiyop, is an admirable example of this kind of African Biblical Theology which is practical, relevant and eminently contextualized. Such a systematic theology is the fruit of a life time of study, teaching, and interacting with the African churches in order to help them grow into maturity in Christ. This is professional theology that is a *task driven theology.* Through his intimate knowledge of his people, Dr. Kunhiyop is able to apply biblical teaching to African believers and for the African Church. Through his knowledge of the biblical languages he is able to exegete Scripture and use biblical tools for interpretation.

In addition to "professional" theologians, however, we also need *task theologians* who are in the battle field of evangelizing, planting churches, pastoring and bringing those churches into maturity, theologians who are able to study the Scriptures and teach biblical truth in a relevant way. Thank God there are many *task theologians* in Africa (pastors, bishops and church leaders). This book seeks to encourage the multiplication of *task theologians* who will take up the challenge to *do theology in the African context*.

What are the basic requirements for a *task theologian*? They are two in number.

First, he or she must know God personally and love His Word as treasured truth. He trusts the Word of God and submits to it. He should be sufficiently trained so that he is able to think and study the Scriptures for himself. In order for him to read the Bible for all its worth, he should be trained in the art of biblical interpretation (grammatical/historical hermeneutics). The "grassroots *task theologian*" should have Bibles well worn, both in the vernacular and the national language, and have access to basic reference books for exegesis and theological study.

Second, *task theologians* must know their people – their worldview, their temptations and weaknesses, their problems and needs, their questions and doubts. *Task theologians* must love their sheep to such an extent that they are willing to sacrifice in order to help them grow into spiritual maturity in Christ.

The grassroots *task theologians* need not be concerned with publication, but only with the application of the truths learned from Scripture to the lives of the flock. The goal is to grow God's people in holiness for God's glory. How exciting it would be for the pastor to lead his elders, and the bishop to lead his pastors, in research of some contextual issue that plagues the church, and then to search the Scriptures together to determine the will of God for their lives. The example of the Theological Advisory Group (TAG) is a wonderful model that can help give direction in the process.

This is the purpose of African Biblical Theology, a theology that has eternal value in building up the Church of Jesus Christ for his glory alone.

BIBLIOGRAPHY OF REFERENCES CITED

Adeyemo, Tokumboh. 1979a. *Salvation in African Tradition.* Nairobi: Evangel Pub.

Adeyemo, Tokumboh. 1979b. "The African Church Struggles into her Third Century." *Christianity Today.* XII (July), 14-17 (1040-1043).

Adeyemo, Tokumboh. 1983. "Towards an Evangelical African Theology." *Evangelical Review of Theology.* VII, 1:147-154.

Adeyemo, Tokumboh, ed. 2006. *Africa Bible Commentary* Nairobi: WordAlive and Zonderrvan Publishers.

Agbeti, J. 1972. "African Theology: What it is? *Presence*, pp. 7ff.

Alliance of Mission Societies, Kenya (A.M.S.). 1922. Minutes of the Representative Council of the Alliance of Missionary Societies in Kenya Colony, Aug. 31 – Sept. 2, 1922. Archives of the National Christian Council of Kenya, Nairobi.

Anderson, Allan. 2001. *African Reformation. African Initiated Christianity in the 20th Century.* Trenton, NJ: Africa World Press, Inc.

Anderson, Gerald H. and Thomas F. Stranskyeds. 1976. *Mission Trends No.3. Third World Theologies*. Grand Rapids: Wm. B. Eerdmans Pub. Co.

Anderson, J.N.D. 1970. *Christianity and Comparative Religion*. London: Tyndale Press.

Andersson, Efraim. 1968. *Churches At The Grass Roots*. N. Y.: Friendship Press.

Appiah-Kubi, Kofi. 1979. *African Theology En Route*. Maryknoll, N.Y.: Orbis Books.

Arthur, John W. n.d. Letter to Bishop Peel, 21st Sept. 15 [sic]. Archives of the Africa Inland Mission, International, Nairobi.

Association of Third World Theologians. 1978. "Pan African Conference of Third World Theologians Communique." *IDOC Bulletin*. 1 (Jan. 1978), pp. 3-6.

Augustine. *Augustine Confessions.* Lib 1,1-2, 2.5,5: CESEL 33, 1-5.

Baeta, C. G. 1964. "The Younger Churches: An African Viewpoint." *Religion in Life*. 34 (Winter 1964-1965), pp. 15-24.

Bares, A. 1978a. *All Africa Lutheran Consultation on Christian Theology and Theological Education in the African Context: Background Materials I.* Geneva.

Bares, A. 1978b. *All Africa Lutheran Consultation on Christian Theology and Theological Education in the African Context: Background Materials II.* Geneva.

Barlow, A. Ruffell. 1925. "Report and Recommendations Regarding Possibilities of Uniformity in Church Discipline in the Native Churches of the Alliance." Prepared for the Alliance of Missionary Societies, August 1925. Archives of the National Christian Council of Kenya, Nairobi.

Barnett, Eric. 1982. A.I.M. missionary, second generation. Personal Interview.

Barrett, David B. 1968. *Schism and Renewal in Africa.* London: Oxford University.

Barrett, David B. 1973. *Kenya Churches Handbook*. Kisumu, Kenya: Evangel Pub.

Barrett, David B. 1982. *World Christian Encyclopedia*. Nairobi: Oxford University Press.

Bauer, Walter. 1957. *A Greek-English Lexicon of the New Testament,* a translation and adaptation of Walter Bauer's *Griechisch-Deutsches Wörterbuch zu den Schriften des Neuen Testaments und der übrigen urchristlichen Literatur* by William F. Arndt and F. Wilbur Gingrich. Chicago: The University of Chicago Press.

Baxter. Jean. 1982. A.I.M. missionary, Kapsabet, Nandi. Personal Interview.

Becken, Hand-Jurgen ed. 1972. *Relevant Theology for Africa*. Durban: Lutheran House.

Bediako, Kwame. 1990: *Jesus in African Culture (A Ghanaian Perspective).* Accra, Ghana: Asempa Publishers, Christian Council of Ghana.

Bediako, Kwame. 1995. *Christianity in Africa: The Renewal of a Non-Western Religion.* Orbis Books: Edinburgh University Press, Edinburgh.

Bediako, Kwame. 2004. *Jesus and the Gospel in Africa,* Maryknoll, NY: Orbis Books.

Bettenson, Henry. 1947. *Documents of the Christian Church.* NY: Oxford University.

Blakeslee, H. Virginia, 1956. *Beyond the Bamboo Curtain.* Chicago: Moody.

Booth, Newell S. 1975. "Time and Change in African Traditional Thought." *Journal of Religion in Africa.* VII, 2, pp. 81-91.

Bosch, David. 1979. “Currents and Crosscurrents in South African Black Theology” in *Black Theology: A Documentary History, 1966-1979,* edited by Wilmore Gayraud and James Cone. Maryknoll, NY: Orbis Books.

Boulaga, Fabian Eboussi. 2002. *Christianity without Fetishes. An African Critique and Recapture of Christianity (1984) with an additional comment by V. Y. Mudimbe and A New postscript by the author.* Translated from Frency by Robert R. Barr in Revue Africaine de Theologie, Kinshasa, 1983. © LIT VERLAG Münster–Hamburg–London. Distributed in North America by: Transaction Publishers, New Brunswick, U.S.A.)

Borchert, Gerald L. 2001. “Demythologization” in *Evangelical Dictionary of Theology,* Second Edition. Walter Elwell ed. Grand Rapids: Baker Academic.

Bowers, Paul. 1980. "Evangelical Theology in Africa: Byang Kato's Legacy." *Trinity Journal.* I (Spring), pp. 84-87.

Bowers, Paul. 2001. “African Theology” by Paul Bowers in *Evangelical Dictionary of Theology.* Second Edition, edited by Walter A. Elwell. Grand Rapids: Baker Academic.

Bowers, Paul. 2001. “Black Theology” in *Evangelical Dictionary of Theology*, Second Edition, edited by Walter A. Elwell. Grand Rapids: Baker Academic.

Bowers, Paul. 2017. Personal Email to Richard J. Gehman.

Breman, Christina Maria. 1996. *The Association of Evangelicals in Africa* Netherlands: Uitgeverij Boekencentrum, Zoetermeer.

Brown, Colin. 2001. “Enlightenment” in *Evangelical Dictionary of Theology,* Second Edition. Walter A. Elwell ed. Grand Rapids: Baker Academic.

Bruce, F.F. 1960. *Commentary on the Book of the Acts.* Grand Rapids: Eerdmans.

Bryson, Stuart M. 1959. *Light in Darkness: The Story of the Nandi Bible.* London: Parry Jackman Scripture Illustrations Ltd.

Bujo, Bénézet and Juvénal Ilunga Muya eds. 2003. *African Theology in the 21st Century: The Contribution of the Pioneers,* Vol. 2. Nairobi: Paulines Publications Africa.

Bujo, Bénézet and Juvénal Ilunga Muya eds. 2003. “Laurenti Magesa: An African Liberation Theologian” in *African Theology in the 21st Century: The Contribution of the Pioneers.* Vol. 2. Nairobi: Paulines Publications Africa.

Buswell III, James Oliver. 1978a. "Contextualization: Is it only a New Word for Indigenization?" *Evangelical Missions Quarterly*. XIV: 13-20.

Buswell III, James Oliver. 1978b. "Contextualization: Theory, Tradition and Method." *Theology and Mission*. David Hesselgrave ed., pp. 87-111. Grand Rapids: Baker Book House.

Buswell, James Oliver. 1962. *A Systematic Theology of the Christian Religion.* Grand Rapids: Zondervan

Buthelezi, Manas. 1973a. "An African Theology or a Black Theology” in *Black Theology: The South African Voice*. B. Moore ed. London: Hurst.

Buthelezi, Manas. 1973b. "African Theology and Black Theology: A Search for a Theological Method." *Relevant Theology for Africa*. H.J. Becken ed. Durban.

Cagnolo, C. 1933. *The Akikuyu*. Nyeri, Kenya: Mission Printing School.

Christian Council of the Gold Coast. 1955. *Christianity and African Culture.* Accra: Christian Council of the Gold Coast.

Church of Scotland. 1926. "African Church Laws, As Revised." Archives of National Christian Council of Kenya, Nairobi.

Coe, Shoki and Aharon Sapsezian. 1972. *Ministry in Context.* Theological Education Fund.

Cole, E. K. 1957. *A History of Church Co-Operation in Kenya.* Limuru, Kenya: St. Paul’s College Press.

Cone, James H. 1970. *A Black Theology of Liberation.* Philadelphia: J .B. Lippincott Co.

Cone, James H. 1986. *Speaking the Truth: Ecumenism, Liberation and Black Theology.* Maryknoll, NY: Orbis Books

Conference of Kikuyu Elders. 1929. Minutes of a Conference of Kikuyu Church Elders, March 8-12, 1929. Archives of the National Christian Council of Kenya, Nairobi.

Continuation Committee of Kikuyu Conference (C.C.K.C.). 1918. Minutes of a Conference of Kikuyu Church Elders, March 8-12, 1918. Archives of the National Christian Council of Kenya, Nairobi.

Continuation Committee of Kikuyu Conference (C.C.K.C.). 1918. Minutes of the Continuation Committee of Kikuyu Conference, Ap. 29, 1918. Archives of the National Christian Council of Kenya, Nairobi.

Coon, Roger. 2016. Email sent to Richard J. Gehman on Nov. 16, 2016.

Coon, Roger. 2016b. Personal Interview by Richard J. Gehman on Nov. 17, 2016.

Cope, T. H. 1979. *The Africa Inland Mission in Kenya – Aspects of its History (1895-1945)* M.Phil. Dissertation, London University.

Covell, Ralph. 1977. Book Review of "Waterbuffalo Theology" by Kasuke Koyama. *Evangelical Missions Quarterly*, Jan. 1977, pp. 55, 56.

Cullmann, Oscar. 1964. *Christ and Time*. Floyd V. Filson transl., Philadelphia: The Westminster Press.

Daidanso, Djongwe. 1983. "An African Critique of African Theology." *Evangelical Review of Theology*. VII, 1:63-72.

Davis, Linnell E. and Martha. 1982. A.I.M. Missionaries, second generation. Machakos, Kenya. Personal Interview.

Deconstruction. 2017. "Deconstruction – Is it a Valid Way of Interpreting Scripture." https://www.gotquestions.org/deconstructionism.html Website: gotQuestions?org

De Gruchy, John and C. Villa-Vicencio, eds. 1994. *Doing Theology in Context: South African Perspectives.* Maryknoll, NY: Orbis Books.

De Vries, Paul. 2001. "Heidegger, Martin" in *Evangelical Dictionary of Theology*, Second Edition. Walter A. Elwell ed. Grand Rapids: Baker Academic

Dickson, Kwesi. 1973. "The Old Testament and African Theology." *Ghana Bulletin of Theology* 4: 31-41.

Dickson, Kwesi. 1974. "Towards a Theologia Africana." *New Testament Christianity for Africa and the World.* M. Glasswell and E. Fashole-Luke eds., pp. 198-207. London.

Dickson, Kwesi. 1975. "African Theology: Origin, Methodology and Content." *Journal of Religious Thought.* 32:34-45.

Dickson, Kwesi and Paul Ellingworth. 1969. *Biblical Revelation and African Beliefs.* London: Lutherworth Press.

Dube, Musa W. 2017. Internet PDF Abstract - Unisa Institutional Repository, Musa W. Dube and the Study of the Bible in Africa.

Edusa-Eyison, Joseph M.Y. 2003. "Kwesi A. Dickson: The Bible and African Life and Thought in Dialogue" in *African Theology in the 21st Century: The Contribution of the Pioneers,* Vol. 2. Edited by Benézét Bujo and Juvénal Ilunga Muya. Nairobi: Paulines Publications Africa.

Ela, Jean-Marc. 1988. *My Faith as an African.* Maryknoll, NY: Orbis Books.

Elwell, Walter A. 2001. *Evangelical Dictionary of Theology*, Second Edition. Grand Rapids: Baker Academic.

Erickson, Millard J. 1998. *Christian Theology*. Grand Rapids: Baker Books.

Ezigbo, Victor I. 2010. *Re-Imagining African Christologies: Conversing with the Interpretations and Appropriations of Jesus in Contemporary African Christianity.* Princeton Theological Monograph Series, KI.C. Hanson, Charles M. Collier, and D. Christopher Spinks, Series Editors. Eugene, Oregon: Pickwick Publications.

Fashole-Luke, Edward W. 1974a. "What is African Christian Theology?" *Communio Viatorum.* 17:97-102.

Fashole-Luke, Edward W. 1974b. "Ancestor Veneration and the Communion of Saints." in *New Testament Christianity for Africa and the world.* Mark Glasswell and Edward Fashole-Luke eds. London: SPCK.

Fashole-Luke, Edward W. 1981. "Footpaths and Sign Posts to African Christian Theologies." *Scottish Journal of Theology.* 34 No. 5, 19-40, Ja-Je 81.

Feinberg, P.D. 2001. "Bible, Inerrancy and Infallibility of" in *Evangelical Dictionary of Theology,* Second Edition. Walter A. Elwell ed. Grand Rapids: Baker Academic.

Ferdinando, Keith. 2007. "Christian Identity in the African Context: Reflections on Kwame Bediako's Theology and Identity" in *Journal of the Evangelical Theological Society*, 50/1 (March 2007).

Fleming, Bruce. 1980. *Contextualization of Theology*. Pasadena: William Carey Library.

Gaussen, L. n.d. *The Plenary Inspiration of the Holy Scriptures.* Chicago: The Bible Institute Colportage Association.

Gehman, Richard J. 1987. *Doing African Christian Theology: An Evangelical Perspective.* Nairobi: Evangel Publishing House.

Gehman, Richard J. 1989. *African Traditional Religion in Biblical Perspective.* Kijabe, Kenya: Kesho Publications.

Gehman, Richard J. 1999. *Who are the Living Dead: A Theology of Death, Life after Death and the Living Dead.* Nairobi: Evangel Publishing House.

Gehman, Richard J. 2005. *African Traditional Religion in Biblical Perspective.* Revised Edition. Nairobi: East African Educational Publishers.

Gelzer, David G. 1970. "Random Notes on Black Theology and African Theology." *Christian Century*. XVI: 1091-1093.

Gibellini, Rosino, ed. 1994: *Paths of African Theology.* Maryknoll, NY: Orbis Books.

Glasswell, M.E. 1975. "Can there be an African or a Black Theology?" *The Modern Churchman*. XVIII, 4:164-172.

Glasswell, Mark and Edward W. Fashole-Luke. 1974. *New Testament Christianity for Africa and the World: Essays in Honour of Henry Sawyer.* London: SPCK.

Goba, Booganjalo. 1979. "An African Christian Theology." *Journal of Theology for Southern Africa*. XXVI: 3-12.

Goba, Bonganjalo. 1987. "A Theological Tribute to Archbishop Tutu" in *Hammering Swords into Ploughshares: Essays in Honor of Archbishop Mpilo Desmond Tutu* edited by Buti Tlhagale and Itumeleng Mosala, Grand Rapids: William B. Eerdmans Pub. Co.

Goreham, N.J. 1975. "Towards an African Theology." *The Expository Times*. 86:233-36.

Gration, John A. 1974. *The Relationship of the A.I.M. and its National Church in Kenya Between 1895 and 1971.* Ph. D. Dissertation, New York University.

Guilding, Mr. & Mrs. W.J. n.d. A.I.M. missionaries and first Principal of Ukamba Bible Institute. Taped Interview by Linnell Davis.

Harjula, Raimo. 1970. "Towards a Theologia Africana." *Student Essays and Religious Workshop Papers*. Limuru.

Hassing, Per. 1971. "Christian Theology in Africa." *Religion in Life*. 40:510-518.

Hearing and Doing. Volumes I - XXI, 1898-1916. Mission Periodical of Africa Inland Mission.

Henry, Carl, ed. 1973. *Baker's Dictionary of Christian Ethics.* Baker Book House Co.

Henry, Carl, ed. 1958. *Revelation and the Bible.* Philadelphia, PA: Presbyterian and Reformed Publishing Co.

Hoffecker, W.A. 2001. "Schleiermacher, Friedrich" in *Evangelical Dictionary of Theology*. Edited by Walter A. Elwell. Grand Rapids: Baker Academic.

Huxley, Elspeth. 1970. *White Man's Country: Lord Delamere and the Making of Kenya.* Vol. 1. London: Chatto & Windus (first printed in 1935).

Idowu, E. Bolaji, 1966. *Towards and Indigenous Church.* Oxford Press.

Idowu, E. Bolaji and Paul Ellingworth, 1969. *Biblical Revelation and African Beliefs.* London, Lutterworth Press.

Idowu, E. Bolaji, 1973. *African Traditional Religion: A Definition.* Maryknoll, N.Y.: Orbis Books.

Imasogie, Osadolor. 1973. *Guidelines for Christian Theology in Africa.* Ghana: African Christian Press.

Jacobs, Donald R. 1966. *Christian Theology in Africa.* Mt. Joy, Pennsylvania; mimeographed.

Kanyandago, Peter. 1978. "Christian Theology in Africa." *African Ecclesiastical Review*. XX, 3:339-348.

Kato, Byang. 1973. "Theological Trends in Africa Today" in *Theological News Monograph,* No. 6, April 1973. This paper was read to the General Assembly of AEAM at Limuru, Kenya, on 4th February, 1973.

Kato, Byang H. 1975. *Theological Pitfalls in Africa*. Kisumu, Kenya: Evangel Publishing House.

Kato, Byang H. 1975. "Christianity as an African Religion." An address given by Rev. Dr. Byang Kato, General Secretary of the AEAM at the National Congress on Evangelisation at Ife University, Nigeria, on August 21st 1975. Typescript.

Kato, Byang H. 1976. "Black Theology and African Theology" in *Perception* No. 6, Oct. 1976. Public lecture delivered at the University of Nairobi, 27th September 1975.)

Kato, Byang H. 1976. "Theological Issues in Africa." *Bibliotheca Sacra.* 133:143-152.

Kato, Byang H. 1985. *Biblical Christianity in Africa*. Ghana: African Christian Press.

Kenya Field Council Minutes, Africa Inland Mission, Kenya, 1930.

Kenya Missionary Council (KMC) 1927. Minutes of the Annual General Meeting of the Kenya Missionary Council. Archives of the National Christian Council of Kenya, NBI.

Kenya Missionary Council (KMC) 1930. Minutes of the Annual General Meeting of the Kenya Missionary Council. Archives of the National Christian Council of Kenya, NBI.

Kinney, John W. 1979. "The Theology of John Mbiti: His Sources, Norms, and Methods." *Occasional Bulletin*. III, 2:65-67.

Kombo, James. 2000. *The Doctrine of God in African Christian Thought: An Assessment of African Inculturation Theology from a Trinitarian Perspective*. A thesis for the D.Th. degree from Stellenbosh University, South Africa.

Kombo, James. 2007. *The Doctrine of God in African Christian Thought: The Holy Trinity, Theological Hermeneutics and the African Intellectual Culture.* Studies in Reformed Theology: Eddy van der Borght, Editor-in-Chief, Volume 14. Boston: Brill.

Kombo, James. 2016. *Theological Models of the Doctrine of the Trinity: The Trinity, Diversity and Theological Hermeneutics (Global Perspectives).* Langham Partnership International.

Koyama, Kosuke. 1976. *Waterbuffalo Theology*. Maryknoll, NY. Orbis Books.

Kraemer, Hendrik. 1963. *The Christian Message in a Non-Christian World*. Grand Rapids: Kregel Pub.

Kunhiyop, Samuel Waje. 1997. "Christian Relevance in Modern Africa" in *Africa Journal of Evangelical Theology,* 16:1, pp. 3-16.

Kunhiyop, Samuel Waje. 2008. *African Christian Ethics.* HippoBooks, an imprint of WordAlive ACTS and Zondervan. African Christian Textbooks (ACTS), Bukuru, Nigeria.

Kunhiyop, Samuel Waje. 2012. Foreword in *African Christian Theology*. HippoBooks, an imprint of WordAlive, ACTS, Challenge Enterprises and Zondervan.

Kunhiyop, Samuel Waje. 2017. "Curriculum Vitae: Samuel Waje Kunhiyop Ph.D."

Kunhiyop, Samuel Waje. 2017b. Email sent to Richard J. Gehman, August 10, 2017.

Kurewa, J.W. Zvumunondita. 1975. "The Meaning of African Theology." in *Journal of Theology for Southern Africa.* 11:34-42.

Kurewa, J.W.Z. 1980. "Who Do You Say that I Am?" in *International Review of World Mission,* World Council of Churches, Ap. 1980, Vol. 69, Issue 274, pp. 182-188.

Latourette, Kenneth S. 1937. *A History of the Expansion of Christianity.* NY: Harper.

Latourette, Kenneth Scott. 1975. *A History of Christianity*. Volume 1: to A.D. 1500. NY: Harper & Row, Publishers.

Lausanne Committee for World Evangelization. 1978. *The Willowbank Report- Gospel and Culture.* Wheaton, Illinois: Lausanne Committee for World Evangelization.

Leakey, L.S.B. 1952. *Mau Mau and the Kikuyu*. London.

Leith, John H. 1977. *Creeds of the Churches.* Atlanta: John Knox Press.

Lewis, Gordon R. and Bruce A. Demarest eds. 1996. *Integrative Theology – Historical, Biblical, Systematic, Apologetic, Practical –* Three Volumes in One. Grand Rapids: Zondervan.

Lewontin, Richard. 2017. "Interview with Richard Lewontin," edited transcript on Internet. <http://www.pbs.org/race/000_About/002_04-background-01-04.htm>

Long, Charles H. 1975. "Structural Similarities and Dissimilarities in Black and African Theologies." *Journal of Religious Thought*. 32:9-24.
Lugira, A.M. 1979. "African Christian Theology." *African Theological Journal*. VIII: 50-61.
Lundblad, Janet. 1978. "Towards an Authentic African Theology." *Covenant Quarterly*. 36:37-47.
Luzebetak, Louis J. 1970. *The Church and Cultures*. South Pasadena: Carey Library.
Maimela, Simon. 1987. "Archbishop Desmond Mpilo Tutu: A Revolutionary Political Priest or Man of Peace?" in *Hammering Swords into Ploughshares: Essays in Honor of Archbishop Mpilo Desmond Tutu*, edited by Buti Tlhagale and Itumeleng Mosala, Grand Rapids: William B. Eerdmans Pub. Co.
Mana, Ka. 2004. *Christians and Churches of Africa: Salvation in Christ and Building a New African Society*, Maryknoll, NY: Orbis Books.
Mary. 1983. A.I.C. Christian, Kyamatu, Kitui. Personal Interview.
Masoga, Magomme Alpheus. 2017. "A Critical Dialogue with Gabriel Molchee Setiloane: The Unfinished Business on the African Divinity Question" Website.
Mbiti, John S. 1966. *Akamba Stories*. London.
Mbiti, John S. 1969. *African Religions and Philosophy*. London: SPCK.
Mbiti, John S. 1970a. "The Future of Christianity in Africa." *Communio Viatorum* XIII, 1-2:32-33.
Mbiti, John S. 1970b. "Sources for the Study of African Traditional Religion." *Student Essays and Religious Workshop Papers*, Limuru, Kenya.
Mbiti, John S. 1970c. *Concepts of God in Africa*. London: SPCK.
Mbiti, John S. 1971. *New Testament Eschatology in an African Background*. London: Oxford University Press.
Mbiti, John S. 1972a. "Christianity and Traditional Religion in Africa." *Crucial Issues in Missions Tomorrow*. Donald MacGavran ed. Chicago: Moody Press.
Mbiti, John S. 1972b. "The Growing Respectability of African Traditional Religion." *Lutheran World* IX, 1:54-58
Mbiti, John S. 1973. "African Theology." *Worldview*. XVI:33-39.
Mbiti, John S. 1974a. "Theological Impotence and the Universality of the Church." *Lutheran World*. XXI, 3:251-260.
Mbiti, John S. 1975a. *An Introduction to African Religion*. London: London University.
Mbiti, John S. 1975b. The *Prayers of African Religion*. N. Y.: Orbis Books.
Mbiti, John S. 1976. "The Theology of the New World. I. Some Current Concerns of African Theology." *Expository Times*. 87: 164-168.
Mbiti, John S. 1978a. "Theology of the New World. Some Current Concerns of African Theology." *Expository Times*. 87: 164-168.
Mbiti, John S. 1978b. "African Theology." *All African Lutheran Consultation on Theology in the African Context: Background Material I.*, pp. 33-38. Geneva.
Mbiti, John S. 1979. "The Biblical Basis for Present Trends in African Theology." *African Theology En Route*. K. Appiah-Kubi and S. Torres eds., op. 83-94. Maryknoll, N.Y. : Orbis Books, 1979.
Mbiti, John. 1979b. "An African Views American Black Theology" in *Black Theology: A Documentary History, 1966-1979*, edited by Gayraud Wilmore and James Cone. Maryknoll, NY: Orbis Books, 1979.
Mbiti, John S. 1986. *Bible and Theology in African Community*. Nairobi: Oxford University Press, 1986.
Mbogu, Nicholas Ibeawuchi. 2012. *Jesus in Post-Missionary Africa*. San Press Ltd.
Mbugwa, Judy ed. 1994. *Our Time has Come: African Christian Women Address the Issues of Today*. Grand Rapids: Baker Book House.
McDowell, Josh. 2017. "Evidence for the Resurrection?" PDF file on Website online.
Miller, Catherine S. n.d. *Peter Cameron Scott*. London: Parry Jackman.
Mosala, Itumeleng J. and Buti Tlhagale eds. 1986. *The Unquestionable Right to be Free: Black Theology from South Africa*. Maryknoll, NY: Orbis Books.
Mosala, Itumeleng J. 1989. *Biblical Hermeneutics and Black Theology in South Africa*. Grand Rapids: William B. Eerdmans Publishing Co.

Mshana, E.E. 1972. "The Challenges of Black and African Theology." *Presence.*
Muema, Joel. 1974. Mukamba Christian, pastor in the A.I.C. and former student at Scott Theological College, Machakos, Kenya.
Muga, Erasto. 1975. *African Response to Western Christian Religion.* Nairobi: East African Literature Bureau.
Mugambi, J.N.K. and Laurenti Magesa eds. 1989: *Jesus in African Christianity: Experimentation and Diversity in African Christianity.* Nairobi: Initiatives Ltd.
Mugambi, J.N.K. 1989: *African Christian Theology: An Introduction.* Nairobi: Heinemann Kenya Ltd.
Murray-Brown, Jeremy. 1972. *Kenyatta.* London: George Allen & Unwin Ltd.
Musango, Jonathan, 1974. A.I.C. pastor in Kitui. Personal Interview.
Mutloatse, Mothobi. 1983. *Hope and Suffering: Sermons and Speeches by Desmond Tutu*, compiled by Mothobi Mutloatse, and edited by John Webster. Grand Rapids: William B. Eerdmans Publishing Company.
McGavran, Donald ed. 1972. *Crucial Issues in Missions Tomorrow.* Chicago: Moody.
McVeigh, Malcolm J. "Sources for An African Christian Theology." *Presence.* V, 3:2, 3.
Neve, J.L. 1946. *A History of Christian Thought*, Vol. 1. Philadelphia: Muhlenberg Press.
Ngewa, Samuel. 1987. *The Biblical Idea of Substitution versus the Idea of Substitution in African Traditional Sacrifices: A Case Study of Hermeneutics for African Christian Theology.* A Dissertation Submitted to the Faculty of Westminster Theological Seminary in Partial Fulfilment of the Requirements for the Degree, Ph.D., 1987.
Ngewa, Samuel. 2009. *1 & 2 Timothy and Titus.* Africa Bible Commentary Series. Nairobi: Word Alive (Hippos Books); Bukura, Nigeria: Africa Christian Textbooks.
Nichols, Bruce. 1979a. *Contextualization: A Theology of Gospel and Culture.* Illinois: Inter Varsity Press.
Nichols, Bruce. 1979b. "Towards a Theology of Gospel and Culture." *Gospel and Culture.* John Stott and Robert Coote eds., pp. 69-82. Pasadena: Wm. Carey Library.
Nichols, Bruce. 1983. *Evangelical Review of Theology.* VII, 1.
Niebuhr, Richard. 1951. *Christ and Culture.*
Nixon, Harmon. 1940. Letter to Ralph Davis, Sept. 6, 1940. File 14, Box 23, Collection 81, Archives of the Billy Graham Center, Wheaton, IL.
Noll, Mark A. 2000. *Turning Points: Decisive Moments in the History of Christianity.* Grand Rapids: Baker Academic.
Nyamiti, Charles. 1971. *African Theology: Its Nature, Problems and Methods.* Kampala: Gaba Publications.
Nyamiti, Charles. 1973. *The Scope of African Theology.* Kampala: Gaba Publications.
O'Donovan, Wilbur. 1996. *Biblical Christianity in African Perspective.* Carlisle, UK: The Paternoster Press.
Oduyoye, Mercy. 1994. "Introducing African Women's Theology" in *Paths of African Theology*, edited by Rosino Gibellini. Maryknoll, NY: Orbis Books (English translation copyright, originally in French).
Ogbonnaya, A. Okechukwu. 1994. *On Communitarian Divinity: An African Interpretation of the Trinity.* NY: Paragon House.
Okeke, George K. 1978. "Indigenization of Christianity in Africa." *Communio Viatorum.* XXI: 49-57.
Oliver, Roland. 1966. *The Missionary Factor in East Africa.* London: Longmans, Green And Co.
Orobator, Agbonkhianmeghe. 2008. *Theology Brewed in an African Pot: An Introduction to Christian Doctrine from an African Perspective* Nairobi, Kenya: Paulines Publications Africa.
Padilla, C. Rene. 1979. "Hermeneutics and Culture- An Anthropological Perspective." *Gospel and Culture.* John Stott and Robert Coote eds. Pasadena: Wm. Carey Library.
Pan African Conference of Third World Theologians. 1978. "Communique." *IDOC Bulletin.* No.1 (Jan.), 3-6.

Parratt, John. 1977. "Time in Traditional African Thought." *Religion.* VII-117-126.
Parratt, John. 1995. *Reinventing Christianity: African Theology Today.* Grand Rapids: Wm. B. Eerdmans Pub. Co.
P'Bitek, Okot. 1970. *African Religions in Western Scholarship.* Nairobi: East African Literature Bureau.
PDF Internet, 2017. "The Medical Evidence: Was Jesus' Death a Sham and his Resurrection a Hoax?" www.outreach.com/media/print/product/pdf/case4easter.pdf
Peterson, Dean A. 1970. "A Summary Report on the 1969 African Theological Faculty Conference." *Lutheran World.* XVII, 1 :65-69.
Pierard, Richard V. 2001. "Romanticism" in *Evangelical Dictionary of Theology,* Second Edition. Walter A. Elwell ed. Grand Rapids: Baker Academic.
Pobee, John S. 1979. *Towards an African Theology.* Nashville, Tenn.: The Parthenon Press.
Pobee, John S. 1992. *Skenosis: Christian Faith in an African Context.* Zimbabwe: Mambo Press.
Ray, Benjamin. 1972a. "Book Reviews: Recent Studies of African Religions." *History of Religions.* XII (Aug.): 75-89.
Roberts, J.D. 1978-79. "Black Theology and African Theology." *INS* 3:14-27.
Roberts, Robert C. 2001. "Bultmann, Rudolf" in *Evangelical Dictionary of Theology,* Second Edition. Walter Elwell ed. Grand Rapids: Baker Academic.
Robinson, Daniel N. 2004. *The Great Ideas of Philosophy,* Second Edition. Published by The Great Courses, Virginia.
Rubingh, Eugene. 1972. "The African Shape of the Gospel." *His.* XXXIII, 2:9-11.
Sandgren, David P. 1876. *The Kikuyu, Christianity, and the Africa Inland Mission.* Ph.D. Dissertation, University of Wisconsin.
Sawyerr, Harry. 1963. "The Basis of a Theology for Africa." *International Review of Mission.* LII: 266-278.
Sawyerr, Harry. 1971. "What is African Theology?" *African Theological Journal.* No. 4, Aug., 7-24.
Schaeffer, Francis A. 1976. *How Should We Then Live: The Rise and Decline of Western Thought and Culture.* Old Tappan, NJ: Fleming H. Revell Co.
Schopp, Ludwig ed. 1947. *The Fathers of the Church: The Apostolic Fathers.* Francis Glimm, Joseph Marique and Gerald Walsh transls. N.Y.: Cima Pub. Co., Inc.
Schultz, Richard L. 2001. "Higher Criticism" in *Evangelical Dictionary of Theology,* Second Edition. Walter Elwell ed. Grand Rapids: Baker Academic.
Setilaone, Gabriel. 1978. *Christianity in Independent Africa.* E. Fashole-Luke, R. Gray and A. Hastings eds. Bloomington: Indiana University Press.
Setiloane, Gabrial. 1980. "Theological Trends in Africa." *Missionalia* 8, 47-53, Aug. 80.
Setiloane, Gabriel. 1986. *African Theology: An Introduction.* Cape Town, S. Africa: Blackshaws Ltd.
Seoul Declaration. 1983. "The Seoul Declaration Toward an Evangelical Theology for the Third World." *Evangelical Review of Theology.* VII, 1:8-12.
Shepard, J.W. 1963. *The Christ of the Gospels.* Grand Rapids: Eerdmans Pub. Co.
Shenk, Wilbert. 2000. "Venn, Henry" in *Evangelical Dictionary of World Missions,* A. Scott Moreau ed., Grand Rapids: Baker Books.
Shorter, Aylward. 1975. *African Christian Theology - Adaptation or Incarnation.* London: Geoffrey Chapman Press.
Smith, Kay Higuera. 2017. "Evangelical Post-Colonial Conversations" edited by Kay Higuera Smith, Jayachitra Lalitha and L. Daniel Hawk. Internet Web site.
Solomon, Robert C. 2000. *No Excuses: Existentialism and the Meaning of Life: Course Guidebook.* Published by The Great Courses.
Spiceland, J.D. 2001. "Tillich, Paul" in *Evangelical Dictionary of Theology,* Second Edition. Walter Elwell ed. Grand Rapids: Baker Academic.
Stauffacher, John. 1927a. Letter to H.D. Campbell, Jan. 17, 1927. File 10, Box 13, Collection 81. Archives of the Billy Graham Center, Wheaton, IL.
Stauffacher, John. 1927b. Letter to H.D. Campbell, Feb. 23, 1927. File 10, Box 13, Collection 81. Archives of the Billy Graham Center, Wheaton, IL.

Stauffacher, John. 1929. Letter to H.D. Campbell, Nov. 19, 1929. File 10, Box 13, Collection 81. Archives of Billy Graham Center, Wheaton, IL.

Stauffacher, John. 1930a. Letter to H.D. Campbell, Feb. 11, 1930. File 10, Box 13, Collection 81. Archives of the Billy Graham Center Wheaton, IL.

Stauffacher, John. 1930b. Letter to H.D. Campbell, Ap. 23, 1930. File 10, Box 13, Collection 81. Archives of the Billy Graham Center Wheaton, IL.

Stauffacher, John. 1930c. Letter to H.D. Campbell, Sept. 17, 1930. File 10, Box 13, Collection 81. Archives of the Billy Graham Center Wheaton, IL.

Stott, John and Robert Coote eds. 1979. *Gospel and Culture*. Wm. Carey Library

Stumpf, Hulda. 1927. Letter to H.D. Campbell, May 3, 1927. File 24, Box 24, Collection 81. Archives of the Billy Graham Center, Wheaton, IL.

Sundkler, Bengt Gustav. 1960. "Towards Christian Theology in Africa." In *The Christian Ministry in Africa.* London: SMC.

Taber, Charles R. 1979. "Hermeneutics and Culture - An Anthropological Perspective." *Gospel and Culture*. John Stott and Robert Coote eds. Pasadena: William Carey Library.

Tenney, Merrill C. ed. 1960. *The Word for This Century.* N.Y.: Oxford University Press.

Thomas, J.C. 1973. "What is African Theology? *Ghana Bulletin of Theology*. IV, 4:14-30.

Tienou, Tite. 1982. *The Theological Task of the Church in Africa.* Ghana: African Christian Press.

Tienou, Tite. 1983. "Biblical Foundations: An African Study." *Evangelical Review of Theology.* VII, 1:89-101.

Tlhagale, Buti and Itumeleng Mosala eds. 1987. *Hammering Swords into Ploughshares: Essays in Honor of Archbishop Mpilo Desmond Tutu.* Grand Rapids: William B. Eerdmans Pub. Co.

Todd, Paul. 2017. Personal Email to Richard J. Gehman.

Torres, Sergio and Virginia Fabella. 1978. *The Emergent Gospel.* Maryknoll, N.Y.: Orbis Books.

Turaki, Yusufu. 1999. *Christianity and African gods: A Method in Theology, and Tainted Legacy.* Potchefstroomse Universiteit Vir Christelike Hoer Onderwys

Tutu, Desmond M. 1975 "Black Theology/African Theology- Soul Mates or Antagonists?" *Journal of Religious Thought*. XXXII: 25-33.

Tutu, Desmond M. 1978. "Whither African Theology?" in *Christianity in Independent Africa.* E. Fashole-Luke, R. Gray and A. Hastings eds. Bloomington: Indiana University Press.

Tutu, Desmond. 1979. "Black Theology/African Theology – Soul Mates or Antagonists?" in *Black Theology: A Documentary History, 1966-1979*, edited by Gayraud Wilmore and James Cone. Maryknoll, NY: Orbis Books, 1979.

Tutu, Desmond. 2017. "Desmond Tutu" in Wikipedia on Internet.

Ukpong, Justin S. 1984. *African Theologies Now - A Profile*. Eldoret, Kenya: Gaba Pub.

United Missionary Society, Kikuyu. 1913. Minutes of the United Missionary Conference, Kikuyu, June 17-22, 1913. Archives of the National Christian Council of Kenya, NBI.

Uzukwu, Eugene. 1977. "Notes on Methodology for an African Theology" in *African Ecclesiastical Review* XIX, 3:155-164.

Wachege, Patrick N. 2003. "Charles Nyamiti: Vibrant Pioneer of Inculturated African Theology" in *African Theology in the 21st Century: The Contribution of the Pioneers,* Vol. 2. Nairobi: Paulines Publications Africa.

Wright, G. Ernest. 1953. *The Old Testament against Its Environment*. London: SCM

Wenham, J.W. 1955. *Our Lord's View of the Old Testament*. London: The Tyndale Press.

Wilmore, Gayraud and James Cone eds. 1979. *Black Theology: A Documentary History, 1966-1979.* Maryknoll, NY: Orbis Books.

Yamaori, Tsunao. 1975. *Christopaganism or Indigenous Christianity?* Pasadena: Wm. Carey Library.

Zacharias, Ravi, and Albert Mohler. 2007. Lectures at the Ligonier Ministries 2007 National Conference.

INDEX OF PEOPLE CITED

AUTHOR
AND HIS OTHER PUBLICATIONS

Rev. Dr. Richard J. Gehman was born in Norristown, Pennsylvania, U.S.A., on December 24, 1935. He earned a Diploma in Theology from Berean Bible School, 1957; a Bachelor of Arts in Anthropology from Wheaton College, 1960; a Master of Arts in New Testament from Wheaton College Graduate School, 1963; a Bachelor of Divinity (MDiv) from Gordon Divinity School, 1963; and a Doctor of Missiology from Fuller Theological Seminary in 1985. He was ordained to the Christian ministry in 1971 by the Bible Fellowship Church.

For 36 years Richard J. Gehman and his wife, Florence (Flo), served in Kenya with the Africa Inland Church as missionaries of the Africa Inland Mission. Throughout those years he became immersed in the rich history of the Africa Inland Church as he engaged in theological education with students, pastors and teachers throughout the Africa Inland Church in Kenya.

After an initial year of orientation in Kenya, Richard and Florence served at Scott Theological College from 1967 to 1984; and 1994 to 2002. For eight years, 1975-1983, he was Principal of the College. He succeeded Dr. Mark Shaw as the Editor of the *African Journal of Evangelical Theology*, 1995-2002.

He served as Assistant Pastor of AIC Embakasi, Nairobi, 1985-1987, and as Assistant Pastor in Maingi, Kijabe, 1987-1994. He launched and coordinated the *Theological Advisory Group* (TAG), 1985-2002, a research and renewal ministry, and served as the manuscript drafter in the composition of the TAG books.

From the first meeting of the Board of Governors for the Nairobi Evangelical School of Theology, February 1980, until 1994, he served as a member of the NEGST Governing Board. He became the first Director of the AIC Training Department, April 1993, and served until December 1994.

In 2002 Richard and Florence retired in the A.I.M. Retirement Center in Florida, USA, where they serve in their local church, in their retirement community and where Richard has continued researching and writing. Their son, Nathan, and his wife, Rosanne, have six children and work in the A.I.M. office in Peachtree City, Georgia. Their daughter, Joy, and her husband, Tom, have four children and live in Wheaton, Illinois.

ADDITIONAL BOOKS WRITTEN BY AUTHOR

Published by Oasis International Ltd.

Distribution Partners:

Oasis Distribution Limited, Lagos and Jos, Nigeria
CLC Christian BookLink (K) Ltd., Nairobi, Kenya
Challenge Enterprises of Ghana, Accra, North Ghana

African Traditional Religion in Biblical Perspective, Revised Edition, 2011.

Learning to Lead: The Making of a Christian Leader in Africa, 2008.

Passing it On: Lessons Learned in Life, 2011 (Memoirs of the Author).

From Death to Life: The Birth of the Africa Inland Church, Kenya, 1895-1945.

The Spreading Vineyard: The Growth of the Africa Inland Church, Kenya, From 1945 Onwards, a Kindle eBook, 2017.

The Spreading Vineyard: The Growth of the Africa Inland Church, Kenya, From 1945 Onwards, a printed shortened version of the eBook, 2017.

Overcoming Fear of Death, 2017.

Published by Africa Christian Textbooks, Nigeria

African Traditional Religion in the Light of the Bible, 2001

Published by Evangel Publishing House, Kenya

Doing African Christian Theology: An Evangelical Perspective, 1987

Who are the Living Dead? A Theology of Death, Life after Death and the Living Dead, 1999.

Published by Mastoff Press, Morgantown, Pennsylvania, U.S.A.

Faith of our Fathers: From Barbarian to Mennonite and Beyond, 2009

Published by Scott Christian University, Kenya

Author served as Coordinator and Manuscript Drafter for the Theological Advisory Group sponsored by Scott Theological College.

The Roots of Christianity in Africa: Prayer in the History of the Christian Church in Africa

'Where Two or Three are Gathered...' Prayer in the Christian Church in Africa (both a Leader's Guide and a Student Workbook)

'Come, Let us Bow Down...' Worship in the Christian Church in Africa (both a Leader's Guide and a Student Workbook)

Worship Guide for Pastors and Elders: How to Improve Worship in the Africa Inland Church

A Biblical Approach to Marriage and Family in Africa

The Holy Spirit and the Church in Africa Today

[illegible]

Overcoming the Flesh, 2012

[illegible]

AFRICA STUDY BIBLE
AFRICA STUDY BIBLE
NLT